Twayne's
Filmmakers Series

74028

Frank Beaver, Editor

‍E:

JP CINEMA

1.95

Oliver Stone on the set of *The Doors*. Copyright © 1991 Tri-Star Pictures, Inc. All rights reserved. Courtesy The Museum of Modern Art/Film Stills Archive.

OLIVER STONE: WAKEUP CINEMA

Frank Beaver

TWAYNE PUBLISHERS • NEW YORK
MAXWELL MACMILLAN CANADA • TORONTO
MAXWELL MACMILLAN INTERNATIONAL •
NEW YORK • OXFORD • SINGAPORE • SYDNEY

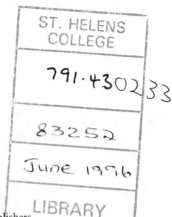
Twayne's Filmmakers Series
Oliver Stone: Wakeup Cinema

Twayne Publishers
Macmillan Publishing Company
866 Third Avenue
New York, New York 10022

Maxwell Macmillan Canada, Inc.
1200 Eglinton Avenue East
Suite 200
Don Mills, Ontario M3C 3N1

Library of Congress Cataloging-in-Publication Data

Beaver, Frank Eugene
    Oliver Stone : wakeup cinema / Frank Beaver.
    p.   cm.—(Twayne's filmmakers series)
    Includes bibliographical references and index.
    ISBN 0-8057-9326-7.—ISBN 0-8057-9332-1 (pbk)
    1. Stone, Oliver—Criticism and interpretation. I. Title. II.
Series.
  PN1998.3.S76B43   1994
  791.43'0233'092—dc20   93-39729
                                      CIP

The paper used in this publication meets the minimum
requirements of American National Standard for Information
Sciences—Permanence of Paper for Printed Library Materials.
ANSI Z3948-1984.

10 9 8 7 6 5 4 3 2 1 (hc)

10 9 8 7 6 5 4 3 2   (pbk)

Printed in the United States of America

CONTENTS

FOREWORD

Of all the contemporary arts, the motion picture is particularly timely and diverse as a popular culture enterprise. This lively art form cleverly combines storytelling with photography to achieve what has been a quintessential twentieth-century phenomenon. Individual as well as national and cultural interests have made the medium an unusually varied one for artistic expression and analysis. Films have been exploited for commercial gain, for political purposes, for experimentation, and for self-exploration. The various responses to the motion picture have given rise to different labels for both the fun and the seriousness with which this art form has been received, ranging from "the movies" to "cinema." These labels hint at both the theoretical and sociological parameters of the film medium.

A collective art, the motion picture has nevertheless allowed individual genius to flourish in all its artistic and technical areas: directing, screenwriting, cinematography, acting, editing. The medium also encompasses many genres beyond the narrative film, including documentary, animated, and avant-garde expression. The range and diversity of motion pictures suggest rich opportunities for appreciation and for study.

The Twayne Filmmakers Series examines the full panorama of motion picture history and art. Many studies are auteur-oriented and elucidate the work of individual directors whose ideas and cinematic styles make them authors of their films. Other studies examine film movements and genres or analyze cinema from a national perspective. The series seeks to illuminate all the many aspects of film for the film student, the scholar, and the general reader.

Frank Beaver

PREFACE

The way we look at the world we live in has undergone significant change since photographic images were first displayed in France in the late 1830s. In her Pulitzer Prize–winning critical study, *On Photography,* Susan Sontag outlined the cultural revolution initiated by the invention of the camera, a reproductive device that permitted instantaneous images of human and material landscapes.[1]

Prior to a system of direct recording of physical presences, the task of image retention had fallen to scenic artists and portrait painters. These imagists—even at their prolific best—were severely limited in output, and their handiwork usually fell into the possession of an elite few. Sontag drew attention to the fact that photographs, in time, gave to all a means of world surveillance as well as personal documentation; she noted that the photograph album eventually supplanted home Bibles and other earlier methods of maintaining family records. At its most immediate level of impact, the photograph provided a universally accessible way of confirming one's existence in either the most serious or the most casual of life's circumstances—fully, from birth to death.

The still photograph, it was said, also held special powers of interpersonal relationship with its possessors. No matter how amateurish, blurred, or distant the captured moment might be, the photograph provided special appeals as an object of inventory for discovery and rediscovery. In *Theory of Film: The Redemption of Physical Reality* (1960), Siegfried Kracauer maintained the retentive nature of photographs as personal archival documents—documents that he said compelled the viewer to "look at them in the hope of detecting something new or unexpected."[2] Similarly, Sontag averred: "Any photograph has multiple meanings; indeed to see something in the form of a photograph is to encounter a potential object of fascination. The ultimate wisdom of the photographic image is to say: 'There is the surface.

Now think—or rather feel, intuit what is beyond it, what the reality must be if it looks this way.' Photographs, which cannot themselves explain anything, are inexhaustible invitations to deduction, speculation and fantasy"[3] (Sontag, 23).

The ability of the camera to apprehend images and preserve them as mysterious souvenirs of personal and public record was further enhanced by the realization of "moving" pictures in 1889—exactly 50 years after the introduction of still photography. Pictures in motion possessed the same mimetic properties as photographs. They could reflect back representations of physical reality with mirrorlike accuracy, but in the new frames-per-second process "cinematography" added dynamism to the effect by allowing photo-images that flowed in time—a significant step beyond the capture of single moments frozen in time.

As a result of their flowing nature, incipient moving pictures offered the simple but immensely satisfying pleasure of images kinetically and rhythmically "alive." Later, with the arrival of film editing, an externally supplied rhythm was supplied through alteration of the recorded material. As the frontier posse in Edwin S. Porter's *The Great Train Robbery* (1903) charged toward its law-and-order mission, intercutting between the good and the bad guys intensified the drama. Film pace moved beyond verisimilitudinous action to rhythms achieved by combining image mobility with regulated "shots" and a fractured narrative structure.

Other film pioneers showed that image dynamics in motion pictures could be altered by a shifting angle of view. The camera could be dollied, panned, tilted, or tracked for instantly changing perspectives of that which was being filmed. Perspective and thus viewer attention remained in a state of potential flux as the creative urge to give moving pictures a "nurtured" life took hold.

In writings first published in the early 1930s, Rudolf Arnheim polemicized that while photography and film reproduced reality "mechanically," they were nonetheless mediums that possessed "artistic resources" and therefore shared resemblance to other art mediums: painting, music, literature, dance.[3] Arnheim attributed photographic and filmic artistry in part to those "surprise" illusions that occurred through the way three-dimensional objects were recorded and projected on a two-dimensional plane. The process in and of itself, Arnheim said, turned the objects into something significantly different from the original. Changes in depth, size, perspective, and the time-space continuum moved the images away from shapeless reproduction and toward artistic effect. According to Arnheim, the film artist's tools of expression were, among others, camera position (angle of view, distance from object), lighting (light and shade), montage (editing), mobile camera, optical effects resulting from special lenses, adjusted frames-per-second camera speeds (slow and accelerated motion), and laboratory devices (dissolves, wipes, superimpositions, fades).

Arnheim argued that the end result of image manipulation should be such "that the character of the objects represented should not thereby be destroyed but rather strengthened, concentrated and interpreted" (Arnheim, 35).

It is not surprising that the earliest responses to motion pictures— offered some decades before Arnheim's—revealed a potentially complex medium of expression struggling for a critical vocabulary. In the early years of moving pictures, film was typically described as "canned drama," "innocent amusement for the masses," or yet another noteworthy example of "scientific marvel" in an inexplicable stage of development. More often than not, the new medium was excused from loftier discussion.

However slow developing, the attention given to the artistic possibilities of motion picture narrative and cinematographic technique was steady and progressive. The aesthetic development of motion pictures and the critical responses they generated were charted by George C. Pratt in *Spellbound in Darkness* (1966), a diarylike accounting of significant early films with concurrent reactions in terms of both story and filmic methods of telling the story.[4] A reading of Pratt's chronology of developing criticism reveals the emergence of traditional approaches to the motion picture as art object—analytical strategies that emphasized the construction of the work and implied that what made the art was not just the story but the methods used in getting the story across. Idea and form came to be viewed as inseparable elements in film art and in the analytical process that followed.

From this "formalistic" stance there developed a greater awareness of the critical link between artistic imagination and film effect, especially the role played by the film director. Treatises written in the 1920s and 1930s by the Russian directors Vsvelod Pudovkin and Sergei Eisenstein offered elaborate theories about how to achieve emotional and political impact through film and in so doing further enhanced the idea of directorial genius as the source of artistic achievement in the motion picture.

A fuller embracing of the idea occurred in France in the late 1940s and early 1950s with André Bazin's "auteur"-inspired analysis. A critical strategy based on analysis of form and idea as viewed through artistic attribution (director as "author") was especially appealing for critics challenged by the knowledge that most motion pictures resulted from team effort geared toward commercial enterprise.

Although often tempted to a priori judgment and overvaluation, the "authorial genius" approach moved the discussion of film artistry into arenas of vigorous discourse and stimulated a reevaluation of the full body of motion picture output.

Nearly simultaneously with the emergence of auteur criticism there surfaced efforts of analysis based on narrative typology, commonly pegged in one form as "genre criticism." Whereas auteur criticism placed its emphasis on uncovering the innate role of directorial vision (personality) in film idea and form, genre analysis shifted the focus to a reading of the film's text. This textual reading, made in relation to well-understood elements of generic formulas (e.g., those of the western and gangster films) and how the text adhered to or deviated from the known elements, implied a participation outside the film itself: that of the audience in interaction with the conventions of the work.

In *Hollywood Genres* (1981), Thomas Schatz assessed the import and methods of genre criticism, summarizing that "both filmmakers and viewers are sensitive to a genre's range of expression because of previous experiences with the genre that have coalesced into a system of value-laden narrative conventions. It is this system of conventions—familiar characters performing familiar actions which celebrate familiar values—that represents the genre's narrative content, its meaningful cultural community."[5]

Observers and advocates of genre analysis noted that the projection of familiar characters and conventions in repetitive film types provided ongoing pleasure to the cultural community. They also noted that in varying the expected conventions, it was possible for the cultural community to detect narrative metaphors that spoke to the social and/or political climate of the times in which the film was made. The text, for example, of Fred Zinnemann's taut western *High Noon* (1953)—a story of the courage exhibited by a frontier sheriff in the face of bullying intimidation—could be read at the time of its release as a pertinent moral reflection on issues pertaining to McCarthy-era America and acquiescence to political tyranny.

Genre analysis was evidence of yet another attempt to confirm the artistic and cultural validity of motion pictures in their most popular and formulaic manifestations. The approach achieved special relevance and import when viewed in the context of studio-dominated Hollywood, where output has favored tradition and convention in narrative storytelling for the screen.

The idea of textual reading as a basis of analysis has conditioned much of contemporary academic film criticism and scholarship. Approaches have ranged from the narrative strategies scheme of genre criticism articulated by Schatz to feminist, cultural, and semiotic, structuralist strategies favored by a host of proponents. Gender, social structure, and semiotic scholars have viewed film as having strong analogies with language where meaning exists both within and outside the text as a result of such factors as cultural, ideological, and mythical predeterminants. Many feminist readings, for example, have examined textual signs with regard to gender emphases, especially the male-oriented sexual instincts in films.

The explosion of discourse strategies for film evaluation has challenged the scholar to broaden the avenue of approach to systematic analysis. Theorists maintain that any strategy can provide a meaningful reading of a film or films, but remains just that—a single reading. A given approach may provide certain "truths," but never all the truth within the film art. A postmodernist philosophy of eclecticism in critical circles has thus gained in validity as the search to expand the range of understanding of a film's meaning has been opened up to all sorts of possibilities of inquiry.

OLIVER STONE

This study of the film work of Oliver Stone takes a decidedly eclectic approach. It nods toward auteur analysis, but it does so through a historical reconstruction that draws on personal background, circumstance, and trial and error within the artistic process. Liberal inclusion of critical reaction to Stone's work is intended to enliven the reconstruction of an emerging career and to illuminate how criticism can in fact help shape the artistic course of an artist's ideas and techniques.

The foundation of this study assumes and attempts to verify a telling symbiosis between critical response and ongoing practice in Stone's emergence as a unique director with an evolved "mission," that is, filmmaking dedicated to what in time he would refer to as "wakeup cinema."

The connections within Stone's films are fascinating, but even more so are the ways he developed his reputation as an unconventional director working within the Hollywood system of filmmaking. Stone burst onto the Hollywood scene in the mid-1980s at a time when many American screenwriters and directors were turning to projects focused more and more on family domestic issues, sentiment, and melodrama, or were being cautiously and conservatively lured to the security blanket of a spinoff or sequel. Stone began to look elsewhere, and it was the time as well as the man that signaled his importance. A product of the 1960s, Stone turned again and again to that decade for stories that reexamined in the 1980s the values of an earlier feverish era. He also questioned 1980s systems: government strategy in Central America, American finance and Wall Street. His were bold "statement films" superbly crafted and told always from a strong male perspective. Stone jarred, provoked, irritated, as he simultaneously captivated. Undaunted by the public ire his films often provoked, he marched on guerillalike—headstrong, blustery—into motion picture history: a finger-waggling filmmaker.

METHOD

The approach of this study has involved close scrutiny of motion pictures Oliver Stone wrote and directed as well as films written by him for other directors. A personal and professional profile—reconstructed from the director's own observations about himself and his work—offers in chapter 1 a prologue to the films themselves. Like most artists of note, Stone has enjoyed introspective self-analysis of the creative urge—evaluation that helps explain a film director of unique impulses and talents.

The film analyses incorporate elements designed to present thorough overviews of production logistics, plot, techniques, thematics, and critical responses to each work examined. As much as any other contemporary director-writer, Stone has generated an extraordinary amount of critical reaction—reaction that has raised discourse not only

on the films but on issues involving American systems, history, politics, and media ethics. The critical response component has involved
examination of thousands of reviews, critiques, interviews, editorials,
newspaper articles, and letters to the editor written about Stone's
films. This discourse is meant to enliven the auteur component in the
study by tracing those stylistic, thematic, and technical elements of
"authorship" which Stone carried with him from film to film.

As the twentieth century moved toward its conclusion, Oliver
Stone's artistic aplomb spurred a significant and timely reconsideration of popular culture's role in a changing, unsettled society. The
conservatism that had entrenched itself in Hollywood during the
1980s and 1990s—dramatically reducing creativity born of imagination, originality, and thought—was met by the even more unsettling
conservative views of art in general by government officials and government support agencies. The final chapter of this study is one of
extended reflection on ideas, issues, and meaning that have developed
from Stone's nontraditionalist exploitation of his medium.

ACKNOWLEDGMENTS

I am deeply grateful for the assistance of Dan Madaj and Jolan Coissart in the preparation of this book, and for the editorial guidance of India Koopman and Mark Zadrozny.

CHRONOLOGY

1946	Born 15 September in New York City.
1957	Enters Trinity School.
1965	Drops out of Yale after one year.
1965	Moves to Vietnam to teach English in Cholon.
1966	Writes symbolist novel—unpublished. Lives briefly in Mexico.
1967–1968	Joins the army, returns to Vietnam as soldier, serving 15 months in the 25th Infantry Division.
1968	Enters New York University Film School.
1973	Directs first film in Canada, a horror thriller, *Seizure.* Released 1974.
1976	Moves to Hollywood.
1978	Hired to adapt *Midnight Express* for the screen. Wins Screenwriters Guild and Academy Awards for best adapted screenplay.
1981	Directs second film based on original screenplay, *The Hand,* another psychological thriller.
1982	Coscripts *Conan the Barbarian* with John Milius.
1983	Writes *Scarface* for director Brian De Palma.
1985	Coauthors with Michael Cimino *Year of the Dragon.*
1986	With David McHenry, adapts *8 Million Ways to Die* for Hal Ashby.
1985–1986	Writes, directs, and releases *Salvador* with backing from the British company Hemdale.
1986	Brings *Platoon* to the screen (first written in 1976). Wins Academy Award for best picture. Stone also named best director of 1986. Film grosses $250 million.

1987   Writes and directors *Wall Street*.

1988   Directs *Talk Radio* and *Born on the Fourth of July*.

1989   *Born on the Fourth of July* wins Academy Award for Stone as best director.

1990   *The Doors* released.

1991   *JFK* creates national controversy.

1992   Stone wins Golden Globe Best Director Award for *JFK*.

1993   *Heaven and Earth*, Stone's first film with a strong female protagonist, is released.

Making Sense of the Oliver Stone Prism

I'm puzzled by life, horrified by the daily newspaper. The only sane response is recreation, drama . . . an ordered series of events that arouse pity and terror, to paraphrase Aristotle. Making movies is my way of exorcising demons, of creating an ethos, a philosophy of life. I'd go crazy without fantasy.
    —Oliver Stone, *Los Angeles Times Magazine,* 17 December 1989

In the first years of his ascendancy as a preeminent motion picture director, Oliver Stone gave hundreds of interviews to film critics and reporters of every persuasion (pro, con, left, right). The scrutiny drove him to an introspective analysis rarely experienced by a still-emerging screen artist. Every path of Stone's life, every up- and downturn was journalistically dissected in the search for clues to a filmmaker seemingly hell-bent on becoming Hollywood's alternative-point-of-view man.

As is often the case in such intensive effort, an impassioned subject—especially one like Oliver Stone—can easily hone and shape a personal and artistic mystique that snugly fits the man to his work. From interview to interview, biographical details repeated themselves as the wellspring of Stone's compulsive inspiration. He sought, for example, to explain both his ambition and his choice of screen material through happenstance of parentage: "My mother was French (having met her husband when he was a G.I. stationed in Paris). I'm half immigrant. I've always felt that urge to risk. . . . And I'm interested in alternative points of view. I think ultimately the problems of the planet are universal and that nationalism is a very destructive force. Just doing provincial American subjects is really boring."[1]

Stone, in interpreting his origins, pointed out that while his mother was French and by religion a Catholic, his father was Jewish-American and that he himself never practiced either of his parent's religions but rather grew up a Protestant. These facts were used to augment claims that his background nurtured universalism and diverse ways of looking at life.

Also, Stone frequently spoke of the impact his father's right-wing politics had on the course of his youth. The elder Stone, except for a brief period as a machete manufacturer, was a stockbroker for nearly 50 years. In talking with Alexander Cockburn of *American Film,* Stone described his father, Lou Stone, as "a Republican," "conservative in an intelligent sense," "an apologist—a defender of the Cold War," "someone who 'created' [the Russians] as a nightmare image for me as a child."[2]

Stone claimed that as a result of his father's views, he developed as a young man into "essentially a torn right-winger" who ultimately would go to Vietnam and be able to react "accordingly," never doubting "that the Communists were the bad guys and we were the good guys, and that we were saving the South from the North" (McGilligan, 16).

Other events from Oliver Stone's childhood were factored into explanations of the development of an increasingly conflicted and unhappy young man. Stone described as a "real cold shower" learning at age 16 that his parents were deeply in debt and divorcing. Illusions of stability were shattered, and Stone found himself restless and ever seeking to turn away from what he has called his conservative upbringing.

Stone was born in New York City on 15 September 1946; his culturally disparate parents sought to raise their son in the best traditions of a northeastern middle-class American family. Lou Stone daily promoted the virtues of discipline to his only child, proud of the boy and intent on keeping him from being spoiled. The father constantly urged writing as a disciplinarian task.

Stone was enrolled by his parents in the prestigious Trinity School, an all-boys institution where strict discipline and academic rigor were the ways of life—an educational experience Stone described as fitting "the reality of schools" in general: "Rigid law, orthodoxy, oppression to some degree . . . rough."[3]

Stone also said that being an only child caused him private anguish, making him feel like an "outsider" at school, and cutting him off from "access to easy conversation" that would have resulted from the presence of another sibling.

Writing was one avenue of escape from the realities of school and youthful insecurity. And so too were the movies. In Stone's recollections, it was his mother—a lover of storytelling, an escapist, and a fantasist—who allowed him to skip school to attend double and sometimes triple features with her. As for his father, also a filmgoer, Stone remembered by contrast a man invariably critical of narrative deficiencies in film plots and therefore a source of "education" in Oliver Stone's own skeptical manner of looking at mainstream motion pictures.

With the announcement that his parents were getting divorced—the message having come by phone to the headmaster at Stone's boarding school and delivered indirectly and impersonally to the 16-year-old—Stone recalled: "I felt like shit; like nothing. Everything was metallic. All the surfaces were metallic. All the adults were dangerous, not to be trusted. The world was a very empty place to me." (Breskin, 40). A variety of other words and phrases were used to describe the feelings and eventual adolescent revolution brought on by the dissolution of his family: "disintegration," "outsider," "disconnected," "on my own," "residing in a new world."

Stone lived in the guardianship of his father until high school graduation, after which he attended Yale University for a year before dropping out in 1965. His young adult life after this can be characterized as that of a restless vagabond-adventurer. After leaving Yale at 19, Stone traveled to Southeast Asia to teach English to Chinese-Vietnamese students at the Free Pacific Institute in Cholon, South Vietnam (the Chinese suburb of Saigon), remaining in this position for more than a year.

The urge to write a novel about his Southeast Asian experiences brought Stone home and eventually to Mexico, where in 1966 he completed 1,400 pages of darkly toned, self-reflective symbolist fiction. Would-be publishers rejected his manuscript, shattering Stone's ego and compelling him to join the army for a return trip to Vietnam and the opportunity for new, complex experiences.

Stone recalled his desire to return to Vietnam as an experience-seeking soldier in ways that tellingly mirrored the compulsive take-me-to-the-edge personae of his later films: "Now I wanted to see another level, a deeper level, a darker side. What is war? How do people kill each other? How will I handle it? What is the lowest level I can descend to find the truth, where I can come back from and say, *I've seen it?*" (McGilligan, 361).

Stone served for 15 months with the 25th Infantry Division in Vietnam in four different combat units where he won the Bronze Star for Valor and—injured in combat twice—the Purple Heart with First Oak Leaf Cluster. Acid and an unending supply of marijuana underscored the craze of his Vietnam adventure. Of the experience Stone remembered: "I walked away from that war, 21 and benumbed, and something of an anarchist. It took me several years to recover some form of social identification."[4]

After returning from Vietnam, Stone wandered aimlessly around the northwestern and southwestern United States, and was jailed for marijuana possession at the Mexican border. As an "overlooked," "chip-on-his-shoulder" Vietnam veteran, he reacted to this event with lingering bitterness. In his own words "benumbed," "lacking social identification," and experiencing culture shock, Stone turned to heavy drug usage. Marijuana, alcohol, and LSD were common sources of alternating solace and mind expansion. That dependence intensified after he relocated back to New York City, where veteran support group opportunities were nonexistent. Lonely, Stone reexperienced the old feelings of being an outsider, and efforts at compensation through drugs continued for years.

At the suggestion of a friend, and using his unpublished novel as evidence of a creative urge, Stone sought and won admission to New York University's film program, which he attended on the G.I. Bill. Under the tutelage of Martin Scorsese and other film instructors, Stone produced three short 16mm black-and-white films at NYU and turned once again to writing for "therapy." Also during the late 1960s and early 1970s, he became attracted to the creative freedom he saw in films coming from France and Italy—in the works of Godard, Truffaut, Fellini, and other directors who were signaling an international explosion of new film talent. The American films of the time that appealed to him were those, not surprisingly, like Martin Scorsese's *Mean Streets* (1972) and *Taxi Driver* (1975)—films about dark tensions within intriguing subcultures and films of personal alienation.

To support himself following film school, Stone drove a cab, and during off-duty hours, living on Houston Street in a "shithole," he continued to write screenplays—nearly a dozen—doing so in part because of his father's lingering charge to discipline and daily commitment. He also married Najwa Sarkis, an Iranian and an executive assistant with the Moroccan Mission to the United Nations. Stone credited Sarkis with helping him through this difficult period when he was attempting to reconnect and find focus in his life. In 1973 Stone secured backers for one of his screenplays, *Seizure,* a thriller about demonic evil. Then 26 years old, he went to Canada to direct the film, a low-budget effort that soon after release fell into obscurity. He continued to struggle.

In 1976, Stone moved to Hollywood to peddle his screenplays. There he was able to obtain an agent who in 1978 got him the job of writing the scenario for a film adaptation of a book by a young American, Billy Hayes. Hayes had been apprehended and jailed in Istanbul, Turkey, in 1970 for drug possession. The book, *Midnight Express,* recounted the treatment Hayes encountered at the hands of Turkish officials, prison guards, and fellow prisoners.

No matter at what angle one might peer through the complex prism Stone constructed of himself over the years, in retrospect the core material of *Midnight Express* appeared as perfectly suited as any might be to a would-be writer of Stone's (at age 32) now hard-edged, dark, visceral sensibilities. The drug-bust aspect fit; so too did the foreign, exotic locales—the mystique of an alien culture—that seemingly had taken Billy Hayes, like Oliver Stone himself, to the end of the world and to the edge of death's precipice.

By the point of writing the *Midnight Express* screenplay, Stone's politics had broadened significantly from those inculcated by his father's narrow, right-wing perspectives. He said his eyes had been opened in observing the treatment of student activists by police at NYU in the early 1970s and by the revelations of Watergate. The "disgust" that developed within him as a result of this awareness of arrogant authority is likely to have fed the angry, one-sided, and often base treatment of Turkish government/prison figures in the script he turned out for *Midnight Express* and its director, Alan Parker.

Parker—British, leftist, directing his second film with *Midnight Express*—proved well suited for interpreting the visceral, go-for-the-craw brutality within the script. The collaboration resulted in a controversial but shockingly compelling motion picture experience—one so engaging that the low-budget effort earned $100 million for its distributor, Columbia Pictures.

Midnight Express brought professional recognition for Stone through a Best Screenplay Award from the Screenwriters Guild, followed by an Academy Award for Best Adapted Screenplay of 1978. Also, *Mid-*

night Express helped pull Stone's artistic vision into sharper focus and in effect launched what in time would come to be known as the prototypical Oliver Stone picture. The shaping of a recognizable screen auteur—an undeniable artist who authors a work through style, technique, and idea—was under way with Stone's success in bringing Billy Hayes's story to light.

Crucial to the typical Stone film has been an antihero protagonist—someone like Hayes with whom Stone can share a strong, symbiotic identification. Stone's second wife, Elizabeth, said: "I don't think Oliver could ever make a movie without being in love with the main character. He gets so involved he takes on the persona of the main character, dressing and talking and behaving like that person. His wardrobe actually changes from film to film."[5]

Also of significance in the *Midnight Express* experience was the discovery of an approach—a bold, dramatic style that no matter how often attacked by critics in this and later films—would move Stone beyond the failure of earlier writing efforts and stasis and into a condition of feeling better about his work and his own self-worth. Addressing an interviewer's statement that a dominant criticism of his films had been a sledgehammer, hit-the-audience-in-the-face approach (charges first leveled at *Midnight Express*), Stone replied:

Obviously I'm aware of that criticism. Possibly I go for the lowest common denominator, in terms of getting the message across, in terms of getting what I want to say across. I think sometimes it's better to be wrong on the side of clarification rather than of obscurity. That's the thing my father always used to beat on me for. Because with all my earlier writing, he'd say, "That's too obscure." And, all my English teachers would drive me nuts: "This is too obscure. What do you mean?" And I wrote a lot of obscure stuff. The novel was mostly obscure, it was symbolist poetry, it was Rimbaud-like. I just want to be clear. Maybe part of going the other way is trying to fight all of those earlier tendencies, where I felt like I was totally irrelevant to the human race, and that I was totally obscure and confused.

(Breskin, 42)

In spite of success, new awareness, and additional writing opportunities in Hollywood as a result of *Midnight Express,* movement toward full control of his ideas—where he would be able to direct his own scripts—would be agonizingly slow. A directorial attempt in 1981 of his screenplay *The Hand* was meant to result in an imaginative psychological thriller involving the mental disintegration of a cartoonist after the dismemberment of his drawing hand. But according to Stone's assessment, so many people interfered with his script that he lost control of the project and the film came out a convoluted horror story that was panned by many critics.

Following *The Hand* and unable to secure backing for additional directing work, Stone sold his writing talents to big-name Hollywood directors with action-oriented projects that involved plotting ingredients he could write about with legitimacy and insight: violence, chaos, drugs, rage, death. Stone coscripted *Conan the Barbarian* with John Milius in 1982, wrote *Scarface* for Brian De Palma in 1983, *Year of the Dragon* for Michael Cimino in 1985, and *8 Million Ways to Die* for Hal Ashby in 1986. These films all generated considerable controversy and further established Stone's reputation as a bombastic blood-and-guts writer. They also led to charges of a right-wing vision bordering on fascism, charges Stone later tried to place in the lap of the films' directors.

Depressed by the way the Hollywood system worked and frustrated at seeing others put their visionary signature on his scripts, Stone stepped up his cocaine habit. For a brief time during this writing-for-others period in the early 1980s, he and his wife Elizabeth felt the urge to escape and moved to Paris.

In this time of restless frustration, Stone saw and took inspiration from Warren Beatty's *Reds* (1981). One of the things that had bothered him most about the Hollywood system had been the recognition of a correlation between the big-budget picture and conservatism, that is, the more money spent on a film, the less daring the ideas. *Reds*, Beatty's account of an American defector in Russia during and following the 1917 revolution, had impressed Stone because, although *Reds* was a big-budget ($36 million) effort, Beatty had dared to make a film with an unlikely protagonist. Stone admired the fact that Beatty had taken the risk because he believed in what he was doing, and this courage led Stone to the conclusion that "you have to make films as an idealist. You've got to make them for the greater glory of mankind. Then, even if you fail, even if the film doesn't work, you do not have to be ashamed, because you tried" (McGilligan, 60).

Having returned from Paris, Stone decided in 1984 to take a trip to Central America to find out for himself if reports were true that the situation there might be leading to another Vietnam. He was horrified at what he saw, especially in El Salvador, and between January and March 1985 developed a scenario for a film based on recent historical

events in the country and on the personal experiences of photojournalist Richard Boyle, who had been covering Central America and
who was Stone's "guide" when he went on his fact-finding mission.
The script also drew on political interpretations in Raymond Bonner's
book *Weakness and Deceit,* a study of the impact of U.S. policy on
events in El Salvador.

Filled with political controversy and populated with two less-than-
wholesome protagonists, the script was rejected by one Hollywood
studio after another. Eventually, in 1985, a fledgling British motion
picture production company, Hemdale, agreed to assist in financing
the film, which would be called simply *Salvador.* Stone and his wife,
by then parents of a baby boy, Sean, agreed that they would also invest all that they had in the project—looking to give Stone the opportunity he had been longing for: the chance to make films with a
difference and the freedom to make them his own way.

Shot in 50 days on a budget so small that production halted when
the money ran out, Stone experienced new invigoration in the making
of *Salvador,* and especially in the fact that in the end he was able to get
his bold political story to the screen. He was particularly proud of the
tone of the film, what he described as its "edge," its "madness," and
its "fury."

Rejected by major American distributors, *Salvador* when released in
1986 reached only a limited audience—a fact that Stone had anticipated
based on earlier reactions to his script as "anti-American." There was
also the complicating factor of videocassette rights, which Hemdale
did not wish to relinquish to another film company; Hemdale wound
up as the sole distributor of the picture, according to Stone handling
the task "badly and unimaginatively" on a limited marketing/distri-
bution budget.

Although *Salvador* died at the box office, impressed filmgoers and
critics (the numbers would grow with the film's release to the home
video market) admired the picture's liberal stance, its humanity in presenting the plight of oppressed people in El Salvador, and its courageous attempt at offering what some called a "bitter pill" of political
truths.

Most significantly, *Salvador* earned Stone the opportunity to make
Platoon—a film about his own Vietnam experiences. The first draft of
Platoon had been written in the summer of 1976, just after his first
wife had left him, and Stone had carried the script around with him
for 10 years.

Convinced of Stone's directorial and narrative capabilities, Hemdale agreed to financial backing ($6 million) of *Platoon*. Hemdale was willing to take its chances on the Vietnam story because, said the company's chairman, John Daly, *Salvador* had "crystallized the reality of war with pathos and passion and was a good indication of what Stone was capable of achieving."[6]

Platoon turned out to be a larger success, personally and financially, than anyone could possibly have imagined. The film ultimately grossed $250 million. Moreover, *Platoon* proved to be unlike any other Vietnam picture. Stone's seemingly choreographed camera had given terror to hostile space in such a way that the unorthodox nature of platoon combat in Vietnam was re-created in horrifying, subjective visualizations. As in *Salvador*, Stone had also exposed hidden realities of war in human terms, notably the internal conflicts and self-struggles that often found the Vietnam combat soldier fighting two wars—the one "out there" in the ambiguous spaces of the VC-ridden jungle, and the other one from within.

Platoon (shot on location in the Philippines) had proved—with autobiographical fervor and candor—the futility of the Vietnam experience as Stone saw it, perhaps purging some of the demons that had been haunting his mind and heart for a decade and a half. At the same time, critics claimed it had achieved universality in its personalization of the potential horrors of war. Some even argued that the film should be mandatory viewing for anyone considering service in the military.

Platoon had made clearer Stone's emerging cinematic style by which he could further stamp his films as those of his tailoring—a peripatetic, often subjectively oriented use of camera; a clear feel for relating popular music and lyrics to ideas and tone; a loud, upfront manner of "pointing" critical thematic details; a fondness for voice-over as a means to character introspection; a facility for quick-cut editing in conveying chaos and upheaval; a fondness for the intensifying big closeup, for the overhead bird's-eye shot, and for a hand-held camera to create immediacy and tension within an event.

Platoon's dramatic achievements led to eight Academy Award nominations—ultimately winning four, including Best Picture and Best Director of 1986.

After *Platoon*, Oliver Stone's importance as a director continued to grow, picture after picture. Detractors would label him a "radical," a "cause freak," a "sensationalist," "excessive" in his self-styled studies of the politics and counterculture of the 1960s. Yet his films managed time and again to generate excitement and to draw large, diverse audiences.

Following *Platoon* came a variety of works of differing subject matter and time periods, but all bearing familiar Stone trademarks. First there was *Wall Street* in 1987, a film that explored the greed-impelled world of American finance, and its challenge to a young man's personal morality. A subtheme of commitment to family *Wall Street*—revealed through a father-son relationship—again hinted at autobiographical reference.

While seemingly quite different from *Salvador* and *Platoon, Wall Street* was in fact ideologically connected to the earlier films. It revealed a young male protagonist being drawn deeply into an involvement with an American "system" of questionable merit: Wall Street trading. As with *Salvador* and *Platoon* the hero eventually becomes tainted and disillusioned by the experience but progresses toward self-knowledge of right and wrong.

Journalist Stephen Talbot, writing for *Mother Jones,* summarized the thematics that connected Stone's films in the following way: "Stone identifies closely with his protagonists, as they struggle with their personal demons torn between self-destruction and salvation. He doesn't have much to say about women. His films explore masculinity: the relationships between men in prison and in war, the conflicts between father and son. If there is a kind of typical Oliver Stone film, it involves a young man—naive, idealistic, patriotic—who undergoes a trial by fire, a rite of passage, that nearly kills him."[7]

An interest in the obsessive, self-destructive side of human nature attracted Stone to the project that followed *Wall Street,* a screen version of Eric Bogosian's one-man stage play, *Talk Radio* (1989). Bogosian's script, which he also performed, was a rhetorical exercise involving an outrageous broadcast "call-in" host who pushes his audience to the brink through cajoling personal and political confrontation, and who in the end is the victim of his own tactics.

Stone would concede that although he was coadapter of the script, *Talk Radio* in film form remained essentially the vision of Eric Bogosian: "I looked at it as more of a technical challenge. It was a bit of an exercise to stretch myself and to try new ways of shooting, working with a very small cast: severe discipline, six people and a limited set, like a submarine film or an elevator film. How to deal with a limited amount of space was very challenging to me after having worked larger canvases. It was like doing a chamber piece."

The adaptation of *Talk Radio* resulted in a microscopically intense screen experience—one clearly different from earlier Stone efforts, but one in which filmgoers and critics would still find in the unwholesome, loud-mouthed radio talk-show host a character of unsavory appeal not unlike that of photojournalist Richard Boyle's character in *Salvador* or the greed-driven Gordon Gekko character in *Wall Street* or perhaps Stone's own real-life persona. Although working in constrained space, Stone had been able to employ familiar cinematic techniques, including a constantly moving camera, bird's-eye-view shots, big closeups, and dynamic cutting.

Still seeking cathartic release from his Vietnam and post-Vietnam experiences, Stone returned after *Talk Radio* to more familiar territory with production of *Born on the Fourth of July*—a project that like *Platoon* had been set to partial script in the late 1970s. Based on the autobiography of Vietnam veteran Ron Kovic, who coauthored the screenplay, *Born on the Fourth of July* recounted Kovic's war traumas, which left him a paraplegic, and his postwar traumas, which resulted in bitter rage, psychological depression, and guilt—concluding with an emerging political consciousness and antiwar stance.

Born on the Fourth of July, the second film coscripted and released by Stone in 1989, constituted a feat Stone said nearly killed him, in part because of his emotional involvement with the material in *Born on the Fourth of July* as well as the epic proportions of the film's plot. The story spanned a 30-year time frame, incorporated 170 speaking characters, and called for the creation of historical facsimiles. Stone's compulsion to make this big film version of Kovic's life story grew from the fact that it took the *Platoon* idea of a patriotic young American man going through war's rites of passage in Vietnam and extended those rites to include the young man's experiences in returning and confronting—which *Platoon* had not done—what his country was going through, politically, back home.

As with all of Stone's films, *Born on the Fourth of July* earned praise for its director (Stone would again win a Best Director Academy Award) while generating considerable debate about its dramatic material and its politics. Many critics expressed admiration of the film's efforts to come to grips with the conflict at home over involvement in the Vietnam War, while others seemed turned off by the "simplistic" use of a paraplegic as a sympathy-evoking figure leading the call for antiwar political conversion.

Also, Stone was criticized for altering or inventing certain "facts" of Kovic's life—a charge heard earlier on the release of *Midnight Ex-*

press, Salvador, and *Platoon* and one Stone again would say was unfair because his films had been intended as artistic "approximations" of historical realities rather than documentary accounts.

With *Born on the Fourth of July,* there began to surface more frequently in critical discussions and interviews an awareness that Stone—accurate or inaccurate—was emerging as a director capable of powerful reinterpretations of recent American history—its politics and its social upheavals, especially the disillusionment of the young that led to the counterculture ferment of the late 1960s and early 1970s. Drugs, music, skepticism, suspicion of authority, and young heroes with emerging leftist political points of view and concluding pacifist stances were fast becoming the stuff of Oliver Stone's backward glances at historical realities.

Observers, aware of the ability of popular motion pictures to re-define history, began to challenge Stone for what they described as his "sixties sensibility" and, in *Mother Jones* writer Stephen Talbot's words, Stone's "alternative, populist vision of recent history." Talbot admitted to finding Stone's films "invigorating" in an industry of "conventional feel good placebos," yet went on to ask:

. . . the question for many of us who are equally skeptical about the government's official stories is how official are Stone's? He sometimes jeopardizes his own credibility when he reshapes the facts into a dramatic structure. . . . I get queasy when Stone says that he feels free to alter facts as long as he doesn't "violate the spirit" of a real event, just as I do when *Rambo* distorts the reality of the Vietnam conflict. If anything I get more upset with Stone, because he is a sixties person, like myself. He was there, an eyewitness, a participant, and as an insider who now has the rare opportunity to tell his stories—our generation's stories, our movement's stories in major Hollywood movies— Stone, I think, must be held to a higher standard of honesty and accuracy.

(Talbot, 49)

Charges to greater responsibility and accuracy in Stone's films were met by responses that were a variation on the old theme of personal challenge: Stone argued "I'm trying to reshape the world through movies" or "I'm trying to keep people from forgetting, trying to help them remember" or "I was trying to tap the American conscience." He defended against attacks on his films as exaggerated and excessive variations of history by arguing that as a film artist striving to make a difference, he had been careful to seek a balanced perspective in how he depicted the past. His obligation, he said, had been to show the "ugly," but also the "good" (Talbot, 49). Frequently he pointed to the last line delivered voice-over in *Platoon,* by the young soldier (Stone himself) played by Charlie Sheen: "Those of us who did make it have a duty to find a goodness and meaning to this life."

Stone had acted on the belief that the "cause" end was justification for the "dramatic" means, and he did so without feeling the necessity of apology. Similarly, he found no need to refute observations that his early screenplays and films possessed an essentially masculine orientation. He attributed this characteristic in part to the fact that he "never had a coeducational experience," having gone from an all-boys school almost immediately into the army, which resulted in more "all-boys" experiences. He confessed, however, to a great personal love of women and to an accompanying sexual desire that he said he could trace back to erotic fantasies that began when he was a child (Breskin, 38).

The reluctance to embrace women on the screen, or the tendency to use them only as sex objects, prostitutes, or "representative" figures, had been, according to Stone, the result of the film opportunities that came his way early on when writing for others or later when able to bring his own cathartic experiences to film—stories of men in prison, men caught up in drug wars and drug smuggling, men in Vietnam, the story of the "men's club" that is Wall Street.

When pushed on the treatment-of-women issue in a 1991 interview for *Rolling Stone,* Stone openly admitted a "failure in the writing" with regard to the female characters in *Wall Street,* who, he did not deny, emerged as little more than "commodities" (Breskin, 42).

This interview perhaps more than any other revealed Stone struggling to address criticisms of female characterizations. It showed him more intent on turning to discussions of his failed effort to make a film version in 1990 of *Evita,* of a future "possible film" with a central female protagonist, of his own adoration of women, and of the important "responses" a beautiful woman generates on the screen. The end effect of the interview was to leave the reader with the impression that Stone might very well have desired early in his career to make films with more proactive, independently motivated women characters, but at the time he was unable to articulate a vision for women in film that did not sound object-oriented.

Stone's success in making motion pictures in which the men were powerful and the women served a one-dimensional purpose corroborated intimations that Stone's masculine sensibilities resulted from deep-seated psychological ties to his father and to the fact that Lou Stone had chastised his son for dropping out of college, going to Vietnam as a soldier, and returning, in Oliver Stone's own words, a drug-ridden, uneducated "bum." The elder Stone (who died in 1985, before *Salvador* or *Platoon*) reportedly never recognized his son's experience as a Vietnam soldier as valid. This refusal remained a painful gesture because, according to those closest to him, Oliver Stone had gone to Vietnam partly to prove himself to his father, a World War II veteran.

It seemed to those on the inside no minor symbolic act that Stone made back to back in 1986 and 1987 *Platoon* and *Wall Street,* the latter dedicated to his dead father. The enormous male energy in these films—one centered on a naive young soldier who had gone to Vietnam because his grandfather and father had fought in World Wars I and II and it seemed "the right thing to do," and the other centered on a naive young man discovering the perils of Wall Street and being saved from his "sins" by an idealistic father—could be seen as artistic angst resulting from father-son competition and from the agonies of a prodigal-son-turned-film-director whose "homecoming" was being sought through the artifice of motion pictures. Charlie Sheen had been selected by Stone to play the naive hero in both *Platoon* and *Wall Street,* a gesture reinforcing the interpretation that the films were essentially about the same character—Oliver Stone's alter ego—being nagged on by a distant father. In an apparent effort to reconcile family differences before he died, the elder Stone had lauded his son's decision to go into filmmaking, seeing it as a good business decision because of the expanding home entertainment market.

Stone's wife Elizabeth often spoke of her husband's "father complex" with regard to *Platoon* and also as part of the impulse behind *The Doors,* the 1991 film written and directed by Stone and based on the music and self-destructive life of 1960s rock legend Jim Morrison.

According to Elizabeth Stone, Morrison, his band The Doors, and their music had meant a great deal to her husband for a number of reasons: "The music of 'The Doors' gave him a contact with the outside world while he was in Vietnam and when he came home he really got into Jim as a person and related strongly to him. They were both poets, both rebelled against their strict fathers—[Morrison's] father was an admiral—and against the suburban life of the Sixties. Oliver saw himself as very much of a rebel" (Miller, 20–21).

Stone frequently referred to Morrison while working on *The Doors* project as "almost an older brother to me," perhaps having seen the rock singer in time as the "conversant" sibling he had longed for as a child. Also, Stone viewed Morrison as a 1960s mythical hero and was fascinated by the singer's self-destructive personality. The combination—the "1960s thing" and a driven, rebellious, self-destructive character—would compel Stone to complete *The Doors* no matter what. His determination was similar to that which would not allow him to give up on his Vietnam films:—the desire to tell the story of someone "who stood for something at a special time in our culture" before he was forgotten forever.

Financed at a big-budget cost of $30 million, *The Doors* followed Morrison's life as a young college-age man on the West Coast (the scenario incorporating evocative flashbacks of a painful childhood memory) up to his death in 1971 in a bathtub in Paris at age 27. Once again, it was a project that called for a broad, demanding dramatic canvas. Interpreting Jim Morrison, clearly Stone's most unsavory and complex screen character to date, would be the film's monumental challenge: creating Morrison's often drug-crazed, anarchistic music performances; visualizing the singer's psychedelic, acid-generated fantasies; making sense of the personal relationships of a man often cruel, someone intellectually and philosophically inclined, haunted by demons, devoid of moral compunction, paranoid, willing to experiment with anything unorthodox, erotic, or destructive. *The Doors* involved heavy, "black" material.

Stone met the challenge with expected aplomb, providing filmgoers with an experience in *The Doors* that was more bombastic, furied, and dynamically charged than anything seen from the director before. As in *Born on the Fourth of July,* Stone rendered—in cinema-verité style—facsimiles that possessed the look and feel of the evolved counterculture world of the 1960s: hippiedom, flower children "living free" on the streets of Haight Ashbury, joints, nudity, cops, the rock concert with its worshiping fans. Stone's facsimile effect was achieved with hand-held camera, overexposed images, and a screen format reduced to look like the less professional, more "innocent" 8- and 16mm film gauges. Short abrupt runs of the camera added spontaneity and a "being there" effect to the evocations.

In another attempt at authenticity, landmark scenes depicting Morrison's professional and personal life introduced, sometimes eerily and surreally, look-alikes for such famous personages as television host Ed

Sullivan and pop artist Andy Warhol, accompanied by familiar members of Warhol's entourage. These scenes assisted Stone in his intended goal of reevoking Morrison and the time and culture in which he lived—not just the counterculture but the mass- and pop-celebrity subcultures the era also embraced.

The Doors was filmed in Los Angeles, New York, and Paris in little more than two months' time on a shooting schedule requiring an unusual amount of night filming. This achievement as much as the film's dramatic accomplishments provided testimony for Stone's strengths as a film director who could be both a determined visionary and an efficient engineer of his craft. This fact had for the most part been overlooked in the rush to deconstruct Stone's films and to discover the relationship of the man to his work. From the completion of *Salvador,* a film with epic qualities made on a shoestring budget, Stone consistently proved himself a director capable of getting the job done. His films revealed a craftsman who could elicit superior acting from his performers in major or minor roles, inspiring fine actors to even greater heights: James Woods in *Salvador,* Tom Berenger in *Platoon,* Martin Sheen and Michael Douglas in *Wall Street,* Tom Cruise in *Born on the Fourth of July,* Val Kilmer in *The Doors.* Producer Ed Pressman spoke of Stone: "To me a great director has to have two important traits—intelligence and an ability to inspire. Oliver has both in spades. People working with him realize something significant is going on, that it's not just another job" (Miller, 21).

Stone had also shown over the years that he not only was drawn to stories about dark exotic environments but had the ability to bring them to credible realization before his camera, whether recreating the body-ridden streets of El Salvador, the insect-infested jungles of Vietnam, or a marijuana-filled arena housing a 1960s rock concert.

Another of Stone's emerging gifts as a director was apparent in his ability to handle crowd scenes and epic details with unusual skill. The assassination of Archbishop Romero and the panic brought on by his in-cathedral killing in *Salvador* offered a near-classic illustration of Stone's capability for re-creating historical incidents in the presence of fictional characters. Arguably, the Romero assassination was as masterful and electrifying as D. W. Griffith's precise re-creation of Abraham Lincoln's assassination in Ford's Theater for *The Birth of a Nation* (with Lillian Gish as Elsie Stoneman present as a theatergoing witness to the historic incident).

Stone's eye for crowd scenes showed itself to be impressively varied in effect. The VC ambush in *Platoon* had captured with primitive fury both the confusion and the horror of guerilla warfare; the ethereal Fourth of July parades in *Born on the Fourth of July*—filmed in alternating natural and slow motion—conjured up memories of an innocent past; and the rock concert performances in New Haven, Tallahassee, and Paris in *The Doors* depicted crowd mentality in chaotic sync with a deranged performer.

Also, more than any other of his contemporaries, Stone had brought the camera into his films in powerful ways, using it as if it were another character in order to give his stories an extra dimension. He described this special aspect of his work as near intuitive, telling *Rolling Stone* interviewer David Breskin: "I walk on the set—I don't know why—and I see the actor, I see the camera, and I see myself. I see a triangle. So that the camera, although inanimate, is as much a human participant as I am. It's an interesting relationship. So often the camera will speak to me on the day and say: 'No, this. That.' And it will become clear to me. . . . The camera is different in each scene. The camera has an eerie kind of power" (Breskin, 43).

There was, too, the achievement of having been able to direct scripts that he himself had authored, adapted, or coscripted. Except for Woody Allen and a rare few others, the standard operating procedure in American filmmaking had been to use separate writers and directors on a film project, in the belief that an "objective" director brought to the scripted material a critical second voice. Stone had managed writing-directing responsibilities with surprising ease, perhaps due in no small part to his passion for the protagonists he had chosen to write about and to an urgency to get the story told at all costs, out of fear that otherwise it might never get told.

From *Salvador* to *The Doors* barely five years had elapsed, yet Oliver Stone's films had created international interest and acclaim and had brought 18 Academy Award nominations spread among only four films. On the release of *The Doors,* Hemdale executive John Daly said: "If Oliver Stone believes in something, he is unstoppable. He has a single-minded passion."[9]

Even before *The Doors*'s release, Stone had begun to discuss his next project, which he recognized as equally controversial and outside the mainstream of American filmmaking: *JFK.* Long fascinated by Lee Harvey Oswald, the John F. Kennedy assassination, and the Warren

Commission findings, Stone had been collecting material and buying screen rights to books on the subject.

He had come to the conclusion that the Warren Commission had not told the true story, believing instead that a conspiracy was behind the shooting of Kennedy. Stone's approach in *JFK,* he told reporters, would be "*Rashomon*-like"—referring to Akira Kurosawa's 1951 film, which had recounted incidents of a crime from the subjective perspectives of four witnesses, each altering details for face-saving reasons. The central figure in *JFK,* another maverick protagonist of sorts, was New Orleans district attorney Jim Garrison (Kevin Costner).

Production and postproduction of *JFK* was accompanied by an unusual amount of controversy and skepticism, not only by the people of Dallas and New Orleans, where Stone went to film, but from within film and political/historical circles as well. Was Stone now openly, brashly—even exploitatively—giving the finger to so-called official U.S. history? Was he recklessly pushing his luck too far in dealing with controversial historical material from the 1960s?

The prerelease controversy upset Stone, who saw in the furor a plot to kill his film before it got into distribution. Some unadoring critics had in fact urged that *JFK* be boycotted, claiming that Stone had gone far enough already in distorting facts and in making films that "undermined confidence" in America's institutions.

In response, Stone told *Esquire* writer Robert Sam Anson: "There's an agenda here. . . . [Those who challenge me are] controlled in certain ways. . . . Let's not be naive. . . . This controversy is meant to kill off the film, precensor it and maximize negative advance impact. . . . What this indicates is that they are scared. When it comes to President Kennedy's murder, they don't want to open the doors. They don't want the first inch of inquiry to go on."[10]

The Kennedy assassination in 1963 had meant a certain loss of idealism for Stone, but his interest in a film inquiry into the killing did not come until 1988, after he read Jim Garrison's book *On the Trail of Assassins.* The book was an account of Garrison's efforts to convict Clay Shaw, a New Orleans businessman, for conspiracy in Kennedy's assassination. The conspiracy plot had supposedly come on a tip to Garrison after a fight in a New Orleans bar on the night of the assassination that involved, according to the book, an assortment of figures who were extreme right-wingers and Kennedy-Communist-Cuban haters—some alleged to be acquainted with Lee Harvey Oswald. Garrison's work reconstructed details of the conspiracy, profiles of the principal figures, and his own "undermined" attempt to prosecute and convict Shaw.

Stone paid Garrison $250,000 for screen rights to the book, fully convinced that the story of a lone, diligent gumshoe district attorney on a trail that widens and widens "until it's no longer a small-town affair," held the substance of a powerful movie. According to those who followed the development of *JFK,* Stone was undeterred by knowledge of Garrison's less-than-pristine past, including run-ins with the law and ongoing psychiatric therapy. Prototypically, Garrison was seen by Stone as a hero who faces "certain extinction, surrounded on all sides by enemy swordsmen, but, by some shining light of inner force and greater love, turns the tables of fate and triumphs over all odds" (Anson, 97).

The script for *JFK* drew from a large number of published works that had examined with skepticism the Warren Commission findings. Details were gleaned that seemed to prove, logistically, that Lee Harvey Oswald could not have acted alone, as were details that, given events of the last several years of Oswald's life, offered possible explanations for the why and how behind the alleged conspiracy plot. Used extensively as a source of additional details on the assassination was the book *Crossfire: The Plot That Killed Kennedy,* by Jim Marrs. Zachary Sklar, a New York literary editor who had assisted Garrison with his book, coscripted *JFK* with Stone.

Financed with the assistance of $40 million from Warner Brothers, *JFK* challenged to the limits Stone's proven abilities for making big, broad-canvas films. The script was huge, the plot complex; there were nearly a dozen principal players, more than 200 speaking roles; and the pressure for visual accuracy in reconstructing details of perhaps the most familiar incident of notoriety in twentieth-century American history was enormous.

From start to release, the project took one full year of nonstop work—an experience that, with all its investment of time, money, and controversy, would bring Stone to comment: "When you make a movie like this, and you get attacked from all sides, sometimes you don't win. Sometimes you fail. But it is well worth it if you lost in an honorable cause. Pancho Villa, I always think of what he said: 'The defeats are also battles'" (Anson, 97).

The multiangled, *Rashomon*-inspired approach to the Kennedy assassination in *JFK* presented the killing (and alleged conspiracy) from three points of view: Jim Garrison's, Lee Harvey Oswald's, and a collective point of view that saw the assassination as the military-industrial complex's efforts to keep the Vietnam War going for profiteering purposes. Not surprisingly, this latter thesis alone led to a storm of controversy and debate when *JFK* opened in theaters in late December 1991.

Stone defended *JFK* in a way that echoed the feelings he had had for Warren Beatty's *Reds* a decade earlier and the development at that time of an idealist's philosophy of filmmaking that argues if you make films you believe in and they don't work, you don't have to be ashamed. In that sense, Stone offered *JFK* without apology and remained consistent, undaunted, in his avowed goal of making motion pictures intended to reshape the world.

2

Early Efforts: *Seizure, Midnight Express, The Hand*

Although it will not be appreciated by more than a handful of admirers, *Seizure* is nonetheless a film worth watching. And worthy of some attention also is the future of its young creator, Oliver Stone.

—Steve VerHieb, *Black Oracle,* Fall 1975

SEIZURE

Oliver Stone described his first, rather obscure writing-directing effort, *Seizure* (1974), as important training-ground experience. It provided him with opportunities for learning the craft of directing and for testing the "playing" capabilities of his own screen material. The film was an extremely low-budget project ($150,000), pulled together in 1973 by Stone not long after his graduation from NYU's film school. The script called for a fairly small cast, and the action occurred in a single, cost-saving setting. The venture became a family affair of sorts, with Stone's first wife, Najwa, serving as the film's art director.

The project revealed Stone at this time as a still-emerging writer-director who exhibited very different interests from those which would later become the focus of his work. As an imaginative psychological thriller, *Seizure* was essentially devoid of political intrigue. It brought forcefully into play on the screen the mental anguish of a creative artist being driven toward an uncertain end by forces outside his control. The effect was that of a painful nightmare, as reality sank further and further into obfuscation for the terrified protagonist.

Synopsis of *Seizure* (1974)

Cast: Jonathan Frid, Martine Beswick, Joe Sirola, Christina Pickles, Roger de Koven, Mary Woronov, Herve Villechaize, Richard Cox, Henry Baker, Timothy Ousey, Lucy Bingham, Alexis Kirk, Emil Meola.

Credits: Director: Oliver Stone. Producer: Garrard Glenn and Jeffrey Kapelmann. Screenplay: Edward Mann and Oliver Stone, based on a story by Stone. Photography: Roger Racine. Art direction: Najwa Stone. Music: Lee Gagnon. A Euro-American production.

The plot of *Seizure* involves an author (whose horror fiction has been likened to that of Edgar Allan Poe), his wife, son, and five weekend houseguests. In a nutshell, the assembled group is terrorized by a trio of unexpected and bizarre evildoers who announce their intentions of eliminating the household one after another until only one survives. The evil trio consists of the Queen of Evil (Martine Beswick), a sadistic dwarf known as The Spider (Herve Villechaize), and a half-faced black executioner (Henry Baker). A radio announcement heard by the houseguests suggests that the three may be escapees from an insane asylum and former members of a violence-prone, Charles Manson–like gang.

Complicating the plot and adding to its intrigue is the question of whether the terror is real or is the result of the author-illustrator's imagination, aggravated by a bout of recurring nightmares. The three evil figures have been the source of the author's dreams, and he has decided to make them the subjects of the book he is currently working on. He has gone so far as to sketch their images onto his illustration pad.

The film opens with the author, Edmund Blackstone (Jonathan Frid), awakening on the day of his houseguests' arrival and telling his wife (Christina Pickles), dejectedly, "I had the dream again. . . . Same one, same way." Later in the day, Blackstone discovers the family dog hanging from a noose on a tree in the woods of his estate grounds. He becomes perplexed and deeply concerned. At the evening dinner—a contentious affair—Blackstone sees the face of The Spider peering through the dining room window. Later, as he puts his son Jason (Timothy Ousey) to bed, he is asked: "Are you scared? You look scared." The author replies: "I'm scared of something inside me." Still later, the boy tells his mother: "I'm scared of Daddy."

For its initial intrigue *Seizure* continues to set up in careful detail the idea of a creative imagination gotten out of hand. The author, in obvious torment, talks at length to one of the houseguests, the refined Serge (Roger de Koven), and tells him of a dream in which he has seen the entire weekend, the appearance of three "frightening" strangers, and the face of The Spider from one of his illustrations suddenly visible in the dining room window. He says of the face: "I drew it myself before I ever saw it."

The "Is this a dream?" seed has been planted. Stone's film then begins to chart the doing-away-with of the guests by the evil trio, starting with the selfish, self-adoring Eunice (Anne Meacham), whose demise comes through a facial ointment given to her by the dwarf with the promise it will bring eternal youth. Disfigured by the ointment, she commits suicide by leaping from her bedroom window. Betsy, the Blackstones' maid, is murdered on her way home by the executioner. The deaths of Mark (Troy Donahue) and Gerald (Richard Cox) follow. Mark is killed by the Queen of Evil after lovemaking, and Gerald is accidentally shot to death by Edmund during a heated argument that occurs after discovery of the three uninvited "guests."

It is at this point that *Seizure* moves the mystery into philosophical territory by developing a game of death and a pronouncement that only one of those remaining within the house will live until dawn. The Queen of Evil, on announcing the game, says of herself and her two partners: "We are without beginning or end, and our purpose, our only purpose, is death."

The game—an "escape" pretense—is one of physical endurance, a race in the garden wherein the last one to cross the finish line is to die. The dwarf disavows belief in God and therefore rules out any chances of assistance for the participants in the game, other than that provided by the strength in the players' arms and legs. The arrogant and wealthy Charlie (Joe Sirola) loses the race and is executed. Charlie's wife, Mikkie (Mary Woronov), attempts to escape by killing Edmund, but loses the fight and dies.

The plot advances, with the script becoming more verbal and philosophical as the characters react to the terror of death. The wise Serge, oldest of the lot, attempts to explain the trio in mythical and legendary terms, and labels Blackstone the Faust who created "these perpetrators of evil." He urges that they accept their fate: "With all our civilization we must learn to accept that nature holds no special account of our disasters." Serge later tells his host, in what are the film's most optimistic dialogue passages, that his belief in and fear of God, and his own belief in himself, have made death "a companion, not an enemy, to life." He goes willingly to his execution.

For the perplexed Blackstone, host to this weekend of horror and death, the final crisis becomes one of deciding whether to save himself or to sacrifice his life for that of his young son Jason. In the tense, final hours before dawn, the author's wife turns sour and blames what is happening on her husband's intellectual fantasies. She accuses him of inviting the wicked trio "here to destroy me, them, Jason, and finally yourself." She pleads only that her son Jason be spared, then commits suicide-by-razor-blade in the bathroom.

Seizure concludes with an unexpected twist. Blackstone, with his son now the only other person alive, is confronted by the Queen of Evil. She asks for the whereabouts of the child, tempting the author with accounts of the pleasure daylight will bring to him if he chooses his life over his son's. Suddenly believing that it is all a dream and arguing that as an artist-writer he can start over again, Blackstone proclaims that an artist is "without end," "can never die," "is not allowed to die." In this inspired moment of belief in creative immortality, the boy's hiding spot in the upstairs attic is blurted out.

When Blackstone's son is apprehended, the dead wife's ghost intervenes to save the child. Imagining himself being strangled, Blackstone wakens from a nightmare, saying, "I had the dream again. Clearer than ever. It's over." He discovers that the person next to him in bed is not his wife but the Queen of Evil.

An unexpected second climax occurs. Nicole Blackstone sends her son Jason to waken the sleeping author before their guests arrive. The boy goes to his father's room and calls "Daddy." A radio news report follows, announcing the death of the prominent author. The son Jason, the report says, has discovered his father dead of a heart attack at age 47.

Critics had mixed reactions to *Seizure*. Admiration was expressed for Stone's efforts to create a horror film that moved beyond mere theatrics and offered points of rumination on the meaning of life in the face of terror and death. At the same time, criticism was leveled at the philosophizing script for having gone on too long and for bordering on pretentiousness.

On the plus side, there was praise for Stone's casting and for the actors' competence and intensity in working through the script's bizarre turn of events. In spite of a minuscule budget, the cast had been assembled from the well-known and the not-so-well-known: Jonathan Frid, Blackstone, had appeared as Barnabas Collins on television's highly successful "Dark Shadows"; Troy Donahue, Mark, was a former movie matinee idol; the role of The Spider was played by Herve Villechaize (*The Man with the Golden Gun,* 1974); and Mary Woronov, Mikki, had been a staple in Andy Warhol's repertoire of film actors. One reviewer called the cast "for the most part interesting and involving rather than the stock bunch of zombies who usually turn up in these things."[1]

Technically, *Seizure* was rather standard mystery/thriller fare. With little outlay for special effects, Stone depended heavily on quick-cut, obscured visual inserts—shadowy footsteps in the woods, silhouetted figures running in the dark, repeated visualizations of a hanged dog. Low-key lighting schemes predominated in both interior and exterior scenes for the purposes of emphasizing the film's desired eeriness and facilitating the sudden appearance of a menacing character.

In what would eventually be recognized as a familiar Oliver Stone soundtrack convention, tense scenes were accompanied by music that incorporated into the composition the muffled, heartbeatlike sound of a drum. The music quickened and grew louder to key a scene's pace and intensity. The death-race game, for example, contrived by the evil trio for the writer's houseguests, found its primeval, *Lottery*-like qualities in Stone's use of the musical drumbeat effect. The technique (the work of composer Lee Gagnon) was repeated in later scenes, and became one of the film's most useful and effective dramatic devices.

Limited by budget and time, cinematographer Roger Racine managed his camera in ways that put the story onto film efficiently and still offered some visual dynamism in crucial scenes. Moving camera dollies would sometimes take the viewer into the heart of a scene (Eunice before her mirror, longing for her former husband), and a hand-held camera would give frenzied spontaneity to scenes of terror (the heated fight scene in the guest house living room). The pronouncement of doom by the Queen of Evil to houseguests was conveyed in extreme closeups that detailed the lips and eyes of the stunned characters. All these devices—the moving camera, spontaneous hand-held shots, and fragmenting, big closeups—would be carried by Stone to future films.

The script for *Seizure,* cowritten with Edward Mann, presented a variety of intriguing (albeit limited and cursory) points of departure with regard to critical assessment. It was possible to label the film, as most reviewers did, simply as decent double-feature fare or as a standard psychological thriller with an imaginative twist. Vincent Canby offered Stone's picture a four-sentence appraisal in a collective film review titled "Who Says They Don't Make B Movies?" Canby described *Seizure* as a "typical" B picture with "enough gore to keep a 42nd Street audience polite."[2]

Beyond the modest, low-budget genre pleasures of *Seizure,* there resided in the script the Faustian side of the effort—projected through the unrelenting torment of the writer-protagonist, who in the end elects to maintain his power as a creative artist rather than give his life for his son's. In one of his philosophical monologues, Serge had referred to Blackstone as "Faust." The wife's charges against her husband of self-centered power control through "intellectual fantasies" further conveyed the Faustian idea in a more personal way, and the sacrificing of the son rendered the idea in classic fashion.

Just how dramatically effective or structurally sound this subtheme was remained a central question of script credibility. The superimposition of the concept onto a horror film could easily be seen as a pretentious and unnecessary tag-on to a plot already laboring in an excess of weighted verbiage. It could also be argued that the Faust twist, combined with the immediate follow-up revelation of the heart attack death of the protagonist, had created an anticlimax and revealed the script's authors as tentative in bringing their film to satisfactory resolution.

Clearly better integrated into the plot of *Seizure* was the morality subtheme involving the assortment of characters who made up the weekend houseguest list. An intriguing house-of-fools approach emerged as the guests arrived for the weekend and their characters were revealed: arrogant, obnoxious tycoon; playboy; vain, selfish woman; failed, down-and-out businessman; cheating wife; aging sage. The houseguests, save the philosophical Serge, are depicted as tainted and possessed with individual self-interests that have left them ill prepared to go to their ultimate fate—death. That they assemble in one place to meet their fate offered a classic narrative ploy.

Critic Tim Lucas lauded Stone's use of a single, contained setting— the Blackstone home—as an unexpected arena of group challenge:

In *Seizure,* Stone follows the lead of Sam Peckinpah and George Romero in his use of the Blackstone cottage as a barrier, but one that is most easily broken by the forces of evil. It was Peckinpah who illustrated in *Straw Dogs* that a home is not an invulnerably religious symbol of security. Romero did likewise in *Night of the Living Dead,* emphasizing the helplessness of his characters in the grip of an all-pervading horror. Terror becomes a reality only after becoming a possibility. Stone is a valuable find because he removes safety yet a further step away. The horror of *Seizure* is one of severe, curt irrationality: a sense of fear made unrealistic through the eyes of hysteria.[3]

Death is presented in *Seizure* in such a way that it becomes more than the end result of terrorizing evil. It is posited—collectively and individually—as a final act of one's life that, the script says, might hold "answers" regarding the nature of that life or might, as the Queen of Evil suggests, be "meaningless." Serge, with his belief in God, a God who he says is both "good and evil," willingly and fearlessly accepts his death as if "an engagement to keep." By contrast, Blackstone refuses to acknowledge as valid Serge's advocacy of faith in God, interpreting the old man's professions as merely "an illusion to pave [the] way to ashes and dust."

These loftier moments of *Seizure* can be appreciated for what they represent in terms of Stone's formative experience as a writer-director. They reveal a young, untried artist working within a familiar genre but with an eye turned to myth and to issues of personal morality centered on the universal theme of death. At the same time, *Seizure* can be faulted for excessive philosophical ramblings, which, in the context of a psychological thriller, often become muddled and distracting.

Logistically, *Seizure* showed Stone admirably adept in directing a first feature-length motion picture at so young an age (27) and with the experience of only three short 16mm projects behind him at NYU. His lack of intimidation by a seasoned professional cast and his ability to inspire performances—which in their sincerity lifted a modest script above its limitations—surely helped convince Stone of his potential as a director looking forward to other and better films.

MIDNIGHT EXPRESS

In 1976, two years after the release of *Seizure,* Stone left New York, where he had been holed up writing additional screenplays, and moved to Hollywood. He said he did so because that's where the factory was, and he hoped that one of his scripts would catch a producer's eye and that he would again have a chance at directing.

In New York, Stone had become acquainted with the playwright Robert Bolt *(A Man for All Seasons),* who helped him secure an agent. The agent showed Stone's work around Hollywood and, while unsuccessful in striking a deal with a studio for production of one of his client's screenplays, got Stone the job of adapting a best-selling autobiography, *Midnight Express.* Columbia Pictures was sponsoring the project.

Midnight Express was a terrifying account of life in a Turkish prison for a young American student, Billy Hayes, who was arrested for possession of 2.2 kilos of hashish at the Istanbul Airport on 6 October

Billy Hayes (Brad Davis) just after capture in *Midnight Express* (1978). Courtesy The Museum of Modern Art/Film Stills Archive.

1970. Turkish authorities originally sentenced Hayes to a prison term of 4½ years on the charge of possession. Two months before completion of the term, Hayes was retried and convicted of a new charge of smuggling. The young student this time was handed a 30-year prison sentence.

Hayes's book (coauthored with William Hoffer) recounted in visceral detail his arrest, trials, legal maneuvers, treatment by prison guards, and ultimate escape through Greece to freedom in October 1975. The book's title came from the prisoners' code words for an act of escape, that is, "taking the 'Midnight Express.' " Hayes said he wrote of his experiences as a means of calling attention to Turkey's brutal penal system and its unjust penalties. He hoped his efforts would assist other Americans still incarcerated in foreign prisons for drug smuggling—at the time estimated to be around 300.

Stone's screen adaptation played up the more violent aspects of Hayes's story, while also altering some incidents and inventing others for a dramatically streamlined account of the alleged inhumanity that forced the young American's escape. The script was essentially bereft of any evidence of sympathy or justice on the part of Turkish officials. Hayes was drawn as a character stripped of civil and human rights, and someone subjected to all sorts of physical, psychological, and sexual atrocities. The tone of the screenplay was grim and the ultimate dramatic effect that of sadistic entrapment by subhuman forces.

Stone wrote his first draft of *Midnight Express* in six weeks, then was joined by Alan Parker, assigned by Columbia as the film's director, who sat down with Stone and, page by page, went through the draft until the two had achieved a shooting script that in no way, Parker said, had "compromised the integrity of the book."[4]

Both Parker and Stone had undertaken the *Midnight Express* project with conviction; they strongly believed in their approach. Parker said that he had every intention of making a very violent, uncompromisingly brutal film after reading the book and realizing it was a true story of "man's inhumanity to man." Having previously directed only the innocently childlike, G-rated musical film *Bugsy Malone* (1976), Parked looked to the *Midnight Express* material as documentarylike, with possibilities for "a bizarre theatrical edge," saying: "I would like the audience to be shaken and shocked that such things happen almost to the point of disbelief—but never to lose them."[5]

Stone supported the Parker vision as a collaborator, fully willing and able to turn *Midnight Express* into a dramatically brutal but heroic plea for penal reform and justice for Americans in alien cultures. It became, significantly, Stone's first produced screenplay written with the essence of "cause" behind it. And in using highly telescoped visceral incidents to convey politically potent ideas, Stone was discovering in the *Midnight Express* experience the loud, disarming method for provoking larger issues that would eventually typify his most memorable and controversial work.

For these reasons, *Midnight Express* stands out, arguably, as the script that launched the unique Stone vision of screenwriting/filmmaking "with a difference." Highly praised, sometimes condemned, enormously controversial, financially successful beyond expectations, *Midnight Express* signaled an important moment of emergence for Oliver Stone.

No other film of the 1970s (not even Michael Cimino's highly controversial Vietnam metaphor *The Deer Hunter,* 1978) generated the

---

Synopsis of *Midnight Express* (1978)

Cast: Brad Davis, Irene Miracle, Bo Hopkins, Paolo Bonacelli, Paul Smith, Randy Quaid, Norbert Wiesser, John Hurt, Mike Kellin, Franco Diogene, Michael Ensign, Peter Jeffrey.

Credits: Director: Alan Parker. Producers: Alan Marshall and David Puttman. Screenplay: Oliver Stone, based on the book by William Hayes with William Hoffer. Cinematography: Michael Seresin. Music: Giorgio Moroder. Columbia Pictures Release.

Plotting details in the opening sequence of *Midnight Express* are developed swiftly and deftly. A young American student Billy Hayes (Brad Davis) prepares to leave Istanbul on a night flight with his girlfriend, Susan (Irene Miracle). In Istanbul's Yesilkoy International Airport, he hyperventilates in the washroom, splashing water on his face, taking deep breaths—obviously terrified that he has hashish wrapped in tinfoil packets on a belt strapped to his waist for smuggling out of the country.

Outside the toilet, Turkish authorities examine Hayes's belongings, focusing their curiosity on a Frisbee™ carried in the student's hand luggage. The detail is used to point up the culturally different worlds of the Americans and their hosts. A transport van carries the couple and other passengers to their plane, which stands on a lighted area of the airfield. Approaching the portable stairs to the plane, Hayes is motioned aside by Turkish enforcement authorities, who search him and discover the drug belt. Hayes is suddenly surrounded by security police with drawn guns, and is arrested. He is led away as his distraught girlfriend enters the plane.

This swift, economic flow of details propels the plot forward in a way that efficiently signals the unrelenting, nightmarish pace of the film as a whole. In the ensuing interrogation scene, the officials speak in Turkish, adding further to the effect of a sudden, terrifying isolation in an unknown and culturally different world. At first Hayes is led to believe that if he cooperates with Turkish officials in their efforts to fight the drug trade, he will be on his way home. An early attempted escape during efforts to locate the cabdriver who sold him hashish lands Hayes in a rathole cell in Istanbul's bleak Sagmalcilar Prison.

From here on, Billy Hayes's story is presented like a nonstop rollercoaster ride, taking the young prisoner on an up-and-down journey through a heart of darkness fraught with every imaginable horror and every possible setback. The frustration reaches a peak with the unexpected change of sentence from 4½ to 30 years.

Stone's script alternates the action between accounts of Hayes's frustrating legal setbacks and his developing personal relationships with prison guards and other inmates. Central to the personal side of Hayes's prison life is interaction with a psychopathically inclined American inmate (Randy Quaid), a drug-addicted British prisoner (John Hurt), and a sensitive Swede (Norbert Wiesser) who attempts a homosexual alliance with Hayes and who has himself been convicted of hashish possession. The villainous figures created to depict life in the prison at its worst are Rifki (Paolo Bonacelli), a sleazy fellow-prisoner-turned-informer (who prevents Hayes's second attempt at escape), and Hamidou (Paul Smith), a sadistic, sodomizing head prison guard.

Other characters central to the plot are Hayes's father (Mike Kellin), who is dejected by his helplessness in finding the clout needed to free his son, and Susan, Hayes's girlfriend, who returns to Istanbul, bringing bribe money hidden in a family scrapbook, and who lends herself to one of the script's most wrenching moments, in which Hayes—crying pathetically—masturbates as he looks at the woman through the glass barricade that separates them.

Hayes's escape is plotted by Stone to occur when Hamidou, the sadistic head guard, is lured with the bribe money to a private room. Attempting to sodomize Hayes, the guard is pushed violently away and accidentally killed when the thrust backward impales his head on a metal wall stake. Hayes dresses in the dead guard's uniform and manages to exit the prison, tensely slipping by other guards in his Turkish disguise until he is in the streets of Istanbul. He begins to run. A montage of kinestatic black-and-white images depicts Hayes being reunited with his girlfriend, Susan, and members of his family back in New York.

kind of uproar that accompanied the release of *Midnight Express*. First screened on 18 May 1978 at the Cannes Film Festival as a British entry (Parker and his crew were British), the film caused an instant furor while winning considerable praise. The Cannes festival had had a long-standing policy of not screening films that might offend the "political sensitivities" of a particular country. Many argued that *Midnight Express,* in its one-sided attack on the Turkish penal system, had done just that.

Shortly after the Cannes showing, a statement of protest was released worldwide by the Turkish Ministry of Foreign Affairs. The document asked that other countries deny exhibition rights to the film.

Most likely because of continuing controversy and efforts to have the film banned, *Midnight Express* played to record attendance in the Netherlands, England, France, and Finland before opening in the United States in mid-October 1978. U.S. audiences and critics alike were openly stunned by the hellish tone of the film and its blood-and-gore rendering of prison details. Some filmgoers were invariably reported to have walked out early rather than to continue to subject themselves to the brutality on the screen.

Much attention was paid to Stone's script and to the way it had been ingeniously "calculated" to build sympathy for Hayes, especially the liberties taken in altering the facts of Hayes's book so that they worked to draw audiences more deeply into an identification with the protagonist.

Beginning with the film's tense opening sequence—concluding with Hayes's arrest—key changes were made. In the book Hayes is naively confident in the Istanbul Airport—he does not hyperventilate in fear of possible capture—and is caught by guards who are on the lookout for possible hijackers, not drug smugglers. The alterations, combined with the use of untranslated Turkish dialogue spoken by the airport guards, create the impression of a frightened young American being pounced on by lurching, sinister figures—not a foolish and brash young student being accidentally caught in the process of a serious illegal act. Stone's reworking stirred sympathy.

Other facts were altered to build a more heroic persona for the Hayes character. In the course of Stone's script, Hayes is depicted wreaking revenge on the informer Rifki by biting out the man's tongue, then killing his main prison tormentor, Hamidou, with the help of a metal stake. Neither actually occurred, according to Hayes's book. Nor did the ultimate escape happen as a result of the fortuitous availability of a Turkish officer uniform that permitted disguise and easy departure from the prison fort. Rather, Hayes's escape as described in the book took several days and involved strenuous passage by dinghy from an island where he had been taken after being in two other prisons, followed by a perilous walk through a Greek minefield.

Hayes himself accepted the script changes, including the addition of violent acts he never committed. He said these invented acts were like things he had wanted to do and no more brutal than things he had seen in his five years of prison life—things "you couldn't show on screen. You couldn't watch it."[6]

The most widely discussed change in the screenplay occurred in Hayes's refusal of homosexual advances by the Swedish inmate. In the book Hayes had consented, but studio executives sought a compromise rather than run the risk of having a homosexual encounter diminish the hero's otherwise "all-American" appeal.

The script and film, in what Hayes himself would describe as a "cop-out," depict the two men bathing with suggestive intimacy, then exercising in rhythmic unison, and briefly kissing in a shower. The interaction concludes with Hayes shaking his head no to halt the Swede's advances. Critics called the pullback approach perverse romanticism, hypocritical, and unconvincing. One said it suggested a vice best left to "the terrible Turk," Hamidou. David Ansen, *Newsweek* critic, wrote of the scene's projected hypocrisy: "The filmmakers . . . evidently felt that we could sympathize with a hero given to biting another's tongue off (an invented episode) but not with one given to physical affection for a man. After a titillatingly lyrical build-up to a kiss between Billy and his Swedish friend, our hero draws back from any further contact—like an old-fashioned Hollywood virgin. Given the setting, the sudden squeamishness is momentarily hilarious."[7]

Another scene viewed as a heroic contrivance by Stone was also the film's most politically inflammatory moment. The scene involved Hayes's impassioned pleas to the Turkish court following the announcement of a new life sentence (later changed to 30 years). In his fury Hayes screams: "For a nation of pigs, it sure is funny you don't eat them." The racist slur was not a part of the speech Hayes had recounted in his book—a speech less emotional and focused more on the argument that a society's maturity can be measured in the ways it punishes its criminals and imbues its justice system with a sense of mercy.

New Yorker critic Pauline Kael called the screenplay outbursts "cheap grandstanding—indicting a whole people on the presumption that the brutality of prison guards represents the national way of life." Kael argued that Hayes's book had stirred up genuine feelings for someone who, having nearly completed his 4½-year sentence for a crime, is suddenly sentenced to a much harsher term for the very same infraction. These strong feelings, she said, had been "destroyed" by the film's "victimization" of Billy and his "messagy speech to the court."[8]

Comparative analysis of the original source material in Hayes's book with what Stone and Parker had done in the film version met with as many judgments as there were responses. *Village Voice* critic Andrew Sarris in his review had been quick to note that alterations "are standard procedure for adaptation" and that it "is boring to carp over every little discrepancy between a book, or 'real life,' and a movie." Sarris then proceeded to list discrepancies and declare the film one in which "everything has been hyped and hoked up to intensify feelings of helplessness and self-pity."[9]

Rather than simply attacking differences as the basis of critical response, it was possible to see the book and the film as necessarily separate entities of different requirements and values. Chris Hodenfield of *Rolling Stone* said: "Hayes' book is about a struggle. The movie focuses on decay."[10] Steve Umberger wrote: "Scenarist Oliver Stone's adaptation activates [Hayes's story] with a drive and continuity that recall *One Flew over the Cuckoo's Nest,* but with a pulse twice as adamant. . . . Stone's relentless script propels the epic story with refulgent expedience by compacting events into a cohesively heightened retelling of the original. . . . The film is still more about what happens than who it happens to, but Stone's choices give his work a personal structural duality that allows emotional investment by both actors and audience."[11]

Umberger argued that *Midnight Express* was part melodrama, part escape film, part individual statement film, part character study, and part documentary, which together put forth the theme of a young man's recognition of and charge that "the concept of a society is based on the quality of its mercy." Umberger added: "The film must evoke that, not through suggestion or portraiture, but head on through specific actions spanning four years. It does so by defining its characters only in terms of that action" (Umberger, 66).

Other critics reacted in a similarly positive manner to *Midnight Express*'s dramatic success in driving home in no uncertain terms its argument for justice. *Los Angeles Times* critic Charles Champlin wrote enthusiastically: "Indeed, for all the horrors of the prison scene *Midnight Express* is in the end exhilarating and affirmative, an object lesson in the joys of freedom and in the value of due process of law."[12]

The rousing aspects of Stone's script and Parker's interpretation were enhanced by realistic and evocative cinematic treatment. For visual credibility Parker had taken his British crew to Malta, where the abandoned army barracks at historic Fort St. Elmo were transformed to resemble Istanbul's Sagamilcar Prison. A third wall, constructed with stone, was added to the fort to provide authenticity and the look of a huge complex of cell blocks and corridors in which to stage the film's action. Other sites in the fort were redesigned as courtrooms, a mental asylum, and sewer tunnels needed for a scene involving an attempted underground escape.

In order to authenticate the location as Turkey, Parker sent another film crew to Istanbul (on the pretense of shooting a cigarette commercial), where crucial establishing shots of Istanbul's hazy skyline were taken. These evocative shots are used to open *Midnight Express* and are intercut with shots of Hayes's hands wrapping hashish into tinfoil packets. The meaning is clear—establishing at once the idea of an exotic location where unusual and dangerously seductive things occur. A certain aura of beauty combined with danger is deftly realized.

Michael Seresin's cinematography and lighting designs for the film's interior prison scenes were equally compelling—achieving the look of "theatrical realism." This look, according to Parker, was meant to emphasize the idea that *Midnight Express* was no "straight, ordinary" prison film.

The effect of theatrical realism was achieved through several devices, including lighting and a hand-held camera. Soft filters were used throughout the shooting to give the prison images a graphic, slightly surreal quality. The theatrical effect of the lighting was particularly evident in the homosexual encounter scenes between Hayes and the Swede, and in the scenes in the prison's mental asylum corridor, to which Hayes is confined after his second breakout attempt fails. The soft lighting in the bathing-exercise-shower scenes with Hayes and the homosexual Erich poeticized the sequence in clearly sensual

36

Brad Davis (Billy) and Norbert Wiesser (Erich) do a form of yoga exercise in a controversial scene in *Midnight Express* (1978). Copyright © 1978 Columbia Pictures Industries, Inc. All rights reserved. Courtesy The Museum of Modern Art/Film Stills Archive.

ways—so much so that Hayes's pullback seems to belie the truth of what the two men were actually feeling for each other. However wrongheaded the decision to stop short of sexual consummation, it was the lighting that gave these short scenes the film's most tender moments.

By contrast, cold blue lighting in the mental asylum corridor was intensely surrealistic, adding a ghoulish feel to the deranged world depicted in this latter part of the film. To complement the film's theatrical realism, supplied in part by lens filters, Parker used smoke extensively in interior prison scenes to diffuse and soften the lighting. The intended effect was to create visual impressions of a horrified, unknown world being viewed for the first time by the filmgoer. The atmospheric achievements of *Midnight Express* intensified the nightmarish aspects of action and setting in Stone's screenplay.

Another form of surreality and theatrical realism was realized in the mental asylum scenes by intermingling real patients—hired and transported from a Malta hospital—with the film's actors. The approach demanded spontaneous filming without the benefit of careful rehearsal and resulted in unpolished, slightly off-rhythm action that abetted the desired surreal quality.

Effective use of hand-held camera shots is evident in intense action scenes, particularly those involving emotional and physical violence. The scene in which a berserk Hayes attacks Rifki for informing on his escape plans—following a whole series of other personal atrocities committed against fellow inmates—is rendered with frantic hand-held camera work that conveys revenge with rousing impact. The explosive scene concludes in slow motion as Hayes bites off and spits out Rifki's tongue—an act often greeted by applause from stirred-up filmgoers.

The hand-held camera was not as obvious in other scenes, but was equally important in helping realize the full potential in dramatic action requiring more subtle, tense visualization. Hand-held camera shots—with the camera filming from in front of the action—were well utilized for the scene in which Hayes and other prisoners make their way through a narrow tunnel shaft to the prison sewers for an attempted underground escape. The claustrophobic life of this scene emerges from the hand-held camera.

Hand-held camera work throughout *Midnight Express* is successful in alternately underscoring a scene full of action and fury or one demanding immediacy and suspense. It, as much as the film's graphic lighting, gave Parker's interpretation of Stone's screenplay its unusual, emotional edge. Lighting helped emphasize the idea of involuntary dislocation; intensive hand-held camera work helped convey the heightened experiences of characters so dislocated.

Stone's script for *Midnight Express* incorporated its own conventions for emphasizing character isolation and agony. The device of a voice-over reading of letters written home by the protagonist was employed as a means of character introspection and self-analysis. The convention also served as a transitional mechanism for incorporating factual details and advancing the plot. These voice-over passages were especially crucial in adding psychological dimension and humanity to Hayes's on-screen character, played by Brad Davis in his first major film role.

The first voice-over heard is a letter written to Hayes's parents, asking their forgiveness. Hayes, seen for the first time inside Sagamilcar Prison, is having his hair shorn off by a prison guard. Read by Davis with a quiet, softspoken sincerity and juxtaposed against the image of a dehumanizing haircut, the voice-over works its sympathy-building effect economically and swiftly. Later voice-over readings to girlfriend Susan speak of loneliness, recount acceptable and unacceptable rules of prison life, and express a building resentment of Rifki. Each comes at an interval indicating either the passage of another year or a major event of new meaning to Hayes as he struggles with his inner emotions and with what is going on around him inside the prison walls.

The voice-over served other critical functions. It added a sense of poignancy and self-reflection to what is otherwise essentially a script full of hotheaded outrage. The device also acted as a caesura, providing a much-needed slowing of pace in a streamlined, pumped-up flow of events.

Stone's screenplay for *Midnight Express* was especially impressive for its dialogue. A particularly memorable scene occurs when Hayes and two other inmates gather to talk in the prison courtyard about the untrustworthiness of other prisoners, their own crimes, and their chances of beating their sentences. It is a scene of apparent small talk but one richly textured to convey, simultaneously, comradeship and alienation, optimism and pessimism. It is a human scene that very early on in Hayes's captivity delineates prisoner ennui growing from mental ups and downs. Stone's sense of an all-boys world—in this instance a prison—comes through in the scene's psychological soundness.

An ability to employ dialogue in rhythmically powerful ways was evidenced in the scene where Hayes's father returns to Istanbul to visit his son for the first time. The dialogue begins with small talk about Hayes's mother and his girlfriend back home, moves on to discussions with a legal counselor and Turkish lawyer, then returns to small talk when the father and son are again left alone. Neither man seems able to express his real feelings and to say what he really wants and needs to say. Finally letting loose, the father shouts: "Billy, why did you do it?" Billy replies that it was a stupid act, then shouts: "Dad, get me out of here!" The rhythmic control and flow of dialogue in the scene define characters experiencing a variety of complex, painful emotions that involve guilt, frustration, sorrow, and love. They were feelings between a father and son that would have been well known to Stone through his own strained relationship with his father.

Other scenes and other characters were written and developed with similar credibility: those involving the drug-addicted Max (John Hurt), the courtroom scene of outrage where Hayes both forgives and attacks his captors, the asylum scene where deranged inmates mutter incoherently about "circles," "bad machines," and "the factory"—metaphors all the more terrifying in their meaninglessness.

Together Stone and Parker, for better or worse, turned *Midnight Express* into an unforgettable motion picture experience. And both men would be significantly influenced in their professional careers as directors by the film's methods and consequent success with audiences. Parker had brought *Midnight Express* in for $2.4 million; it earned $100 million. Critics complained of the film's rawness, its sensationalism, its racism. But controversy and word-of-mouth response to the film's vitality and heroic ending proved stronger than the negative criticism aimed at Stone and Parker.

Parker would continue to make motion pictures that were dynamically charged and shaped by theatrical realism for audiences who (apparently large in number) liked their films loud, tinged with emotion, and larger than life: *Fame, Mississippi Burning, The Commitments,* and others.

Oliver Stone would carry forward successful dramatic elements in the *Midnight Express* script to his future work, for example, the voice-over letter home convention, the validation of father-son relationships, and a special feeling for male-oriented worlds and dislocated characters gaining new knowledge in an alien culture.

Stone also took from Parker important directing techniques—knowledge of the power of the hand-held camera, slow motion, diffused lighting, and the effect of authenticity combined with surreality.

Perhaps more important than any other was the fact that *Midnight Express* had not wavered in achieving what it set out to do. The line of action in realizing its effect was pure, the message unencumbered by pretentious and obscuring philosophy. Oliver Stone in time would come to see the approach as necessary for lifting his own work to the same level of directness, however controversial.

THE HAND

The phenomenal success of Stone's *Midnight Express* collaboration brought a second opportunity to direct one of his own screenplays, *The Hand* (1981). The film possessed striking similarities to *Seizure*— being another horror tale about the mental anguish of a creative artist who is destroyed by forces outside his control.

Synopsis of *The Hand* (1981)

Cast: Michael Caine, Andrea Marcovicci, Annie McEnroe, Bruce McGill, Viveca Lindfors, Rosemary Murphy, Mara Hobel, Pat Corley, Bill Marshall, Charles Fletcher.

Credits: Orion Pictures, released through Warner Brothers. Director: Oliver Stone. Producer: Edward R. Pressman. Screenplay: Oliver Stone, from the novel *The Lizard's Tail,* by Marc Brandel. Photography: King Baggot. Music: James Horner.

The Hand recounts the story of a comic-strip artist, Jon Lansdale (Michael Caine), who has his drawing hand sliced off when the car in which he is riding with his wife (Andrea Marcovicci) in rural Vermont sideswipes a passing truck. Efforts to relocate the hand at the accident site for possible surgical reconnection fail, and the cartoonist is left unable to resume his work.

Attempts are made to continue the syndicated comic-strip with Lansdale serving as narrative plotter and another artist moving in to draw the daily panels. It is also hoped that in time, a newly fitted mechanical hand will enable Lansdale to draw once more. Neither works. The young artist hired to render Lansdale's plots chooses to soften the persona of the comic-strip hero—a macho, Superman-like character called Mandro—and Lansdale in a fit of anger walks out on his New York agent and his job. And attempts to train his new artificial hand to do the work of the original also meet with futility.

As a further complication in his life, Lansdale finds his marriage—which had begun to deteriorate before the accident—now at a frustrating impasse. Desperate, he decides to accept an offer to teach art at a small alternative college in California's Sierra Mountains—with his wife and daughter remaining in New York City in a trial separation.

Once at the college, an institution called Saraville, Lansdale finds himself isolated with a group of rather listless students—save one sexually promiscuous and seductive woman (Annie McEnroe), who suddenly appears at her instructor's rustic abode with a sketchbook thought to have been mistakenly left behind. An affair is launched in the encounter.

As coincidence might have it, Lansdale's other adult acquaintance at Saraville—a rough-hewn psychology professor and bar-drinking companion named Brian (Bruce McGill)—is also the artist-turned-teacher's competition for the sexually inclined student, Stella. In the course of their conversations, Lansdale confides in Brian, telling him of his apparent blackouts and of the mysterious appearance and disappearance of personal objects: a signet ring from his lost hand, the sketchbook returned by Stella containing a pornographic drawing.

Brian, being the psychology professor that he is, warns Lansdale that "blackouts are nothing to fool with," and ominously plants the idea that in a blackout "you could do anything you ever dreamed of" and still not "know who . . . you really are." As in *Seizure,* the protagonist-artist becomes an increasingly depressed, perplexed, and tormented figure.

The Hand's plot leads to a series of violent incidents and accompanying revelations that suggest all that has been happening in the course of the film might have to do with a profound, repressed rage seething within the comic-strip artist, who has been deprived of both profession and family.

The film's ambiguities are borne through periodic inserts of the dismembered hand, seemingly having taken on a life of its own—journeying from the field in Vermont where it fell at the time of the accident, to New York City, to the mountains of California. In the course of its travels, the hand appears to be on a revenge mission, doing damage to all those who have hurt Lansdale: the young artist who sought to humanize Mandro, the comic-strip hero; a bothersome street bum; the rival psychology professor; the promiscuous student; the independence-seeking wife. In the end, the hand turns on Lansdale himself as a final gesture of resentment. A concluding sequence occurs in the lab of a psychoanalyst (Viveca Lindfors), who seeks to convince Lansdale that what has happened to him is the result of an "ancient rage," causing him to commit murder in his blackouts. He has been wired for shock therapy when the hand suddenly reappears to strangle the psychoanalyst. *The Hand* ends with a freeze frame as Lansdale releases himself from the shock treatment chair.

Like the film *Seizure, The Hand* created uncertainty as to whether the terrorizing acts were real or acts of aggression committed by the protagonist during blackouts. Rage and anger are used to propel a psychological horror story that Stone clearly meant to possess extra dimensions, again as he had sought to convey in *Seizure.* In an interview with the *New York Times,* Stone interpreted the message of *The*

Hand as meaningfully human: "Sometimes I feel like the bad luck will catch up. You look over your shoulder. That's what *The Hand* is about. That unconscious state, that time you do something you're not even aware of."[13]

Critics paid significantly more attention to *The Hand* than they had to *Seizure.* Vincent Canby, *New York Times* film critic, was especially appreciative: "Mr. Stone's screenplay is tightly written, precise and consistent in its methods, and seemingly perfectly realized in the performances of the very good cast headed by Mr. Caine. It approaches its revelations in the self-assured way of a film made by someone who knows exactly what he's up to and has no need for red herrings."[14]

Rolling Stone magazine was not as impressed, accusing Oliver Stone of having stuffed "the story with queasy Freudian innuendos until . . . the hero becomes a sexually threatened jackass."[15]

David Ansen in *Newsweek* wrote that while *The Hand* had tried "for something other than cheap thrills . . . [the exercise] ultimately doesn't seem worth the effort. Connoisseurs of schlock shock effects will not be satisfied by its tony illusion/reality games, and those looking for psycho/sexual illuminations will be one step ahead of the Freudian clichés."[16]

A good deal of the negative critical reaction to *The Hand* also drew on comparisons of what Stone had done in his script with what had happened in Marc Brandel's novel *The Lizard's Tail,* on which the film was based. Considerably more subtle and complex in analyzing the cartoonist's deterioration, Brandel's book had located the hand entirely in the protagonist's mind.

Variously, Stone's visualization of an ambulatory, revengeful hand was described as producing "giggles," "working against the film's enjoyment," capable of destroying "the atmosphere of the rest of the film," and "more painful than entertaining."

Whether it would have been at all possible for Stone to win with a film like *The Hand* is questionable. An "interior" novel such as Brandel's, kept in its cerebral form in a film adaptation, would probably have been equally disastrous. Film, like theater, is to a significant extent bound to dramatic action.

There was also the fact that the plot of *The Hand* was not original. A number of motion pictures had used the idea of a living, violent hand before Stone: *The Hands of Orlac* (1926), remade as *Mad Love* in 1935, and as *Hands of a Stranger* in 1960; *The Beast with Five Fingers* (1946). *Boxoffice* magazine, referring to these earlier efforts, began its review: "*The Hand* is a movie everyone has seen before. They may not be quite sure where or when. But they know they've seen it." The review—one intended for film exhibitors—concluded: "The best course of action in selling *The Hand* may be to forget all the pretentious psychology the movie has to offer, and just camp it up like you're selling a Boris Karloff midnight show. Scatter rubber hands throughout the theater, concession stand and box-office, and have the ghoulish fun the movie should have had with its topic."[17]

The Hand in the end suffered the same critical fate as *Seizure*—attacked for its pretentiousness and for having diminished the expected pleasures of a horror film experience. The major fault with Stone's approach, most critics concurred, resided in the script's failure to create a more sympathetic, dimensioned protagonist whose inner anguish and ultimate punishment come more from fate and social circumstance than from arrogance, insensitivity, and chauvinism. The Jon Lansdale created by Stone and actor Michael Caine was far too abrasive, it was felt, to make the film work on the level of psychological rage, sympathetically viewed. Better to have left the genre effort "ghoulishly" fun.

On the technical side, *The Hand* had much to recommend it. Stone's work was undeniably stylish, and the film contained well-developed suspense and excellent performances.

Especially impressive was the visual mise-en-scène, which served as a match for the protagonist's progressive deterioration. Opening sequences in rural Vermont, Lansdale's "ideal" environment for living and working, were photographed by King Baggot to project the idyllic: lush green grass, deep blue skies, warm earth colors, sunshine. The atmosphere suggested innocence—an innocence that would turn to ironic horror with the sideswipe accident on a peaceful rural road that cost Lansdale his hand. (Later, directors like David Lynch would employ the effect, e.g., the opening of *Blue Velvet*.) With similar effectiveness, *The Hand*'s shift of location to a SoHo loft in New York City—a place detested by the protagonist—was met with visual treatment that conveyed a sense of cramped, bohemian living interiors and pushy, dirty, wino-infested streets.

Capping the atmospheric achievements of *The Hand* were the California mountain scenes—created in dark, rain-soaked space that is isolated by hills and valleys and populated with people who all appear slightly off-center. Scenics again complemented the now depressed, increasingly obsessional world of the protagonist's mind. Night

scenes—interior and exterior—were superbly lighted to achieve max-
imum suspense and psychological inference.

The Hand also revealed Stone's gift for working details into a film
with memorable effect. In an early scene, as Lansdale is chopping
wood, an ax blow leaves a lizard chopped in half, its two parts still
animated with life. As the protagonist's daughter pokes at the lizard's
moving tail, the family cat suddenly leaps in to eat the remains. The
incident foreshadows the car accident and the slicing away of a human
body part that will also refuse to die. The sudden appearance of cats
as a fright technique is repeated (sometimes unconvincingly) throughout the film.

Another scene notable for its foreshadowing details occurs when
Lansdale—back home in Vermont after his hospital stay—goes searching for his dismembered hand at the site of the accident. As Lansdale
walks in tall grass, Stone employs an extremely low-angle long shot
showing the hand—an insect clutching to it—in the immediate fore-
ground. Lansdale is visible some distance away in the background.
The in-depth composition conveys the impression that the hand now
possesses its own singular presence—ominously so in its continuing
separation from Lansdale. Lansdale never sees the hand, finding instead his signet ring, bearing his initials, JL, which he was wearing
when the accident occurred. The signet ring will disappear and reap-
pear throughout the film as a motif for increasing Lansdale's concern
about his blackouts.

Clearly the film's most memorable and terrifying scene is the one
involving the automobile accident. Stone's work in this scene offered
a near-model example of how accumulative, fast-paced narrative details can build to a horrifying screen event: small talk between husband
and wife leading quickly to a heated argument; the wife angrily floor-
ing the gas pedal; a passing truck approaching; the cartoonist sticking
his arm out the window to wave the truck back over; the automobile
brushing by the side of the truck, its wooden-frame edge acting with
the effect of a guillotine blade to slice the man's hand away; blood, as
from a spray gun, showering the scene. Stone's deft, economic handling of these details resulted in a scene that appeared real as well as
psychologically sound and horrifying.

The soundtrack for *The Hand* was another of the film's technical
strengths. Stone had been successful with this element in *Seizure* by
using drumbeat musical accompaniment for suspenseful scenes. *The
Hand* was impressive for its effective use of noise: heavy breathing
during closeup shots of the disembodied hand; the sudden, passing

screech of a cat; the sounds of wind, thunder, and rain; insect sounds; the shattering of a glass window; and especially the sounds accompanying the hand's attacks on its victims—sounds of primitive, indeterminate origin that conveyed the horror of the attacks more fully than the visuals. The substitution of sounds for visuals in conveying the hand's dispatching of its victims more fully approached the subtler, keep-it-in-the-mind-of-the-protagonist treatment that had been hoped for.

Also as a means of keying the hand's attacks as another form of reality, Stone employed the convention of shifting from color to black-and-white images. The approach worked on two levels: it served as an alert mechanism for the attacks, and it carried a visual correspondence for the protagonist's blackout periods, when the revengeful deeds occurred.

Stone focused considerable attention on the quality of the acting in *The Hand,* and clearly performance was a plus. He had shown with *Seizure* a gift for inspiring his actors to new heights, and this was again evident in *The Hand.* Michael Caine was pushed to do things he had never done before, including allowing himself to look unkempt and physically unattractive for greater psychological realism. Vincent Canby said, "[Caine's] performance is scary for being so utterly reasonable" (Canby, 8).

Stone won praise for his success in drawing fresh, offbeat performances from the actors playing laid-back Californians in the Sierra Mountains college town of Saraville, especially Annie McEnroe as the sexually promiscuous Stella, and Bruce McGill as the bearded, jeep-driving, bar-drinking psychology professor. This offbeat approach to characterization and performance supplied needed texture.

In another innovative casting angle, Stone himself appeared briefly in the role of a wino street bum who is attacked in a New York alley in the film's first black-and-white scene. The practice of making a cameo appearance would become a standard element in later films.

The nature of the material in *The Hand* showed Stone once more grappling with ideas that involved the recesses of the mind, placed within a melodramatic horror film in which the protagonist earns his living through a type of storytelling. Evil, fear, rage, self-doubts, and drug-induced-like movement between illusion and reality are the central ingredients, as they were in *Seizure.*

It would be impossible not to see these efforts as somehow connected to Stone's own troubling years as a young man, and during and following Vietnam. Stone's alter egos in *Seizure* and *The Hand*

Michael Caine as the tormented cartoonist Jon Lansdale in *The Hand* (1981). Copyright © 1981 by Orion Pictures Company. Courtesy The Museum of Modern Art/Film Stills Archive.

were not as obvious as in later works, but the inclination for purging one's demons and looking for proof of one's artistic and personal worth seem as evident in the early "failed" work as in the later, more acclaimed effort. Opting for the horror film made perfect sense for Stone at the time, as he was not yet powerful or lucky enough to treat personal history openly and honestly in his screenplays.

Artistically, *The Hand* was a mishmash of good and bad—evidencing the work of a director with clear talent, but not yet the work of a talented, focused writer. The urgency to create something that would make a difference, even in a horror film, was admirable, but it had led Stone to misstep. *The Hand,* in its attempts to deal obliquely with some heavy issues, failed. The *Christian Science Monitor* reviewer, the most direct and succinct of all, said of *The Hand*: "Total it up, and you have another loser in the overcrowded horror market."[18]

Oliver Stone, understandably, was upset and depressed by the negative responses to his second directorial effort. He believed he had turned out a challenging piece of high-level entertainment that would lead to more directing assignments. Also believing his career was on an upturn, Stone had asked Elizabeth Cox, his assistant on *The Hand,* to become his second wife. They were married in June 1981—a month after the film's release.

Blame for *The Hand*'s deficiencies was placed on backer and production management interference in the project. It was at this juncture that Stone, to support himself and his new wife, was compelled to return for nearly five years to writing scripts for other, established Hollywood directors. It would be a productive but not a happy time of his life.

Arnold Schwarzenegger in *Conan the Barbarian* (1982). Copyright ©
1982 Universal City Studios, Inc. All rights reserved. Courtesy The
Museum of Modern Art/Film Stills Archive.

3

Writing for the Establishment: *Conan the Barbarian, Scarface, Year of the Dragon, 8 Million Ways to Die*

Conan the Barbarian turns out to be muscle-bound moviemaking—all grunt and sweat and grim ambition in the void. Were it not for heavy doses of violence, its lumpy narrative would put the audience to sleep.
—David Denby, *New York,* 24 May 1982

In the five-year period Oliver Stone spent performing writing chores for violent action pictures, his career as a screenwriter took a seesaw ride. Some of the work was commendable; some of it was bad. Working relationships with established figures on the Hollywood scene (John Milius, Brian De Palma, Michael Cimino, and Hal Ashby) resulted in both challenging and frustrating experiences. Creative input varied from picture to picture. In effect Stone was earning a living, albeit somewhat haphazardly.

CONAN THE BARBARIAN

The first project of this period (1982–86), *Conan the Barbarian* (1982) had come Stone's way after the success of *Midnight Express* in 1978. Paramount Pictures—with access to movie rights for Robert E. Howard's comic-book character, Conan—put up the money and hired

Stone to produce a screenplay based on the adventures of the prehistoric barbarian character. During the 1930s and 1940s, Howard had written 13 stories centered on Conan's adventures, which had been published in the magazine *Weird Tales*. A budget of $2.5 million was allocated for what was initially to be a fantasy quickie-film, designed to capitalize on Conan's sizable cult following.

Drawing on two Howard stories, "Black Collossus" and "A Witch Shall Be Born," Stone constructed an action adventure fantasy of epic proportions and big-budget cost. The screenplay called for massive battle scenes, mechanical chariots, and mutant armies attacking one another (10,000 mutants altogether). The script strongly emphasized violence, and in an act of dramatic departure from Howard's work, Stone had set the action not in the past but in a futuristic, post-holocaust time. Conan, the pagan hero, was depicted as waging a valiant, lonely battle against life-threatening forces that roamed a future world.

Estimates for producing Stone's script were placed at somewhere between $30 million and $40 million. Edward R. Pressman, securer of the rights to the Conan stories and original producer of the film, briefly considered Stone as the director of the project but backed down because, according to Stone, "I had no clout." Stone tried to talk Ridley Scott *(The Duellists, Alien)* into directing, but Scott declined.

Pressman, recognizing the magnitude of the screenplay, enlisted the financial and production assistance of epics producer Dino De Laurentis and daughter Raffaella De Laurentis. John Milius, who at the time was working on an ill-fated De Laurentis project, *Half of the Sky,* became interested in the Conan film and agreed to direct—with the stipulation that he be allowed to write his own scenario. Milius was a highly regarded, macho-style writer *(Dirty Harry, Magnum Force)* and had been the scenarist for Francis Ford Coppola's epic Vietnam film, *Apocalypse Now* (1979). He had also previously directed *Dillinger* (1973) and *The Wind and the Lion* (1975).

Milius in time wrote four drafts of *Conan,* incorporating elements of Stone's screenplay into his own but completely altering the nature of the plot. Where Stone's script had envisioned an epic spectacle based on Conan's adventures—playing up the heroic gallantry of the character—Milius's account emphasized swordfighting, sorcery, and the supernatural and drew on cult aspects (snake and death rituals) of a prehistoric world 12,000 years in the past.

Synopsis of *Conan the Barbarian* (1982)

Cast: Arnold Schwarzenegger, James Earl Jones, Max von Sydow, Sandahl Bergman, Ben Davidson, Cassandra Gaviola, Gerry Lopez.

Credits: Director: John Milius. Screenplay: John Milius and Oliver Stone. Photography: Duke Callaghan. Production design: Ron Cobb. Art design: Pierliugi Basile and Benjamin Fernandez. Music: Basil Poledouris. A Dino De Laurentis presentation of an Edward R. Pressman production.

Milius's plot told of Conan's origins (also in Stone's script but expanded) and the destruction of Conan's family and village by Vanir raiders, who steal a sword made by Conan's weapons-maker father and bequeathed to his son. Conan (Arnold Schwarzenegger), enslaved and chained to a wheat-grinding wheel ("A Wheel of Pain"), grows into a powerful man and in time becomes a skillful gladiator. He eventually escapes during an earthquake and ventures into the wilds.

A lengthy, peril-filled journey in search of the man responsible for the killing of his family follows—leading Conan to an inevitable showdown with snake-cult followers and their evil leader, Thulsa Doom (the family murderer). Along the way, Conan acquires two companions—Subotai (Gerry Lopez), a thief and skilled archer, and Valeria (Sandahl Bergman), a beautiful female mercenary—who later save Conan from crucifixion. In the end, Thulsa Doom (James Earl Jones) is beheaded by Conan and the snake cult destroyed. Witches, wizards, quasi-religious death cults, giant serpents, and voice-over intoners of wisdom-filled oracles pepper the fantastically inclined story.

On the release of *Conan the Barbarian* in 1982 Stone was listed in the credits as coscenarist with Milius, although Milius had taken full control of the project and made the film his own way, without regard for Stone's input. According to Stone, the most significant changes came in developing the snake-cult motif and in rewriting the film's ending. Somewhat intact were elements Stone had taken from Howard's story "A Witch Shall Be Born." Stone summed up his involvement in the following way: "It was the least successful collaboration I ever did. . . . There was no collaboration essentially. I wrote my stuff and I never really got a second pass. John rewrote. I gave notes, he tore up the notes, and then we never talked about the movie again" (McGilligan, 13).

Conan, which was filmed primarily in Spain in 1981, did not set well with film reviewers, who—uninformed as to who had done what—would ally Stone with the film's scripting deficiencies. The screenplay's minimalist approach to dialogue was cited as having produced an action-oriented film, but one without a core and one devoid of character development and motivation.

Another criticism was that the script had taken itself too seriously, had not had fun with the material the way comic-book adaptations were supposed to. *Time* magazine's Richard Schickel referred to the film as "a sort of psychopathic *Star Wars,* stupid and stupefying."[1] The script had included a Nietzsche quote—"That which does not kill us makes us stronger"—in an apparent effort to lend an air of importance to myth and the Conan tale. The gesture was seen as unwarranted inflation within a rather trivial and meaningless adventure film.

There were also charges of an unfortunate fascist tone to *Conan.* Of this stance the *Maclean's* magazine reviewer wrote: "The director John Milius, who co-wrote the grunting and belching script with Oliver Stone, has already identified himself as the monarch of macho with *Dillinger* and *The Wind and the Lion.* Opening with an appropriately fascistic quote of Nietzsche's, *Conan* proceeds to tell its audience that nothing can be trusted in the world other than the power of might and then supplies as many examples as it can. Men, the movie suggests, should pump iron and fight; women are either sluts or child-bearers and should be loyal to their death."[2]

The cult aspects of *Conan*—admittedly Milius's own invention—also came under attack with their suspiciously contemporary associations with a Reverend Jim Jones–Guyana/Charles Manson type of disciple mentality. Thulsa Doom's dedicated Cult of Set followers are depicted as behaving in a self-sacrificing manner. Vincent Canby of the *New York Times* argued, "Though Mr. Milius asks us to make such associations, he doesn't reward us for making them." Canby said *Conan,* in its "overexercised" seriousness, did not win the commitment of the audience and had the "curious effect of inhibiting the imagination."[3]

Removed from any creative interaction with the makers of *Conan,* Oliver Stone later spoke critically of the film, focusing his reactions on stylistic changes made by Milius in production and on the visual look of the picture: "I think he masculinized it and went more with his friends—more with the bodybuilding aspect of Arnold Schwarzenegger [Conan]. I think Arnold has a more romantic side. John populated the movie with surfers and bodybuilders. And the look—he made it look like a Spanish western. . . . The picture should have been green; John made it rocky desert yellow, more a [Sergio] Leone western. It was all cheap—they cut back on the extras, the fights were done on the cheap, the rocks looked like cardboard boulders" (McGilligan, 13).

It is clear from these comments that Stone would have made a different *Conan the Barbarian* from the one turned out by John Milius. He in fact had written his script as the first in an intended series of films on the Conan character. As it was, Stone's work on *Conan* was at best frustrating and in the end—perhaps mercifully—little more than an abortive enterprise. Milius's own projected sequel to *Conan*—for reasons of common sense—never materialized. In the meantime, Stone had undertaken the writing of *Scarface* for producer Martin Bregman.

SCARFACE

The screenplay for *Scarface* (1983) holds some special significance for Stone's developing career because of the importance of the film project and because Stone was the script's sole author. The picture—a quasi-remake of Howard Hawk's 1932 classic—cost $27 million to produce, and in its final edit ran for 2 hours and 50 minutes. Because of its many complex characters and its abundance of intense violence, *Scarface* can be more accurately tied to Stone than was the case with *Conan the Barbarian*. Unlike Milius, director Brian De Palma had remained largely faithful to Stone's screenplay—one that incorporated a great deal of dialogue (again, unlike *Conan*) and episodic action.

The idea for a remake of *Scarface* had come from producer Martin Bregman, who envisioned the project as offering another powerful gangster role for *Godfather* actor Al Pacino. Bregman had also seen compelling connections between the old Prohibition bootlegger dealings that had been the subject of the original *Scarface* and a contemporary underground drug world of Cuban origin. To Bregman the times seemed ripe for an updating of a shifting but ongoing story of illegal enterprise and gangsterism in America.

Stone was engaged to write, Pacino would star, and initially New York–based director Sidney Lumet *(Dogday Afternoon, Prince of the City)* was to direct; Bregman would produce.

The *Scarface* project seemed especially well suited to Stone. It contained potential elements of excessive violence, perversion, and death, combined with unsavory characters—the same elements that had propelled *Midnight Express* to success. Stone was also well known as someone familiar with the drug scene and had a reputation as the master of the visceral detail.

On reading Stone's original draft of *Scarface*—more than four hours long in playing time and filled with boldly explosive action and dialogue—Bregman decided its material was better suited to the cinesensibilities of Brian De Palma than to Sidney Lumet's more cerebral, reserved style. De Palma was a director with a reputation for turning out peculiarly engrossing films containing oddball characters and spine-tingling violence, for example, *Carrie, Dressed to Kill,* and *Blow Out.*

With De Palma as director and Stone as writer, *Scarface* emerged a film with extraordinary displays of insensate violence, initially earning an X-rating and generating a great public and critical flap over both the film's style and its content.

Synopsis of *Scarface* (1983)

Cast: Al Pacino, Steven Bauer, Michelle Pfeiffer, Mary Elizabeth Mastrantonio, Robert Loggia, Miriam Colon, F. Murray Abraham, Paul Shenar, Harris Yulin, Angel Salazar, Pepe Serma.

Credits: Director: Brian De Palma. Producer: Martin Bregman. Screenplay: Oliver Stone. Photography: John A. Alonzo. Art direction: Ed Richardson. Music: Giorgio Moroder. Universal Pictures.

Stone's plot for *Scarface* begins in Cuba in 1980, where Tony Montana ("Scarface") and 125,000 other refugees (including 25,000 criminals) are released by Fidel Castro for relocation to Florida. In a Cuban detention camp in the United States, Montana (Al Pacino)—one of the ex-criminals—assassinates an ex-Castro collaborator in return for his release. Unhappy with the menial jobs handed him in Miami, Montana stumbles into the drug trade through a botched and bloody deal (involving a chainsaw murder) that leaves Montana holding both the purchase money and the cocaine he had gone to buy from Colombian drug peddlers.

Impressed, Miami drug king Frank Lopez (Robert Loggia) takes Montana into his Babylon Club crime organization. There Tony Montana learns the ins-and-outs of gangsterism—how the system works, its women, the value of violence in tight situations. As his brazenness increases (he oversteps the boundaries of his role in the organization, establishes a critical tie with a Bolivian cocaine manufacturer, and becomes attracted to the boss's woman), efforts are made to eliminate Montana but fail. Eventually, Montana kills Lopez and assumes command of the Babylon Club and its illegal activities.

The plot in its second half recounts Montana's success in building up the crime-based empire, his marriage to Lopez's ex-girlfriend Elvira (Michelle Pfeiffer), and his seemingly incestuous obsession for sister Gina (Mary Elizabeth Mastrantonio). Stone's script delineates Montana's evolution into a pathological monster—withdrawing; raging; succumbing to cocaine (as earlier had his new infertile wife); killing his own best friend, Manny (Steve Bauer); and being wiped out in the end in a drawn-out hit squad attack that also kills his sister.

Stone's script had developed the principal character of Tony Montana (Pacino), without making concessions to sympathy-building details. Its dramatic action followed the wily progress of an icy killer— from ex-Cuban criminal looking for the American dream in the drug-trade underworld of Miami to a totally unlikable monster. Sideline players who figured into the antihero/hero's rise and fall met the same kind of cynical, unsympathetic treatment. *Scarface* was a narrative without positives, without redeemed characters.

The unrelieved "black" qualities of *Scarface,* viewed beside the rather genteel fun and sometimes funny nature of the original, led to an outpouring of unfavorable reaction. The most positive responses seemed to come from critics who felt some need to defend the film as antidrug in stance or who saw its extreme uses of violence and unsympathetic characters pointing in that direction. The original X-rating, later changed to an R, had stimulated defensive responses from liberal-minded critics. Vincent Canby of the *New York Times* argued: "This *Scarface* is too good—too rich in characterizations and too serious in its point of view—to deserve to be classified with the porn movies that glory in their X-iness."[4]

With similar reasoning, *Newsweek's* David Ansen wrote positively of the De Palma–Stone film: "Is *Scarface* as violent as its reputation? . . . Yes and no. The violence is constant (as are the four-letter words), the body count astronomical, the infamous chain-saw scene unnerving. But De Palma doesn't linger on gore. Any recent horror film is more graphically grisly. If *Scarface* makes you shudder, it's from what you *think* you see and from the accumulated tension of this feral landscape. It's a grand, shallow, decadent entertainment which, like all good Hollywood gangster movies delivers the punch and counter-punch of glamour and disgust."[5]

Its occasional apologist aside, *Scarface* took a critical beating. De Palma's directing was criticized for its "trademark operatic flourishes" and for its unusual excesses. Summarizing—in order to attack—Karen Jaehne wrote in *Cineaste:*

De Palma's violence does not seek stylistic excuses or social justification: be-cause his vision eschews elegance in favor of exaggeration, and the pop-artsy knowing wink by pushing each violent scene just beyond the brink of credi-bility, he has created a special cinematic niche for the one-upmanship of the emergency room. . . . In fact, nobody was surprised to hear that the director of the *Scarface* remake was Brian De Palma: they were perhaps surprised to see a theme that had obsessed an entire generation of young American direc-tors to make arguably great films like *The Godfather* and *Mean Streets* turned into pure panache and tasteless titillation.[6]

Critics of Oliver Stone's script found two avenues of attack: the screenplay's failure to achieve cohesiveness, variety, and motivational soundness, and the failure of the remake writing to come up to the Howard Hawks–Ben Hecht original. In the first area, the Stone–De Palma collaboration was criticized for its repetitive use of bombastic dialogue that drew heavily on four-letter words for its impact—the result being tedium and the eventual loss of any impact at all. The Tony Montana/Al Pacino character was said to be similarly repeti-tious—"without internal contradictions or shading," said Pauline Kael in her *New Yorker* review.[7] Other critics called the development and progress of the Montana character "ponderous," "predictable," "limp," without depth, "sillier and sillier" as the film "plods" toward its "overwrought, drawnout" conclusion.

Others argued the failure of *Scarface* by comparing and contrasting the dimensions of the Hawks-Hecht protagonist, Italian Tony Ca-monte, with the De Palma–Stone protagonist, Cuban Tony Montana. As analyzed by David Chute in *Film Comment:*

A crucial distinction between Montana and Camonte is that Camonte at least had some clumsy high cultural pretensions and a yen for self-improvement. He lived in a pre-pop period when distinctions between high and low society still meant something; one reason Tony Camonte wanted money was to buy quality. Tony Montana craves only quantity. . . .

Al Pacino ("Scarface" Tony Montana) in *Scarface* (1983). Copyright ©
1983 Universal City Studios, Inc. All rights reserved. Courtesy The
Museum of Modern Art/Film Stills Archive.

Every great movie gangster (someone said) is Richard III in a double-
breasted suit; getting there is all the fun but being there is a drag. Even the
Godfather saga says more or less the same thing. But Tony [Montana] isn't
tragic by a long shot because he's too narrowly defined in terms of appetite.
Neurotic obsessive hunger is not a tragic flaw. It's a sickness like bulimia.[8]

While both Stone and De Palma proclaimed to interviewers that
Scarface carried a moral about capitalism, money, and business ethics
in the extreme, the lack of a projected complexity of character in the
rendering of Montana proved alienating and boring. The film simply
did not captivate or work well enough to make its intended message
seem relevant or compelling. Some called the film's closing credits'
dedication to Howard Hawks and Ben Hecht a self-serving, grandiose
gesture and an insult to the memory of the original work.

In a convincing analysis of Stone's own failures in the scripting of
Scarface, *Village Voice* critic Enrique Fernandez saw as problematic

Stone's inability to fully identify with a character like Montana. Fernandez argued this had not been the case with the more successful *Midnight Express* screenplay: "His Oscar-winning *Midnight Express* is a sexy story: drugs, exoticism, violence, perversion, torture, tribal bonding, heroic struggle, freedom. It also boasts a level of jingoism rarely seen in American films anymore. . . . His *Scarface* is less chauvinistic, only because, after all, the central character is not an American innocent abroad but a Latin malevolent stateside. But *Scarface* is shallow precisely because Stone is unable to project himself into any kind of otherness. *Midnight Express* works because it's told from the protagonist's p.o.v. *Scarface* fails for the same reason."[9]

Coming just after *Conan the Barbarian,* Stone's involvement with *Scarface* brought further charges of fascistic instincts. The world depicted was again one in which power, control, and attainment come through brute force—a bravura machismo rules. The film's Cuban protagonist also added to Stone's growing reputation (after treatment of the Turks in *Midnight Express*) as a screenwriter whose work carried racist overtones. Subsequent collaboration with Michael Cimino on *Year of the Dragon* in 1985—Stone's next project—intensified these claims of a fascist/racist perspective.

YEAR OF THE DRAGON

With *Year of the Dragon,* Stone entered into yet another creative (and unfortunate) partnership with a director known for making violent, controversial films—Michael Cimino. The endeavor also involved writing again about largely unpleasant characters—many being immigrants to America—who have connections to the drug trade. It would be another adaptation for Stone of a story filled with exoticism and moral ambiguities. Actors have been known to fall into typecasting ruts; Stone appeared suddenly cast in the rut of screenwriter playing brutal melodramatist.

Dino De Laurentis, with whom Stone had been marginally associated in the making of *Conan the Barbarian,* was the producer of *Year of the Dragon,* and Stone said he agreed to cowrite (with Cimino) the screenplay—based on a novel of the same name by Robert Daley—because De Laurentis had promised financial support for *Platoon,* a project on which Stone was working at the time and one he intended to direct himself. According to Stone, De Laurentis later reneged.

Year of the Dragon was viewed by everyone in the film industry as a "comeback picture" for Michael Cimino, a director both praised and reviled for the alternating success and failure of, respectively, *The Deer Hunter* (1978) and *Heaven's Gate* (1980). *Heaven's Gate,* a box-office critical bomb, had been produced by United Artists at a swollen cost of $44 million, the budget getting out of hand in part because of over-confidence in the Best Picture Oscar Cimino had won for *The Deer Hunter,* and in part because of United Artists' long-standing policy of noninterference in the creative filmmaking process. *Year of the Dragon,* it was felt, could be the film that would repair Cimino's shattered reputation.

When all was said and done, *Year of the Dragon*—variously retitled "Hell's Gate" and "a Chinese *Godfather*" by the skeptical—offered it-self up as an oddly styled police action melodrama with a displaced Rambo-style attitude of correction and revenge.

Synopsis of *Year of the Dragon* (1985)

Cast: Mickey Rourke, John Lone, Ariane, Leonard Termo, Ray Barry, Caroline Kava, Eddie Jones, Joey Chin, Victor Wong.

Credits: Director: Michael Cimino. Producer: Dino De Laurentis. Screenplay: Oliver Stone and Michael Cimino, based on the book by Robert Daley. Photographer: Alex Thomson. Music: David Mansfield.

Year of the Dragon's protagonist is Stanley White (Mickey Rourke), a Vietnam veteran and a highly decorated member of the New York City Police Department. The plot is launched with the assassination of a Chinatown figurehead by street gangs during Chinese New Year celebrations. White, a captain, is given the task of clearing out the street gangs and returning the Chinatown sector to normalcy.

In his campaign to set things right, White is drawn as a proud, second-generation Polish-American. Disdainful of Asian-Americans, he sees his assignment as comparable to winning the war in Vietnam. White embarks on a crusade that pits him against the ambitious young Joey Tai (John Lone), who is seeking to take over Chinatown's heroin drug trade and racketeering market from the established crime families: Chinese Triads. Tai's eventual goal is to seize control of the crime business and move it away from existing arrangements with the Italian mafia.

Although cautioned by his superiors for overmeddling, White lunges hotheadedly forward in his crusade, stirring up the Chinatown community and calling media attention to his efforts to undermine the gang's base of power. White uses a beautiful young Chinese television reporter (Ariane) to aid his cause, while entering into a love affair with the woman. Tai, ruthlessly striking back, orders White's estranged wife (Caroline Kava) killed, and his television-reporter girlfriend is gang-raped after a shipment of heroin is revealed by an undercover agent hired by White.

The obligatory showdown takes place at a shipyard dock, where Tai has gone to pick up the heroin shipment. In an intense chase and shootout, the young Chinese crime boss is wounded and White (also wounded) allows Tai to commit suicide. White is reunited with his girlfriend, who offers solace to the injured but victorious police captain.

Any notable appreciation mustered for *Year of the Dragon* often took a halfhearted turn, such as the back-handed accolade that proclaimed Cimino's film the "most exciting bad movie of 1985." There was some admiration for the action—which was said to have been skillfully choreographed—but on the whole the film was widely criticized for being pretentious, uneven in dramatic flow, and questionable in its development of the central character, Stanley White (Mickey Rourke).

The unevenness of the script and the film derived from a tendency to shift rapidly between scenes of explosive action and scenes of raw, emotional reaction played out in overly long conversations. The pumped-up nature of the dialogue—particularly White's crusade rhetoric—had what was referred to as a ludicrous, unbelievable quality about it. *Year of the Dragon* possessed its moments of exhilarating visual power, but its aural text was regarded as an unconvincing mess.

Tied to the film's vacillating qualities were the peculiar and unappealing character traits of Stan White, the protagonist. Stone and Cimino had constructed White as a Dirty Harry/Rambo amalgam, a returned Vietnam veteran with an obsessive demeanor for getting the job done. White, in his determination to clean up Chinatown at any cost, was meant to be the mythical lone frontier hero bravely setting out to correct crime. At the same time, White's character contained perplexing contradictions—he was racially concerned at one moment, racist at the next; his interpersonal skills with colleagues and women were clearly lacking; his persona was self-centered, sexist, foulmouthed—adding up to a generally unlikable "cause freak" hero.

Particularly nagging with regard to the White characterization was the fact that Stone had made the protagonist hero a second-generation Polish-American, a reinvention of Daley's novel character (who was

Micky Rourke on a mission of revenge in *Year of the Dragon* (1985). ©
1985 Dino De Laurentis Corporation. All rights reserved. Courtesy
The Museum of Modern Art/Film Stills Archive.

not Polish). The depiction, critics said, further muddled Stone and
Cimino's intentions and offered an immigrant hero going after other
immigrants. The creation, therefore, did not entirely ring true. Stone
had also made the female television reporter Chinese, which she was
not in the novel, leading to more questions about why a racist—compelled by an anti-Asian attitude—would love and be solaced by an
Asian-American woman.

Critics were especially perplexed that White—a member of one
American immigrant group—would wage a war of vindication
against another. Richard Combs of *Monthly Film Bulletin* summarized
the contradictions:

That the vehicle for this vindication should be a Pollack cop who has returned
from a tour of duty in Vietnam with a chip on his shoulder about the Oriental

race (Rambo come home) is a contradiction that Cimino takes in his stride—that in fact powers the film. White is a racist; then he is one with a peculiar racial conscience—as he demonstrated in his lecture about the Chinese who built the Western railroads, and were buried, forgotten, beneath their tracks. In terms of character and experiences, Stanley has to be racist (though the film is no more undivided about this than, say, *Dirty Harry* was) but in terms of his drives, and Cimino's larger scheme, he is trying to redeem America for all Americans.[10]

What exactly, critics asked, were filmgoers supposed to make of such contradictions in a morally crusading character? Whatever the intentions, the approach distracted and ultimately led to a dissipation of interest in the film.

There were other elements of racism. The Chinese mafia plotting details, the racist remarks spouted by the central character, and the tendency to lump all Asians together as alike in order to engineer the hero's crusading as an extension of a Vietnam, anti-Asian attitude resulted in an outpouring of public antipathy against *Year of the Dragon*. Stone and Cimino had made limp attempts to counterbalance the hero's jeering attitude by incorporating dialogue about the achievements—past and present—of the Chinese people as well as "knowledgeable" discussions of media stereotypes such as Charlie Chan. But the script's counterattempts at a more elevated view of the Chinese people had not satisfied Asian-Americans. The film was widely picketed, and briefly its distributor, MGM-United Artists, considered placing a disclaimer in the opening credits. Novelist Robert Daley publicly denounced the screen adaptation of his book.

The outcome for *Year of the Dragon* was not a particularly happy one, although the film in its run abroad scored much better with European critics than with U.S. reviewers. The unfortunate conclusion was that Cimino had not reclaimed his stature lost in the making of *Heaven's Gate*. Put tersely by Janet Maslin in reviewing *Year of the Dragon* for the *New York Times*: "It is no pleasure to report that Mr. Cimino's reputation as the man who best exemplifies what can go wrong with big-ego, big-budget filmmaking remains unchallenged."[11]

Because Oliver Stone had worked in intense, close collaboration with Cimino ("He breathed me," Stone said), the ill-received film's faults were Stone's as well as Cimino's. Dino De Laurentis, as producer, had also been involved—insisting on plot changes that affected the final results. Recognizing the inextricable contributions of Stone and Cimino, Pauline Kael leveled a particularly vituperative attack on the team:

In terms of any kind of controlling moral intelligence Oliver Stone and Michael Cimino are still living in a cave. Stone, whose credibility as a writer is based on his having taken an Academy Award (for *Midnight Express*), and Cimino, whose first movie credit was for the script that John Milius and he wrote for *Magnum Force,* the seamiest of the Dirty Harry movies, are evenly matched. *Year of the Dragon* suffers from a form of redundancy. One brazen vulgarian working on a movie might enliven it, but two—and both xenophobic—bring out the worst in each other. They're bouncing their ideas off a mirror, so neither one knows when he has become a public embarrassment.[12]

8 MILLION WAYS TO DIE

Against such attacks Stone went on to write the screenplay for Hal Ashby's *8 Million Ways to Die* (1986), an insignificant police action thriller that was a forerunner to the *Lethal Weapon*–style melodrama that builds sympathy for a down-and-out ex-cop who is pulled—against his desire—back into the line of duty and, coincidentally, up from the doldrums. The arena of action was again illegal drug trade, but in a more personal, intimate setting than the worlds entertained in *Scarface* and *Year of the Dragon.* (Only eight people die in the course of the film's action.) The project was an adaptation of a series of novels by Lawrence Block and coscripted by Stone with David Lee Henry— a novelist-turned-scenarist who had written the screenplay for *The Evil That Men Do* (1984).

The promise of the film came in the expectation that director Hal Ashby *(Shampoo, Harold and Maude, The Last Detail, Coming Home)* possessed the wherewithal to take the standard thriller story and— with Stone's drug-trafficking screen experience—elevate it to a new level of entertainment.

Disappointingly, *8 Millions Ways to Die* was universally regarded as a failure. The Stone-Henry screenplay had provided mustily familiar material: drugs, loud and foul-mouthed dialogue, chases, shootouts. Plot development was either clichèd or full of inexplicable connections. Character motivation could only be guessed at. The film was labeled a tired and listless repeat of *Scarface* (Andy Garcia's Angel character in *8 Millions Ways to Die* was also of Cuban extraction). Nothing

Andy Garcia (Angel Maldonado), Alexandra Paul (Sunny Hendryx), and Jeff Bridges (Matt Scudder) meet at a party in *8 Million Ways to Die* (1986). © 1986 Tri-Star Pictures, Inc. All rights reserved. Courtesy The Museum of Modern Art/Film Stills Archive.

Synopsis of *8 Million Ways to Die* (1986)

Cast: Jeff Bridges, Rosanna Arquette, Alexandra Paul, Randy Brooks, Andy Garcia, Lisa Stone, Christa Denton.

Credits: Director: Hal Ashby. Producer: Steve Roth. Screenplay: Oliver Stone and David Lee Henry, based on the novels by Lawrence Block. Photography: Stephen H. Burum. Music: James Newton Howard. Distributor: Tri-Star Pictures.

Matt Scudder (Jeff Bridges), a drug-bust police officer, participates in a squad raid in which he kills an unarmed man in the house under seizure. Scudder is shown drinking during the raid and later is seen out-and-out drunk. Recognizing that his alcoholism is interfering with his police duties (he's already been reprimanded), Scudder requests a medical leave.

After six months of AA meetings, the ex-cop is revealed speaking to his group about the costs of his alcohol problem—job, health, family. At the end of the AA meeting, Scudder is handed a note by a stranger soliciting his assistance in helping a beautiful young prostitute, Sunny (Alexandra Paul), escape her pimp. The note leads Scudder to a fancy Los Angeles hilltop house, where he meets Sunny, her prostitute pal Sarah (Rosanna Arquette), and an assortment of sleazy-con types, including Chance (Randy Brooks), manager of a gambling-and-sex club, and Angel (Andy Garcia), a drug dealer.

Scudder agrees to help Sunny out of Chance's sex ring and takes her into his protection. On the way to an airport, Sunny is kidnapped and murdered, causing Scudder to start drinking again. The ex-cop eventually decides to sober up and seek the prostitute's murderer. Scudder discovers through the woman's address book and a phone number on a bracelet that Sunny was involved in Angel's cocaine operation and that he is the murderer. Realizing that Sarah is probably also in danger, Scudder takes her away, and the two, who have previously seemed to dislike each other, discover some mutual interests and concerns.

Scudder presses the nervous, neurotic Angel regarding Sunny's murder; Sarah is lured back into the drug kingpin's entourage; Scudder has a fortuitous run-in with Chance and engages his help in getting Sarah away from Angel and busting the cocaine drug operation, which works out of a supermarket warehouse. In an encounter with Angel, the drug baron admits killing Sunny as "advertising" in the cause of preventing more killings.

In the showdown, Scudder draws Angel to the warehouse, where a drug-bust squad lies in waiting. Sarah, used as a hostage, is freed when Scudder threatens to set fire to the cocaine supply. The bullets fly, killing Chance and most of Angel's henchmen—but the drug czar is able to escape. Returning home with Sarah, Angel waits in ambush but is shot and killed by Scudder. The film ends with Scudder and Sarah walking, kissing on a beach while Scudder's pep lecture to an AA group about his hopefully successful battle with booze is heard voice-over.

---

had seemed to jell in production; story, acting, directing—all fell flat. Hal Ashby had in fact withdrawn from the project before final shooting was completed, nearly aborting the project altogether.

Looking for explanations, Rita Kempley of the *Washington Post* surmised: "The movie's a mixed bag, probably because the script was written by drug-traffic expert Oliver Stone of *Scarface* and *Midnight Express* and David Lee Henry of *The Evil Men Do* on the one hand, and directed by sensitive guy Hal Ashby of *Harold and Maude* and *Coming Home* on the other. It's an unhappy hybrid, a valiant but impractical attempt to upgrade the genre."[13]

Oliver Stone's four writing assignments between 1982 and 1986 had resulted in disillusionment and frustration. Two of the projects *(Conan the Barbarian* and *8 Million Ways to Die)* so mangled the writing that Stone's efforts were considered wasted. He refused afterwards to even discuss *8 Million Ways to Die.* The claims of a racist/ fascist attitude and inauthenticity in *Scarface* and *Year of the Dragon* fell Stone's way—and appropriately so—as much as to their directors, both De Palma and Cimino being known for tendencies toward excessive violence. Stone saw himself as someone unable to control his own destiny, constrained by a necessary commercial sellout while he waited for the chance to direct his own screenplays that stood more firmly on the left side of the political fence than on the right.

And yet Stone, an educable filmmaker, took what he could from the experiences. The documentary footage used at the beginning of *Scarface* to reveal the release of Cuban refugees had been declared a powerfully effective device for authenticating a dramatic story. The device would become standard in his own later backward scans of American history.

There was also an interesting fact of discovery in the creation of the Stanley White/Mickey Rourke character in *Year of the Dragon.* The charges of having constructed a sexist, brutish hero, full of contradictory attitudes and questionable values, would not deter Stone from creating such characters again; nor would they intimidate him from treating the unwholesome side of humanity.

Stone's maverick, innovative nature—waiting to fully emerge—had been given some valuable testing ground.

4

Salvador

How does an ex–Vietnam veteran like Oliver Stone end up making one of the most hard-hitting condemnations on film of American policy in El Salvador?
—Sally Hibbin, "Blood from Stone," *Films and Filming,* January 1987

The above question was asked not only by Hibbin but others who knew Oliver Stone and had followed his much-discussed screenwriting jobs between 1978 and 1986 for pictures like *Midnight Express, Conan the Barbarian, Scarface,* and *Year of the Dragon.* As Stone's first directorial effort after writing this body of films, which critics had frequently referred to as nihilistic and fascist, *Salvador* did appear politically anomalous with what had just gone before.

There was also the oddity of Stone's first two directing efforts, *Seizure* (1973) and *The Hand* (1981), both rather standard horror films. Although philosophically inclined, those works gave no hint whatsoever of a writer-director interested in turning out films with political themes. That *Salvador* was altogether political was a surprise; that the film was powerfully and adamantly leftist came as a shock.

Stone saw the movement from *Seizure* and *The Hand* to *Salvador* as easily explained by his progress as an artist whose work changed as his personal life changed. Stone said, "What you do at 33 you don't do at 39. *The Hand* [as was *Seizure*] was something I did at a much darker phase of my life. Horror seemed to me an apt reflection on my inner turmoil. I was happier when I turned to the social themes of *Salvador.* . . . Each film for me was a breakthrough, an education. Each film was a product of time and place, a year of my life."[1]

The shift to a hard-hitting political stance in *Salvador* did not just happen but occurred over a period of time. Stone's original intention

James Woods as photojournalist Peter Boyle in *Salvador* (1986). Courtesy The Museum of Modern Art/Film Stills Archive.

in writing a film about El Salvador was to produce a character-focused study of photojournalist Richard Boyle. Boyle was someone Stone had come to know in California in the late 1970s, and he had become increasingly intrigued by the photojournalist's lifestyle. According to Stone, "[Boyle] was always broke, always needing to be bailed out of jail, always on drunken driving charges. He was a womanizer and a drinker, yet he would always be popping off to these small places, like Ireland or Lebanon, and doing these stories" (Hibbin, 18).

There was also the fact that Boyle had worked in and written about Vietnam, another attraction for Stone. Boyle's Vietnam experience resulted in a book, *Flower of the Dragon,* that recounted in detail an incidence of troop resistance to combat within an American unit stationed in Southeast Asia. Boyle had also covered the fighting in Cambodia.

After Stone met Boyle in 1978, the photojournalist shifted his work as a stringer largely to troubled Central America, traveling to and from the area as often as he needed to support himself and his wife.

Between 1979 and 1982—Boyle plagued by financial and marital difficulties—made seven trips to El Salvador, sending back stories and becoming romantically involved with a Salvadoran woman, Maria. Boyle witnessed the political turmoil that at the time entangled the United States and its ambassador, Robert White, in a violent civil war between the centrist government (U.S.-backed) and leftist guerilla troops. The activity of right-wing death squads also accelerated in this period. The conflict resulted in the deaths of thousands of Salvadoran citizens; the assassination of Salvador's liberal archbishop Oscar Arnulfo Romero; and, most shockingly, the rape/murder in 1980 of an American Catholic lay worker, a friend, and two nuns traveling by van from El Salvador's major airport.

Boyle had kept a diary of his visits to El Salvador and of the events he had seen (and heard of) occurring around him, including the death of girlfriend Maria's brother, Carlos, by a right-wing death squad. Oliver Stone, already fascinated by Boyle's "rascally" character, became even more intrigued by the drama going on in El Salvador and decided to go see for himself, accompanied by Boyle as a guide.

Early in 1985 the two traveled to El Salvador, Honduras, and other areas of Central America. Stone said he was struck by how much his visit brought back memories of Saigon in 1965: "It's 20 years later, but you see the exact same environment of militarization and corruption of the populace. . . . It goes all the way back to the '60's when we actually trained the original members of the Salvador death squads in Vietnam. They studied our counterinsurgency techniques and brought them to El Salvador. That's part of the whole tragedy here—that what started out as idealism turned into torture."[2]

What had started as interest in Richard Boyle as a kind of gadfly journalist drawn to the brink of violence and death began to change for Stone into a story that would include Boyle's autobiographical material along with an analysis of U.S. involvement and policy in El Salvador. Stone described the transformation as such:

I was interested in Boyle as this sort of renegade journalist, a selfish rascal who through his exposure to the country, becomes more unselfish, and who, through his love for the woman [Maria], starts to become something he wasn't in the beginning. . . . In following that intention, however, I got very involved in the background story of El Salvador. To be frank, when I first went down there I didn't know anything about the 1980–81 period. I had really been confused by the American press reports and the situation seemed to me very ambiguous. When Boyle introduced me to El Salvador, I was quite shocked to see how really black and white it was, because everybody always tells you the grey, and it was at that point that we really tried to tell more of the Salvadoran story than the Boyle story, and we tried to blend the two together.[3]

For the Salvadoran side of the story, Stone consulted Raymond Bonner's 1984 book, *Weakness and Deceit: U.S. Policy and El Salvador,* using Bonner's interpretations to help explain the why and how of actual incidents, such as the assassination of Archbishop Romero.

Stone pulled together his screenplay for *Salvador* during a three-month period after returning from El Salvador early in 1985. The script took the anecdotal incidents as described by Boyle and blended them into a screenplay that was bold in both its characterizations and its political attacks. Stone said he had wanted to create a different film on both accounts, capturing in a no-holds-barred approach the political realities of U.S. involvement in El Salvador, and at the same time presenting the journalist-protagonist Boyle in a nitty-gritty, realistic manner—in ways that would "work against the conventional grain of those types of movies where the journalist has to be pious and saintly and dignified. A lot of these war junkies are really fucked-up people," Stone said.[4]

The political material in *Salvador*'s script, plus the presence of an unsavory antihero protagonist, made Stone's project unsalable in conservative Hollywood. Responses were said to be highly negative. Stone took the script to the British-based Hemdale Corporation, which had just registered a big success with *Terminator* (1984) and was looking for additional American properties in which to invest. Hemdale agreed to put up $6 million, and additional backing was secured from Gerald Green of Mexico's Pasta Producciones. Mexican backing came after Stone's decision to make *Salvador* in Mexico in a small village outside Cuernavaca. To assist his efforts in winning financial support, Stone had agreed to invest his own money in the production and to direct without salary.

Salvador was shot in Mexico, California, and Nevada over an eight-week period, with Stone able to film his script as he had written it, without so-called front-office interference: "I was able to state my point of view politically. I think that's possibly because it's English money. They view the situation in Central America with a little more irony than the American film people do. It would not have been made had it not been for the English."[5]

What filmgoers would see in *Salvador,* in its limited commercial release in 1986, was a highly streamlined film (Stone having taken his dramatic cues from *Midnight Express*) in which events occurring over a two-year period in El Salvador were condensed into a period of several months. The film, with its explosive ideas and oddball characters, offered original and compelling fare.

Synopsis of *Salvador* (1986)

Cast: James Woods, James Belushi, Elepedia Carrillo, Michael Murphy, John Savage, Tony Plana, Cynthia Gibb, Colby Chester, Will MacMillan, Jorge Luke, Valerie Wilman, Jose Carlos Ruiz, Juan Gernandez.

Credits: Director: Oliver Stone. Screenplay: Oliver Stone and Richard Boyle. Photography: Robert Richardson. Music: Georges Delerue. Production: Pasta Productions, Hemdale. Distributor: Virgin.

The plot of *Salvador* begins in San Francisco, where photojournalist Richard Boyle (James Woods) is seen in a swift flow of details: in a domestic squabble with his Italian-born wife (Maria Rubell); being harangued about past-due rent; phoning a news service for money to finance a trip back to El Salvador to shoot photos of the violent uprisings there. Unsuccessful on the phone, Boyle goes out to look for work and is stopped for speeding. He is hauled off to jail for an excess of motor offenses and for not having a valid driver's license. After being bailed out by an out-of-work disc jockey friend, Dr. Rock (James Belushi), Boyle returns to his apartment to find that he has been evicted and that his wife has left for Italy with their baby son.

Now desperate but free, Boyle talks Dr. Rock—whose girlfriend has also just walked out—into fleeing south to Guatemala with him, fully intending all the while to travel to El Salvador in his beat-up but serviceable Ford Mustang convertible, which he has named the "Deathmobile."

On the way Dr. Rock sees a road sign reading El Salvador and discovers the ruse; he becomes irate. Boyle calms his traveling companion with promises that the country holds access to easy sex and cheap drugs. Traveling on, the two are taken hostage at a road block by sinister-looking men who have just destroyed a truckload of "suspicious *compañenos.*" Boyle claims to be friends with Colonel Julio Figueroa (Jorge Luke), after which the two Americans are seen being taken by jeep—through streets strewn with dead bodies and burned-out cars—to Figueroa's quarters, where the colonel greets the journalist boisterously. The dialogue reveals that Boyle had once done a story praising the officer as a hero, and Figueroa anticipates that Boyle will continue to give him favorable press in American newspapers.

With this reception Boyle is able to reclaim his convertible and is free to do what he has returned to El Salvador to do: to carouse; to drink; to reunite himself with his girlfriend, Maria (Elepedia Carrillo), in the coastal town of La Libertad; and to seek out combat situations that will make good photo stories and earn him the money needed to continue his carousing ways.

Boyle seeks out old friend and fellow journalist John Cassady (John Savage), a writer supplying stories to *Newsweek,* who takes Boyle for a photo shoot to "El Playon"—a body dump for Salvadorans killed in the right-wing and military skirmishes that escalated in 1980. The two journalists climb among the mass of burned bodies, photographing the eerie scene while chatting in journalese: "You have to get close to the truth. You get too close you die," Cassady says.

Salvador encapsulates the reign of terror of 1980–81 by depicting the engineering of death squads by right-wing party leader Major Max (Tony Plana). In Stone's story the squads are blamed for the disappearance of tens of thousands of Salvadorans and Major Max is shown plotting the assassination of Archbishop Oscar Romero—a powerful liberal and church leader who has spoken out against right-wing repression of his people.

Boyle himself is depicted as a target of the Major Max squads, as is Carlos, Maria's brother, who is arrested and disappears. Accompanied by a Catholic lay worker in a local war orphanage, Cathy Moore (Cynthia Gibb), Boyle seeks to involve the U.S. ambassador, Tom Kelly (Michael Murphy), in the search for Carlos. Kelly is evasive, reminding Boyle that he once wrote a story in which he called the Khmer Rouge "the good guys."

Salvador places Boyle, Maria, and Cassady in the cathedral when Romero (José Carlos Ruiz) is assassinated—Boyle having gone to confession and then communion in a ploy to improve his image with Maria and convince her to marry him. The mutilated, beheaded body of Carlos (Martin Fuentes), Maria's brother, is discovered shortly after the Romero assassination, quickly followed by the atrocious rape/murder of Cathy Moore, a friend, and two nuns, apparently at the hands of a death squad. Boyle and Ambassador Kelly are shown observing the scene (while Cassady photographs it) as the women's bodies are dug up at the murder site, off a Salvadoran highway.

The infuriated Ambassador Kelly cuts off military aid to the right-wing Salvadoran regime at the very same time Boyle and Cassady leave to interview and photograph left-wing guerillas high in the mountains. They learn of a planned offensive attack on Santa Ana.

Back in the capital, Boyle reveals his guerilla photographs to American advisers, who say their own evidence tells them the left-wing guerilla activity is part of a Communist insurrection, not a revolution. Boyle—who sides with the guerillas—passionately challenges the advisers' interpretation, but gets no-where. He turns his attention to efforts to secure official papers, a *cedula,* for Maria so that she and her children can leave the country and return with him to the United States.

As American soldiers begin to arrive in El Salvador, the rebel offensive against government troops begins—a fierce civil battle in which government forces are driven by the rebels out of the city. The rebels are then themselves driven back by Colonel Figueroa's forces after aid is restored by Kelly. In the course of covering the battle—presented with the guerilla rebels on horseback charging the streets and government tanks—Boyle is wounded and Cassady is killed as he photographs his own death (by machine-gun fire from an airplane above).

Salvador concludes with Boyle and Maria—assisted by Ambassador Kelly—managing to get out of El Salvador, only to have Maria and her family taken from a bus and turned back by U.S. immigration officials. Protests by Boyle fail, and he is driven away in an immigration official's car. Final explanations by way of end titles report that Maria was sent to a refugee camp in Guatemala, that Boyle continues to search for her, that Dr. Rock is back in San Francisco, and that the murderers of Archbishop Romero have not been found.

The political details in the Stone-Boyle script were powerfully un-compromising by themselves, but what propelled *Salvador* to both acclaim and controversy was Stone's energetic, quasi-documentary translation of events for the screen. *Los Angeles Times* critic Michael Wilmington wrote: "Whatever may be flawed in Oliver Stone's searing, full-torque new war movie *Salvador,* one thing about it is burningly right. It's alive. It broils, snaps and explodes with energy. The events (condensed from two years of battles and political upheaval in El Salvador) fly past at a murderous clip, hurtling you along almost demonically."[6]

The unrelenting pace of *Salvador* (again not unlike that achieved by Alan Parker in *Midnight Express*) resulted in a film experience critics variously described as "gutsy," "disturbing," "left-wing machismo," and capable of pulling the viewer into its "crescendoes of violence" with jolting effect. Stone had translated Boyle's anecdotal material with impressive control, achieving variety in the film's flow by inter-mingling humor, suspense, action, passion, and historical facsimiles. His work with his cast—from principles to extras—once again re-vealed him capable of deriving credible, texturally dimensioned performances.

Of equal note, and inextricably bound to *Salvador*'s visceral impact, was the way Stone had imbued his political story with a sense of heightened realism—another cue taken from the *Midnight Express* association. The film begins with newsreel footage of violence in El Salvador, and a slightly grainy overall look is applied to the remainder of the film to sustain its quasi-documentary properties. The docu-feel effect is reinforced by the periodic use of captions—also common to the documentary film—to explain and punctuate events developing within the narrative. The sudden appearance of an explanatory caption simultaneously works to suggest factual authority in what is happening on the screen and to lend an aura of ominous significance to the developing events.

The visual design of scenes in *Salvador,* especially those depicting death and its sinister origins, also heightened the reality of the film. A hazy, surreal quality dominated Robert Richardson's cinematography in his Mexican-based revisualizations of El Salvador. Night scenes and interiors are invariably film noir—supplying the atmosphere with suspenseful ambiguity. Smoke (à la *Midnight Express*) is everywhere—shrouding death-strewn streets, rising from El Playon's death mound—and it becomes a primary element in the battle of Santa Ana, obscuring the images and adding to the sense of confusion and futility in the film's most epic and dramatic scenes.

Stone achieves additional dramatic impact by giving his film the constant feel of spontaneity. A hand-held camera is used to record most of the intense action. In the scene of panic and violence following Romero's assassination, the camera is so spontaneously free that the film resembles a cinema verité evocation of the event.

Even more jolting in their spontaneity were Stone's depictions of the death squad incidents that had helped call worldwide attention to the violent upheaval in El Salvador: the assassination of Archbishop Romero and the rape/murder of the four church women. These events were included in the plot of *Salvador* in a cleverly glib manner, but in a way that electrifies them with new impact.

The scene in which Romero is killed at the communion rail is introduced by Stone with near-comic and sacrilegious playfulness. In one of the film's funniest moments, Boyle confesses his sins to a priest—receiving a penance of 12 Our Fathers, 10 Hail Marys, and an Act of Contrition. Boyle, "renewed" and cockily relieved, exits the confessional and rejoins Maria and John Cassady in a pew in the cathedral, where Romero is presiding at the Mass. They listen to the prelate's impassioned homily about "the right" and the tragedy of political repression. As Romero later distributes communion, moving down the communion rail to Maria and Boyle, then to his kneeling killer, the assassin suddenly spits at Romero before killing him with several shots to the chest. In the presence of well-developed screen characters who are "innocent" witnesses to an act of historical notoriety, the shock of the assassination is powerfully conveyed.

In a seemingly uneventful bit of plotting detail, Cathy Moore—the caring lay church worker who has been assisting Boyle and Dr. Rock in their run-ins with the law and Maria in her efforts to locate her missing brother—brings a bottle of Irish whiskey to Boyle as a Christmas present. In an exchange of small talk, Boyle seeks advice from Moore about marrying Maria. The domestic discussion ends with Moore—needing to get home—telling Boyle she has agreed to drive some nuns from the airport the next day. She kisses Boyle goodbye and says "Merry Christmas." The following day Moore and her riding companions are raped and murdered, their bodies tossed into a shallow roadside grave.

Once again the handling of this notoriously familiar detail, as with Romero's killing, achieves a chilling effect through the insertion of sudden, abrupt violence into what seems innocent, commonplace narrative action. These two events, along with the unexpected disappearance of Maria's brother, Carlos, significantly abet Stone's goal of presenting El Salvador as a place where awful things just happen— without expectation, without development. In this manner Stone intensifies the deadly atmosphere he had sought to convey throughout the film.

Music composed by Georges Delerue provided another kind of intensifying accompaniment to what went on on the screen. While still employing the suspense-building drumbeat sound favored by Stone in *Seizure* and *The Hand*, *Salvador*—with its broad ambitions and rapidly changing moods—offered a pastiche of musical underscoring that was varied in style and impact. Religious choral music accompanies the photo shoot at El Playon; dissonant, blaring trumpets and staccato drumrolls propel scenes of chaotic disorder; a Latino folk song with men's chorus plays beneath the guerilla fight scenes during the Battle of Santa Ana, striving to ennoble the action and build thematic empathy for the guerilla efforts.

In his professed attempt at creating in *Salvador* a film of heightened reality, Stone had, as in *Midnight Express,* telescoped events and taken significant dramatic liberties in altering and embellishing factual details. Most notable in its change was the fact that Romero had been killed in a small church—not a cathedral. Boyle had not been present. The sermon speech had been given by Romero in a larger church, a few days before his assassination, and the violent panic scene had occurred not at the time of the killing but at Romero's funeral a few days later. The rearrangements, Stone said, had not violated the truth and had been necessary to condense time, provide dramatic cohesiveness, and supply the sought-after heightened realism.

Other liberties taken to give *Salvador* a special dramatic edge included decisions to put the guerilla rebels on horseback and to send Dr. Rock along as a traveling companion of Boyle's. The intended effect of these changes was explained by Stone:

At the Battle of Santa Ana I have a cavalry charge against the tanks. In fact the rebels didn't have that kind of cavalry. They were on foot. But I put that in because to me it symbolized the overwhelming odds against their success [horses against tanks]. Probably the biggest liberty I took was that Dr. Rock never went to El Salvador. He's a San Francisco friend of mine and Boyle's, a rock disc jockey. But he's been a friend of ours for years; his character is an appendage to Boyle's, and we hypothesized—if he went to El Salvador—we would see the country through an ordinary American's point of view, from a man who is not an exotic foreign journalist.

(Gordon, 40)

The plotting details involving the Dr. Rock character in essence provided the kind of "layman's journey" effect Stone sought in the ploy of a traveling companion for Boyle. The events that befall Rock in El Salvador served to reveal in crass terms a neophyte's growing awareness of a world overcome by all sorts of life-threatening dangers and political perversions: the initial impact of arriving in El Salvador and immediately coming upon the aftermath of a death squad attack, the contracting of a venereal disease, the observance of evasive U.S. government and media rhetoricians, a jailing and a run-in with a death squad about to kill Boyle, and the discovery of war's effect on innocent children.

The accumulation of these events lead Rock to his own conscientious understanding of human and political realities in El Salvador. And in an ironic change-of-heart conversion, Rock is revealed as willing to remain in the country at the moment a fully disheartened Boyle has decided he must leave. The Belushi-rendered Dr. Rock character-ization—obese, bawdy, and unscrupulous—also provided a large part of the film's crude, Falstaffian-like humor.

Altogether the major elements in *Salvador* had culminated in a unique, widely debated film experience. Clearly among the many fas-cinating elements in Stone's work—and at the core of many of the film's most heated debates—were the offbeat characterizations created for Boyle and Dr. Rock. On the surface there appeared to be little or nothing to like and admire in the personae as outlined. The two men were failures in their interpersonal relationships with women; were heavy drinkers and drug users; were money-obsessed but financially incompetent; used foul, often sexist language ("The best thing about Latino women is they don't speak English"); and seemed to be sadly displaced carryovers from the 1960s counterculture—unable to get on with their lives. (In San Francisco, the two men, riding in Boyle's Mustang, anachronistically shout at passersby: "I hate yuppies!")

Depending on one's critical point of view, the Boyle–Dr. Rock characterizations had either made *Salvador* "unbearable" or provided one of the film's most distinguished, laudable qualities. Movie critic Gene Siskel, writing for the *Chicago Tribune,* called *Salvador* more "in-sult than message," and discredited the film's suggestion—through Boyle's character—"that you have to be half-juiced up to do war-zone journalism," adding: "That's an insult to the courageous men and women who regularly perform the media's most dangerous job—that of foreign correspondent." Siskel went on to criticize Stone for "the need to jazz up his action with wacked-out characters who belong in a *"Saturday Night Live"* sketch."[7]

Pauline Kael in the *New Yorker* saw little redeeming value in either Boyle's character or *Salvador,* saying bluntly, "The movie is as screwed up as its hero."[8] *Maclean's* reviewer admired *Salvador*'s "gripping ac-tion" but described the film as "the victim of an artistic war—between repugnant farce and historical tragedy."[9] *New York Times* critic Walter Goodman declared the Dr. Rock character "irrelevant as well as repulsive."[10]

Other analytical voices reacted to the crudities of character in dif-ferent ways, many seeing the Boyle depiction as essential to the film's theme of personal discovery, redemption, and conversion. (At the end of the film, Boyle shouts at the immigration officials who are hauling Maria away: "You don't know what it's like in El Salvador. You have no idea!")

Charles Champlin of the *Los Angeles Times* argued: "Those hints of a complexity of character—the conniving survivor coexisting with a capacity for loving concern—are absolutely essential to the intentions of *Salvador*. . . . [Boyle], having taken the audience near to an uneasy contempt at the outset, becomes a man of courage and humor (life size, not larger than life; no incredible heroics) and the contempt changes to admiration and, I think, a profound sympathy."[11]

In a similar line of argument, *Washington Post* critic Paul Attanasio wrote: "Rock keeps to his straight line (for him *Salvador* is just a kind of barroom brawl). But Boyle struggles to go on beyond that—he's a habitual jerk, but the country peels away his hustle. The emotional thrust of the movie comes in Boyle's odyssey from a sleazy operator to a sleazy operator with a conscience, and it's because he remains distasteful that the conversion carries such oomph. Boyle embitters what might otherwise be sentimental about *Salvador,* makes it believable."[12]

In his interpretation of the Boyle character, actor James Woods was credited with great skill in the way he had developed a multidimensioned human being with a complex value system. Critics called the performance "mesmerizing," "full of nervous energy," "one of the driving forces of the film."

The *Washington Post* critic saw Woods's performance as Boyle and James Belushi's interpretation of Dr. Rock as meshed with Stone's desire for alternative, nonromanticized heroes: "it's a terrific role for Woods, a nervous, fast-talking actor with a long pock-mocked face and shrewd eyes. Woods' work is chaotic and undisciplined, and in another context he might seem hit or miss; but his anything-goes style melds perfectly with what's messy and lunatic about *Salvador*. Stone isn't interested in polish, but authenticity. . . . Belushi gives a believable performance as a drug fiend; he doesn't romanticize Rock—he's mostly brooding, sluggish and depressed" (Attanasio, D11).

Another aspect of the *Salvador* debate focused on Stone's scripting of the scene in which Boyle takes a stand against the U.S. position in El Salvador—launching into a highly emotional, rhetorical debate with the two American military/CIA advisers over the pros and cons of the political situation in Central America. Some called Boyle's sudden leftist outburst—in which he uses such phrases as "in the name of decency," "a just society," and "everybody on this planet"—the work of a "bleeding heart" screenwriter and too didactic to be effective. Christopher Hutchins in *Commentary* claimed that the dialogue did not ring true and detracted from Boyle's otherwise credible character: "He

sheds the gross and very fluent vernacular that he employs the rest of
the time and becomes sententious and verbose."[13] The dialogue written by Stone for the two advisers was also criticized for the way it
drew on loaded counterattack clichés, such as the statement to Boyle
"I never understood why you guys like Commies so much."

Apologists for the scene said they did not hear Boyle's sympathetic
speech as Stone interrupting the action for a message. Charles Champlin argued: "[Boyle] begins to sound off as imprudently as he's done
everything else in his life and the passion of his protest to some of the
U.S. brass is the more compelling because it is an outburst, not a
doctrinaire sermon to the already convinced in the audience" (Champlin, 8).

Critic Paul Attanasio excused the "message" aspect of *Salvador* because of its cinematic style: "But if Stone's métièr is a brand of left-
wing machismo that's nearly extinct, it's also a style you wish were
around more these days, especially when it results in movies like *Salvador*. You might think it's preachy; you might think it's messy, but
when you leave, you won't doubt that you've seen a real movie" (Attanasio, D11).

The importance of *Salvador* to Oliver Stone's emergence as a flamboyant screenwriter-director cannot be overstated. While the film's
energy might be likened to that in *Midnight Express* and while Boyle's
offbeat, antihero character could be compared with the Mickey
Rourke character in *Year of the Dragon*, *Salvador* was entirely Stone's
own achievement, in so many ways a remarkable leap from the small-
cast, simple-setting efforts of *Seizure* and *The Hand* and from the
entertainment-oriented action thrillers he had been writing for mainstream Hollywood.

Stone's directing skills were also undeniably obvious. He had credibly re-created El Salvador in Mexico, including the staggering Battle
of Santa Ana, staged with cavalry charges, tanks, and air warfare. The
production for *Salvador* involved nearly 100 speaking roles, 1,000 extras, a crew of 200, and 40 different shooting locations. Stone handled
his management chores efficiently and economically, completing the
film at a cost of $4.5 million—well below the $6 million backing al-
located by Hemdale. *Salvador* proved that Stone was more than capable of realizing a broad-canvas film and of doing so with authentic
force.

Salvador also moved Stone closer to the discovery of his creative
voice—to that narrative and visual style by which his work would
become distinguishable from that of other American directors of the

Elepedia Carrillo (Maria), James Woods (Peter Boyle), and James Belushi (Dr. Rock) caught up in the furor of political upheaval in *Salvador* (1986). Courtesy The Museum of Modern Art/Film Stills Archive.

1980s. On the release of *Salvador,* Stone spoke about what he saw as the film's special qualities: "It has an edge to it, it has a madness and a fury. I like anarchy in films, and this one has plenty of anarchy—that's what I'm proud of. My heroes were Buñuel and Godard, and *Breathless* was one of the first pictures I really remember being marked by, because of the speed and energy."[14]

The driving force of *Salvador* had not gone unnoticed as the primary strength of the film. George Robert Kimball, critic for *Films and Filming,* cited Stone's work as an "astounding visual and narrative feat, [with its] machine-gun editing, a sometimes unbearably realistic use of special effects make-up, perfectly handled sound, and perhaps most important, a restless almost tormented camera that seems never to stop hunting through the unfolding scenes of chaos as if frantically searching for some 'truth' it believes must be there but simply cannot find. That, in the end, was what really did it for me, I think. That stunning use of frenetic camera movement as a visual correlative for the mass insanity being dramatized."[15]

Charles Champlin labeled *Salvador* "a thrilling movie-movie (a test not many films of advocacy pass). It is fast, eventful, varied, exciting (the battle scenes are concise but amazing), passionate, often funny, suspenseful, and, in the end, potently affecting" (Champlin, 8).

Salvador revealed other important traits of the emerging Oliver Stone narrative and visual style. In his approach to war, Stone was eschewing the faddish heroic *Rambo/Delta Force/Top Gun* style of war picture that had swept into American filmmaking of the 1980s. Stone saw war as ugly, bloody, hard, unresolving. Picking up on these qualities, *Boxoffice* critic Tom Matthews said: "*Salvador* is an engrossing drama that has a subject matter that can't help but make one feel angry and frustrated. Like Boyle, the viewer quickly gets a sense that this is a war with no clear good guys and bad guys and with no apparent solution, and it makes the film a maddeningly involving experience."[16]

Reviewer Michael Wilmington referred to Stone's alternative approach to war in *Salvador* as "violent, gutsy, brainy, occasionally annoying and hellishly exciting," calling the film a "man's movie" and citing Stone for his abilities to show "the grungy depths of male camaraderie" (Wilmington, 6).

The dominant male qualities of *Salvador* had in fact significantly favored men altogether. Journalists Cassady and Boyle were drawn as striving to get "close to the truth," willing to move to the very center of war's death, while female journalist Pauline Axelrod (Valerie Wildman) was depicted as a vain television reporter parasitically and safely allied with the U.S. government-military corps in Central America. Axelrod—in contrast with Boyle and Cassady—is shown in her reports helping the U.S. officials cover up what is happening in El Salvador. Church lay worker Cathy Moore and "love interest" girlfriend Maria are essentially idealized, passively rendered women. The heroic, proactive, nitty-gritty provocations of *Salvador* had been worked through Stone's male personae altogether.

Salvador served as a primer for *Platoon*—Stone's next film, another war story, and this time his own. The mad fury, the violence, the grungy male camaraderie, the loose edges, the blood, the truth-seeking camera, a reluctance to resolve—all would show up again. Hemdale, so impressed with Stone's abilities, had given the go-ahead for *Platoon* even before the release of *Salvador*. Confidently, Stone was ready for the task.

Tom Berenger (Sgt. Barnes), left, and Willem Dafoe (Sgt. Elias), right, square off against each other in *Platoon* (1986). © 1986 Orion Pictures Corporation. All rights reserved. Photo by Ricky Francisco. Courtesy The Museum of Modern Art/Film Stills Archive.

5

Platoon

He's got power and force. It's good to see our country can still produce directors like him. He has a unique style and he's become a real, personal filmmaker. No one else is doing the things he's doing. He's out there by himself.
—Martin Scorsese on Oliver Stone, after the release of *Platoon*,
December 1986

Oliver Stone's preparation for what many consider to be his magnum opus, *Platoon*, began when he was a 19-year-old youth teaching English to Chinese-Vietnamese students in South Vietnam. After a year at Yale, Stone had quit college and in June 1965 moved to Saigon, where he taught school in the city's Chinese sector and worked briefly as a wiper in the merchant marine. Two years after this first "civilian" stint in Southeast Asia, he went back as a U.S. combat soldier.

Stone's recollections of his two Vietnam experiences were to a significant degree sensory—the natural result of an impressionable young man experiencing a world entirely different from that of his own limited past. He said it was in Southeast Asia that he became a man—the East becoming his "orphan home" and a place where images sharpened and where he realized that what he was seeing, feeling, and enduring he would someday tell as his own special story.

During his 15 months of military service (September 1967–November 1968), Stone was assigned to four different units—suffering two wounds while in combat and encountering the soldiers who would serve as the prototypes for *Platoon's* assortment of characters. As a naive ex–New York City boy, he was especially taken with two men of different but superb soldiering instincts—one a 23-year-old in the First Cavalry's Long Range Reconnaissance Patrol, who was turned on by the dangers of war but still could draw a moral line when it came to killing. The other was a sergeant—an angry loner and the "best soldier" Stone ever met—who had a near-obsessive penchant for killing and getting even. These two men would become, respectively, Elias and Barnes in Stone's imaginative retelling of his Vietnam experiences.

The first draft of *Platoon* was written in New York City in the summer of 1976, in the period following NYU film school when Stone wrote more than a dozen screenplays with an eye toward Hollywood and directing his own films. The idea for a Vietnam film had been germinating since his release from the army, but Stone confessed that postwar anxieties and drugs retarded the effort. When he finally sat down to write *Platoon* at age 30, he shaped his story into what he felt was a classic framework—using himself, and his memories of Elias and Barnes—two opposites in war—to construct the narrative conflict.

It was from these roots that the essential conflict between Elias and Barnes grew in my mind. Two gods. Two different views of the war. The angry Achilles [Barnes] versus the conscience-stricken Hector [Elias] fighting for a lost cause on the dusty plains of Troy. It mirrored the very civil war that I'd witnessed in all the units I was in—on the one hand, the lifers, the juicers, and the moron white element . . . against, on the other, the hippie, dope-smoking, black and progressive white element. . . . Right versus left. And I would act as Ishmael, the observer caught between those two giant forces. At first a watcher, then forced to act—to take responsibility and a moral stand. And in the process grow to a manhood I'd never dreamed I'd have to grow to. To a place where in order to go on existing I'd have to shed the innocence and accept the evil the Homeric gods had thrown out into the world. To be both good and evil. To move from this East Coast social product to a more visceral manhood where I finally felt the war not in my head, but in my gut and my soul.[1]

Initially, Hollywood producers showed little interest in Stone's dark, archetypal war story. Then in 1984, when the financial backing expected from Dino De Laurentis (in return for writing *The Year of the Dragon*) fell through, Stone thought for certain he would never see *Platoon* on film. Adding to his frustrations was the fact that he had to sue De Laurentis to win back property rights to the screenplay. De Laurentis had apparently been sincere in his desire to finance the picture, but had temporarily withdrawn support when no distributor could be found.

The rather unexpected and fortuitous achievement of *Salvador* in 1985 finally brought Stone his chance, and *Platoon* went into production in the Philippines in the spring of 1986. Charlie Sheen, 19-year-old son of actor Martin Sheen, was cast as Stone's fictional on-screen persona, Chris Taylor, with Tom Berenger as Sergeant Barnes and Willem Dafoe as Elias. Against the odds of a demanding script and an alien environment, and complicated by the historic overthrow of the Marcos regime, remarkably, shooting of *Platoon* was completed in 54 days—precisely the same time it had taken to film *Salvador.*

The realization of *Platoon* had special meaning for Oliver Stone, and in the public arena the motion picture's release was met with unusual anticipation and interest because it was the first Vietnam film written and directed by a Vietnam veteran. Audiences expected something different from an "insider" drawing on personal experience.

What *Platoon* projected through its evocative story was both the authentic revisualization of historical realities and the gut-and-soul feelings of youth transformed. The literal—expected by many—was not as evident as the visceral and the spiritual, resulting in an innovative, challenging exercise that bombarded the senses. As a result it became one of the most attended, debated, and written-about motion pictures ever made. The film's popular reception was especially significant when viewed in the context of mid-1980s film enterprise—a time when audiences were responding most favorably to films with upbeat endings, including fantasy-inspired inversions of the U.S.–Vietnam War outcome in the form of the Sylvester Stallone *Rambo* films. There was a widely held theory that filmgoers were tired of Vietnam films altogether and wished the subject put to rest once and forever.

Synopsis of *Platoon* (1986)

Cast: Tom Berenger, Willem Dafoe, Charlie Sheen, Forrest Whitaker, Francesco Quinn, John C. McGinley, Richard Edson, Kevin Dillon, Reggie Johnson, Keith David, Johnny Depp, David Neidorf, Mark Moses, Chris Pedersen, Corkey Ford, Corey Glover, Bob Orwig.

Credits: Director: Oliver Stone. Producer: Arnold Kopelson. Screenplay: Oliver Stone. Photography: Robert Richardson. Music: Georges Delerue. Art direction: Rodel Cruz and Doris Sher Williams.

The action of *Platoon* begins with a superimposed biblical quote from Ecclesiastes: "Rejoice, O young man, in thy youth." Raw recruits, Chris Taylor (Charlie Sheen) among them, are seen disembarking from a military transport plane into a parched yellow-orange world. Taylor, stunned, observes body bags being unloaded from the plane that has brought him to the jungle outpost. Another caption appears: "September 1967—Bravo Co., 25th Infantry. Somewhere near the Cambodian border."

Via a compilation montage with accompanying actor credits, the secondary, then principal, characters are introduced, followed by production credits and a sequence of shots showing the men of Company B entering a dark, dense jungle. The new recruits, disoriented and fatigued, are prodded on and cajoled with debasing labels—"fatso," "lardass."

Arriving at camp, the soldiers go about their tasks of unloading war materiel, digging foxholes, and writing letters home. The company appears to be predominantly black in population. In a voice-over, a softspoken Chris Taylor is heard reciting a letter written to his grandmother a week after arriving in Vietnam. He tells of his point duty, confusion over jungle combat, fatigue, all-night ambushes, and what it's like to be a new guy in Vietnam. Taylor says: "I don't think I can keep this up for a year, Grandma. I think I made a big mistake coming here."

From these introspective observations of an innocent, *Platoon* develops a larger picture of the grueling, tense life of soldiers in Company B. News comes of another distant platoon, "blown to pieces" by the North Vietnamese Army (NVA); factions are revealed between officers and NCOs and between whites and blacks as plans are made for an ambush attack.

With the ambush patrol moving forward in heavy rain into the jungle, Taylor's voice-over letter continues, recounting how he came to Vietnam against his middle-class parents' wishes—feeling a need to break away from his sheltered existence and to "do my share for my country—live up to what Grandpa did in the first war and Dad did in the second." Taylor tells his grandmother he's come to realize that his fellow soldiers are "guys nobody really cares about," "the end of the line," "the bottom of the barrel"—self-aware men, however, who call themselves grunts "because a grunt can take it." Taylor expresses his admiration for these people and says he hopes he can see something in Vietnam he doesn't yet see and learn something not yet known. His letter ends with a reminder of how much he misses his family.

The plotting details of *Platoon,* which will lead Taylor to the knowledge he seeks, activate with haste. In a shootout with the NVA that occurs during the patrol, Taylor is grazed by a bullet, panics, observes the driven Sergeant

Barnes (Tom Berenger) finishing off a wounded NVA enemy soldier, then witnesses the death of two of Company B's own men. No sooner is this patrol trauma ended than Taylor is seen back in camp on latrine duty, emptying and burning toilet feces and telling his short-timer supervisors how he dropped out of college for voluntary duty in Vietnam.

Barracks life introduces Taylor to the "druggies"—the dope-smoking faction of Company B, men who dance to "Tracks of My Tears." Sergeant Elias (Willem Dafoe) spearheads this more laid-back group of soldiers, whose primary goal is simply to do their duty and get out of Vietnam alive. Elias offers Taylor his first dope, ominously compelling the wide-eyed young soldier to smoke from a rifle barrel. Elias, dutiful but disillusioned by the war and its seemingly endless futilities, eventually wins the respect of Taylor, who simultaneously comes to resent Barnes.

New Year's Day 1968 finds Taylor's letter home calling the occasion "just another day . . . staying alive." From here *Platoon* moves episodically to develop the conflict between Elias and Barnes—a conflict born of and nurtured by the unorthodox, no-rules-apply nature of Vietnam guerilla warfare. Combat patrols are depicted as deadly, frustrating missions, with Company B men dying by booby trap and sinister crucifixion. An increasingly irate Barnes strikes back, compulsively gunning down a Vietnamese villager and killing a woman who protests the violent treatment of Vietnamese civilians by the frustrated American soldiers. Taylor himself momentarily loses control in a fit of rage, shooting his rifle at a villager's feet.

When Barnes puts a gun to a hysterical child's head, Elias intercedes and a fight breaks out between the two men. Elias intends to expose Barnes's atrocity in killing the Vietnamese woman. Barnes dares to challenge the company officer who stops the fight. The ambiguous war goes on. Villages are torched, Vietnamese women are raped, the competition between Elias and the gung-ho Barnes grows. In a letter home Taylor writes about "a civil war in the platoon: half the men with Elias, half with Barnes. There's a lot of suspicion and hate. I can't believe we're fighting each other when we should be fighting them."

A lengthy, frenetic ambush by the NVA leads *Platoon* toward a violent and surreal conclusion in which the external conflict of enemy battle and the internal conflict involving Barnes, Elias—and now Taylor—are merged. The shootout becomes a dizzying, bloody affair that shows charred bodies strewn about like fallen leaves. Barnes and Elias, in acting to repel the surprise attack, compete for the last time as Barnes uses the distracting furor of the battle to seek out and shoot ("frag") Elias, who—rendered helpless—later dies in an onslaught of enemy bullets.

Taylor—aware of Barnes's actions and unable to tolerate any longer someone who goes "on making up the rules" anyway he wants—kills Barnes after he is wounded during a raging battle that occurs on the second day of the attack. Wounded himself, and badly burned, Taylor is carried by stretcher to a waiting helicopter. Rising above an open mass grave—a common dump for the enemy dead—and the now-still battle plain, Taylor's final thoughts are heard:

> I think now, looking back, we did not fight the enemy, we fought ourselves and the enemy was in us. The war is over for me now, but it will always be there the rest of my days, as I am sure Elias will be fighting Barnes for what Rhah called possession of my soul. There are times since I have felt like a child born of these two fathers. Be that as it may. Those of us who did make it have an obligation to build again—to teach to others what we know. And to try with what's left of our lives to find a goodness and a meaning to this life.

Platoon concludes with a screen wash to white and an end title that reads "Dedicated to the men who fought and died in Vietnam."

Platoon performed the unexpected not because of universal acclaim and approval—although the film won wide praise—but because of its peculiarly diverse appeals. As a combat war film—an American genre form with numerous built-in attractions—*Platoon* was both adventuresome and introspective, hell-bent and morally inclined. Its tone seemed to deglamorize war, while the charged action and intense conflicts undeniably provided steamrolling entertainment.

In its approach *Platoon* had also admirably skirted the distracting obliqueness of films like *The Deer Hunter* and *Apocalypse Now*. The straightforward presentational style of delivering the rite-of-passage, loss-of-innocence theme through simple statement and the letters home device offered a certain directness that added to the film's accessibility, especially for younger filmgoers.

In incorporating its well-articulated ideas of "knowledge gained" about good and evil—first learned by Taylor in his observance of Barnes and Elias, then made incontrovertibly real in his act of retribution against Barnes—*Platoon* effectively operated on two levels: the realistic and the spiritual. Richard Combs in *Sight and Sound* argued that the dual approach gave *Platoon* novelistic properties and abetted its acceptance: "It's perhaps this split between 'how it was reportage' and blinding spiritual truth that has made *Platoon* so appealing, that accounts for its critical elevation. . . . There is something less conspicuously film-like and 'effected' about *Platoon's* operations, something closer to the model of the Great American Novel, the

Willem Dafoe (Elias), center, the disillusioned sergeant in *Platoon* (1986). Courtesy The Museum of Modern Art/Film Stills Archive.

combination of how–it–was (or how–to–do–it) narrative and spiritual testament exemplified by *Moby-Dick* (a comparison the film explicitly conjures, by referring to the relentless Barnes as the platoon's Ahab)."[2]

It was generally conceded that *Platoon's* achievements resided to a large extent in the clarity of its ideas, which held not "the truth" about Vietnam but certain truths about moral ambiguities, human nature, violence, and initiation—forcefully and artfully presented in the uniquely textured landscape of Vietnam. *Platoon* was both spiritual and spatial mystery—with Stone rendering the dense and ambiguous rain-soaked jungle in alternating images that were at one moment surreally beautiful with their patches of light and dark and at the next moment menacing and deadly. The ill-defined space was presented through a moving camera that scanned and probed the jungle like the eyes and bodies of the soldiers themselves.

Stone's power as an energetic film director—affirmed by *Salvador*—was reaffirmed in *Platoon*. Ed Kelleher of the *Film Journal* wrote: "From *Platoon's* opening minutes, Stone plunges the viewer into the chaotic landscape of a reality gone unhinged. Thanks to some extraordinarily mobile camera shots, we get a very real sense of what it must be like to be in a nighttime firefight, with confusion and death at every turn. The director also tantalizes us with the fearful beauty of such skirmishes, with the arcing tracers and billowing flares almost hypnotizing to the eye."[3]

Other critics referred to *Platoon*'s fluid pace as "terrifying momentum," "fiery ambiguity," "lightning-fast mayhem," and "adrenaline-rush chaos." Terrence Rafferty in the *Nation* said, "Stone's directorial style, which is fast, kinetic and rather literal, serves him well in the action scenes; there are few battle sequences on film as tense and frightening as these."[4]

Enhancing the film's terrifying chaos were tight, cluttered camera compositions in the fight scenes; numerous overhead air shots; and quick-cut, frenetic editing. *Platoon*'s effect was just what Stone had envisioned on writing his screenplay—a visceral, gut-felt film experience that pulled the filmgoer into its story with stimulating and moving impact.

The appeal and success of *Platoon* could be attributed, too, to Stone's growing skills as a first-rate director: his camera-eye, his control of pace and rhythm, his ability to direct his actors to brilliance—this time is ensemble performance—and his sense for the texturing detail. Conveying the terror of the Vietnam landscape as effectively as *Platoon*'s rendering of ambiguous space were its unforgettable visual moments: a mosquito on a soldier's neck; clinging leeches; red ants; a poisonous snake slithering across a combat boot; an abandoned, steaming teapot; a suffocating underground NVA bunker that in a glance heightened the mystery of the unseen enemy; the wind of a helicopter lifting a tarpaulin from American corpses. Stone—as he had in *Salvador*—proved himself a director capable of gathering up details to bring his story to atmospheric life.

Because of its rich texturing of the grungy war experience, numerous critics labeled *Platoon* a modern *Red Badge of Courage*. *New York* magazine critic David Denby said that Stone

has put together a classical, Stephen Crane–like account of a young man's initiation in battle. . . . [He] has told the familiar young soldier's story without copping out on the ineradicable bitterness and confusion. The messiness, the weird tensions, the moral ambiguities and disasters of the conflict all come flooding back along with a comforting pleasure in American heroism and endurance. In its combining intimacy and emotional complexity, the movie is charged response, on the one side, to such grandiose and impersonal art visions of the war as *Apocalypse Now* and *The Deer Hunter,* and on the other to such dumb-whore movies as *Rambo*. One comes out excited yet shaken and close to tears.[5]

Stone had scored a major victory with *Platoon* because, as Denby had found it, the film was an affectively moving event. In the rush of critical responses to the picture, no reviewer had claimed to be untouched by Stone's challenging effort. Even his most outspoken detractor, Pauline Kael, admitted that "Stone has talent" and that "*Platoon* has many things to recommend it." While critical of the film's "preppy literary" qualities, Kael's interpretation of Stone's intentions was expressed in terms of the story's narrowly focused personal and emotional bent: "The film is about victimizing ourselves as well as others; it's about shame. That's the only way in which it's political; it doesn't deal with what the war was about—it's conceived strictly in terms of what these American infantrymen go through."[6]

Because Stone had avoided the larger metaphoric ambitions of earlier Vietnam films, critics claimed that *Platoon* went more directly to the heart. And for the critics who approved of the film—a majority— they did so primarily on the basis of emotional impact in a story seen, as had Kael, as essentially personal and nonpolitical. *Commonweal* reviewer Tom O'Brien wrote that *Platoon* "has a heart large enough to cover a multitude of artistic sins. Indeed its frankness and non-ideological approach to the issues place it among the best movies to date about the war in Vietnam."[7]

For those who took issue with Stone's approach or who saw flaws in the film, they did so with either the argument that the script contained bothersome narrative defects among its many strengths or the argument that Stone had been remiss in not treating the politics behind the war.

Those who found *Platoon* textually flawed often argued that the Chris Taylor characterization was "too good" or "too straight" for the ironic conversion (from innocence to guilt) to be taken seriously. Many found this aspect of the story to be overly lofty and obvious, while often saying at the same time that the script was more impressive in detailing the daily lives of grunt soldiers experiencing the internal and external terrors of Vietnam guerilla warfare. There was also ample criticism of the letter home voice-over monologues as clichéd and "oozing" with sincerity, while Stone's grunt soldier dialogue was earning praise for being "painfully accurate [and for illustrating] just how corrupting the experience of war is to language." Some critics found unnecessary, even offensive, the Christ-like, upstretched-arms death of Elias, which occurs, surprisingly, not with Barnes's bullets but the next day by NVA fire. Critics referred to this unexpected plot detail as Elias's "double death."

The more intriguing controversy over *Platoon*'s effectiveness came in discussions of the film's politics or lack thereof. Both what was in Stone's script and what was left out came under political scrutiny. Looking from the left and beyond the script, Sydelle Kramer of *Cineaste* wrote:

The 1980's have witnessed the eradication of national memory. We watch events unfold in a historical vacuum, shaped by men who are unaware of the past. *Platoon* is thoroughly of this tradition. It is a war movie unreflective about the moral nature of war itself, a Vietnam movie undisturbed by the voices of dissent that heated this country in 1967–68, when the film takes place. Stone's soldiers share the drugs of the counter culture, its obscurity, its messianic fervor, but not its questions, not its moral confusions. These soldiers allude to racism, the black man's draft, but never to whether they should be fighting or not.[8]

With another line of argument taken from a politically conservative position, a *New Republic* columnist said the point had been made that in contemporary times "to dramatize the horrors and costs of military action without reference to its value and occasional necessity . . . breeds appeasement, isolationism, defeatism." *Platoon*—cited as war as "existential-nightmare"—was said to have conveyed "an unavoidably left-wing message." This overtly conservative assessment of *Platoon*'s political effect concluded by attaching the film's "message" to such incidents as the Iran Contra Affair: "The relationship between *Platoon* and Iranamok is not that the scandal changed public attitudes and made the movie's popularity possible. It's that the public's true attitude toward war, as tapped by *Platoon,* is what drove the Reagan administration to conduct an illegal war in secret, which led to the scandal."[9]

Such divergent political ruminations as these two touched on long-held theories about the sociopolitical implications of war pictures in general, but they also seemed to play down one critic's arguments that *Platoon* was a film that could be appreciated by doves and hawks alike.

As to charges that his script should have incorporated the politics of dissent and explanations for the war's "why," Stone maintained that in his own experience in Vietnam there had been little political talk—that the experience was more "religious" than political. Charles Krauthammer of the *Washington Post* wrote favorably of Stone's decision, saying "To present combat without context is a classic anti-war technique. In that sense *Platoon* is very much like the Vietnam Memorial. They share the same blankness, the same seeming freedom from politics, the same narrowness. The narrowness is the message. A list of names without context is a memorial to the waste that is war."[10]

There were those who saw *Platoon*'s sociopolitical significance as residing in its authentic rendering of the Vietnam soldier's day-to-day ordeal and the landscape in which the war was fought. *New York*'s David Denby said: "Those of us who opposed the war may not have wanted to experience the fighting man's emotions so directly. But we do experience them, and for us the war has lost some of its comforting remoteness and perhaps for good" (Denby 1986, 88).

David Halberstam, a *New York Times* reporter who covered the Vietnam War in the early 1960s, told *Time* magazine: "*Platoon* is the first real Viet Nam film and one of the great war movies of all time. The other Viet Nam films have been a rape of history. But *Platoon* is historically and politically accurate. It understands something that the architects of the war never did: how the foliage, the thickness of the jungle, negated U.S. technological superiority. You can see how the forest sucks in the American soldiers; they just disappear. I think the film will become an American classic."[11]

To achieve the kind of personal-experience accuracy and historical-landscape authenticity Denby and Halberstam spoke to, Stone had hired retired marine captain Daniel Dye, also a Vietnam veteran, and three additional military advisers, who put *Platoon*'s 20 principal actors through two weeks of jungle training in the Philippines—requiring the cast to carry a full complement of military gear, to dig foxholes and to go without bathing.

Dye appears briefly in the film as a captain calling for air assistance for his beleaguered unit. In his personal pitch for authenticity, Dye is heard during his call for help referring to the enemy as "Zips"—a popular name used for the Vietnamese in the earliest years of the war. Dye had gone to Vietnam in 1965. Stone himself—prior to filming—had visited former platoon buddies, who helped him recall the layout of battle skirmishes experienced in Vietnam and to be re-created in the film.

Vietnam veteran reaction to the authenticity of *Platoon* was understandably mixed. Of the 2.7 million Americans who served in Vietnam, no two had had exactly the same experiences. Too, the film in large part was artifice—a creation of Stone's imagination. Veterans responded most favorably to the realities of the jungle-based, guerilla warfare, claiming that was the way it was and saying the battle scenes brought their experiences back to life. Black veterans and critics regretted that Stone had not depicted blacks in more heroic situations or shown more of them in NCO and officer positions—factors they said caused *Platoon* to be less true and hence less forceful in characterizing a typical American combat unit.

The narrative conflict was also considered troublesome. Veterans argued that open war between two NCOs in front of their men—one of the sergeants brazenly challenging a bumbling commissioned officer—would not have been tolerated. Many also felt that the drug aspects of the Vietnam experience had been exaggerated by Stone. John Wheeler, a Vietnam veteran organizer, defended *Platoon* and Stone against these charges:

There *were* drug cultures, there *were* green lieutenants. Stone wanted to clean out the festering part of the wound. The next Vietnam movie may be the one that tells the whole truth: that we were the best equipped, best trained army ever fielded, but against a dedicated foe in an impossible terrain. It was a state-of-the-art war on both sides. But *Platoon* is a new statement about Vietnam veterans. Before, we were either objects of pity or objects that had to be defused to keep us at a distance. *Platoon* makes us real. The Vietnam Memorial was one gate our country had to pass through. *Platoon* is another. It is part of the healing process. It speaks to our generation. Those guys are us.

(Corliss, 57)

Issues of politics and authenticity aside, *Platoon* pointed to the stylistic, textual, and directorial preferences that were shaping Stone's developing reputation as a screen auteur. In fact the strengths and weaknesses of *Platoon* were quite similar to those of *Salvador*. A vitality within the two films and a nitty-gritty aliveness born of grungy male camaraderie and ritual—offered transfixing cinema even as other elements jolted in their self-consciousness.

Stone had, for instance, almost stubbornly repeated the use of elegiac music to ennoble men in battle. *Requiem*-like choral music had made majestic *Salvador*'s death-strewn images and its fiery rebel attacks; for *Platoon* Stone juxtaposed Samuel Barber's plaintive *Adagio for Strings* against shots of Company B's soldiers marching, heads up, toward their combat missions. Depending on one's critical preferences, the application of elevated music in *Salvador* and *Platoon* either had added a tragic tone to the presentation of men at war or had in its artsiness distanced the viewer from the immediacy of war's fury.

Another common element of nagging proportion occurred in the characterization of the film's two central protagonists—in each case a man who challenges the traditional concept of hero. The Richard Boyle character Stone had drawn for *Salvador* had been so defiantly unattractive and morally repugnant that even the film's most admiring critics had to go to great lengths to explain how such an antihero/hero worked in the end to Stone's (and the filmgoer's) advantage.

The problematic areas for *Platoon*'s designated hero—Chris Taylor—came in the narrative device of having Taylor kill Barnes as a signification of evil overtaking good and the accompanying realization by the hero that at that moment he had, symbolically, been born into knowledge—the product of two father-opposites.

As stated earlier, the conversion act had been challenged on the grounds of dramatic impact, but the larger issue arose from the fact that in the end Taylor was a murderer—perhaps more Barnes than Elias—yet espousing an obligation as a survivor to return to the world and teach others what was learned and to find a "goodness" in life. The juxtaposition of murderous acts and righteous sermon fueled arguments—as had *Salvador*—that the serious moral ambiguities of the alleged hero prevented the film from achieving any credible or satisfying catharsis.

Again Stone argued that he had intentionally developed a tainted hero, one "soiled" by the war, as most veterans, he said, had been—a hero who was both a good man and a murderer. As he had done in explaining the Boyle character, Stone maintained that the moral contradictions in Taylor were more realistic and therefore added to the desired complexities of a film like *Platoon*.

A case could also be made that Stone's creative process in making *Salvador* and *Platoon* showed an artist whose work tended to transform itself from initial responses to a compelling character to larger issues for which the character becomes—perhaps too obviously for some— a megaphone of conveyance. The concept for *Salvador* began in Stone's stated desire to simply make a film about a rascally gadfly journalist, but with creative energies focused, the concept expanded

Charlie Sheen (Chris Taylor) and Keith David (King) in *Platoon* (1986). Courtesy The Museum of Modern Art/Film Stills Archive.

into a journeyman's destiny with a volatile time and place. Stone used his unsavory, rascally character to take a political stand and say what he thought he had learned.

The creation of *Platoon* apparently occurred in a similar manner, with Chris Taylor developing from the simple idea of a "social product" innocent observing and caught up in the grunt experiences of Vietnam to someone of a much more dangerous and wiser screen character than Stone had originally imagined. The device of having Taylor kill Barnes had not been in the *Platoon* script Stone wrote in 1976 but was added when the film was made 10 years later. The transformed character could again be explained as the logical result of Stone's evolved understanding of certain realities and his desire to express them without Hollywood piety.

The process of *Platoon*'s evolution in Stone's mind had been remarkably lengthy: Stone experienced Vietnam at age 19, wrote the first draft of *Platoon* at 30, and directed the film at 40. Of the final result Paul Attanasio wrote: "*Platoon* may be about Chris Taylor, but the point of view belongs to someone older, who has looked back and made sense of it, sorted out the heroes and villains, learned a lesson."[12] Stone's penchant for characters of a morally different sort who take a stand—Stone's point of view—would be carried forward as an essential ingredient of future work.

Platoon contained numerous other elements that could be associated with the achievements of *Salvador,* not the least of which was the fact that both films had sensitively depicted the oppression of people in a country at the mercy of U.S. policy. In showing the Vietnamese villagers as victims of the war also, *Platoon* broadened its vision of war's tragedy and gave more complexity to the idea of how easily evil can overtake good.

Platoon repeated Stone's success in achieving spontaneity and heightened realism, especially in the surreal atmosphere of location. As in *Salvador,* misty, smoke-filled environments and outstanding night photography provided the suspenseful ambiguity of a place where sudden death could just happen and often did. The familiar musical drumbeat sound to signify terror—now pure Stone—was present, as were the foul language and Stone's own obligatory cameo appearance (this time as a major blown up in a bunker).

Platoon's other achievement was that it had been created with—in terms of Hollywood accounting—a minuscule budget: $6 million. Stone once more had proved himself a frugal but masterful engineer of his craft, capable of turning out an exotic, first-rate film with B-picture financing. He was now someone who could no longer be ignored, and the phenomenal success of *Platoon* proved this: $136 million in box-office sales in the United States alone, a Best Director Award from his peers—the Directors Guild of America—and eight Academy Award nominations, resulting in four Oscars, including Best Picture of 1986.

The film touched the nerves of Americans, perhaps coming just at the right moment when the country needed a vehicle of cleansing and purging. Film actress Jane Fonda, who had led a vociferous campaign against earlier Vietnam films like *The Deer Hunter,* saw *Platoon* in a Los Angeles suburban theater and confessed that afterward she met with Vietnam veterans who had been in the audience and wept. The National Council of Churches Communication Commission issued *Platoon* a special award for its "cinematic brilliance" and its "uncompromising portrait" of the Vietnam War.

For those who had not had a chance to see *Salvador* or had not paid much attention, *Platoon* at once signaled the conversion of Oliver

Stone, causing critics to raise their expectations of his work. Terrence Rafferty wrote in the *Nation:*

It's a little ironic . . . that after his manic, hallucinated versions of other people's lives—the feverish caricatured Turks, Chinese-Americans and Miami Cubans of his previous scripts—Oliver Stone has become an honorable and scrupulous artist in dealing with the central experience of his own life. Let's hope that this strong movie isn't just an isolated episode in Stone's career, that he'll be able to carry over his new rigor and generosity from his memory to his imagination. Vietnam seems to have made him a better filmmaker—his next movies should tell us whether, in the best war movie tradition, it's also made a man out of him. (Rafferty, 56)

6

Wall Street

Wall Street is *Platoon* in civvies. Instead of jungle warfare, there's the financial jungle where man eats rather than shoots man. Corporate raiders, hostile takeovers, insider trading, arbitrage—above all, endless computer terminals and telephones bursting like rockets everywhere—create a battlefield as dense, noisy, frantic, and ultimately deadly as anything in Vietnam.
        —John Simon, *National Review,* 22 January 1988

Oliver Stone's creative energy was such that, once the opportunity for writing and directing films had sustained itself, he seemed almost driven toward his next exercise. This was partly due to the uncertainties of Hollywood in the 1980s. Stone said: "There's no security at all. People who were my idols 10 years ago are not even working today. You have to be ruthless in your strategy. The more you want to make something and somebody knows it, the more exposed you are. I keep four or five things in development at all times, projects A, B, C and D at different places. So if a studio doesn't want to make A I go somewhere else and make B."[1] *Wall Street,* a film about the corrupting potential of New York's stocks and securities world, was well along when *Platoon* won its Best Picture and Best Director Oscars in March 1987.

The development of a film in which a young man becomes trapped by the greed of Wall Street through the lure of insider trading also showed a certain desire for symmetry in Stone's creative compulsiveness. *Salvador's* politics-and-war ruminations led forcefully into *Platoon's* achievements, and *Wall Street* owed much of its narrative structuring and conflict to *Platoon.* The idea of a naive young man being born into knowledge of sin by corrupt action, then redeemed—

Platoon's thematic raison d'être—was carried forward in *Wall Street*. *Wall Street* also repeated the narrative device of two "fathers" at opposite ends of the morality spectrum vying for a young man's soul—doing so by taking the antithetical Barnes-Elias approaches to guerilla warfare and extending them into *Wall Street*'s money-greed wars. The issue of conduct of killing was replaced in *Wall Street* by the issue of conduct of business.

Stone's script for *Wall Street* was also impelled in part by an ongoing urgency to use film to come to grips with concerns that were in part autobiographical in their inspiration. *Platoon* had been an artistic attempt at both explanation and self-purging of the Vietnam experience—an experience Stone's father at one time had been unable to validate. *Platoon*'s central character had sought to justify duty in Vietnam by equating his actions with his father's patriotic call to duty in World War II. The hope of validation might be seen symbolically in the "educating" nature of the experience—the claims to new knowledge, initiation, and commitment to do good. Perhaps *Platoon* seemed to say Stone hadn't returned from Vietnam so much the "uneducated bum" he *claimed* his father once thought him to be.

Wall Street grew from similar interests. Stone, whose father was a stockbroker for nearly 50 years, saw the stock securities trade arena as an apt place for telling a story about a son's relationship with his father. In the early 1980s, through a stockbroker friend, Stone had come to see Wall Street and the stock business as being very different from what his father had known, and he recognized that another tale about youth initiation and good versus evil resided in this new investment center. Because of his father's association with a more distant, less selfish business world, Stone began to develop the concept of an onscreen father-son relationship that would be tested by a corrupting surrogate father of the new hyperconsuming, driven Wall Street sort. The screenplay was developed and cowritten with Stanley Weiser.

The intended dramatic result would again come in the son's movement toward knowledge of evil, the act of destroying the bad father and embracing the good one of old-fashioned, hardworking values and ethics.

In an interview after the release of *Wall Street,* Stone said: "I consider my films first and foremost to be dramas about individuals in personal struggles, and I consider myself to be a dramatist before I am a political filmmaker. I think what links all my films—from *Midnight Express* to *Scarface, Salvador, Platoon* and *Wall Street*—is the story of an individual in a struggle with his identity, his integrity and his soul. In many of these movies, the character's soul is stolen from him, lost, and in some cases he gets it back at the end. I do not believe in the collective version of history. I believe that the highest ethic is the Socratic one, from the dialogues of Socrates, which says 'Know thyself.'"[2]

Synopsis of *Wall Street* (1987)

Cast: Michael Douglas, Charlie Sheen, Daryl Hannah, Martin Sheen, Terence Stamp, James Spader, Sean Young, Millie Perkins, John C. McGinley, Hal Holbrook, Tamara Tunie, Franklin Cover, Sylvia Miles, Sean Stone.

Credits: Director: Oliver Stone. Producer: Edward R. Pressman. Screenplay: Stanley Weiser and Oliver Stone. Photography: Robert Richardson. Art direction: John Jay Moore and Hilda Stark. Music: Stewart Copeland.

Wall Street opens with a montage of morning shots of New York City. On the soundtrack Frank Sinatra sings "Fly Me to the Moon." Constantly moving Steadicam shots follow Bud Fox (Charlie Sheen) from elevator to brokerage office, where the clock reads 9:29:58. As Fox shouts, "And they're off and running," a title super indicates "1985." Camera pans, zooms, and dolly and tracking shots reveal the chaotic world of broker dealing. Assigned a nonpaying client, Fox seems frustrated that he isn't able to make as much money as others before him have made. He has to borrow $5 from Marv (John C. McGinley), a low-key broker pal at the next desk.

Following work, Fox meets his father, Carl Fox (Martin Sheen), in a New Jersey blue-collar bar, where the two eat and talk about their jobs. The father—an airline machinist and union boss who makes $47,000 a year—tells his son, who can't make it on $50,000, that he should not have gone to work on Wall Street, should have been a salesman and living at home. The father tells about an expected favorable FAA ruling that will make expanded routes possible for his company, Blue Star Airlines, and dramatically improve its stability. As he leaves, Bud Fox asks for and receives a $200 loan from his dad.

The next day the young broker manages to get a meeting (after calling "59 days in a row") with powerful, wealthy corporate raider Gordon Gekko (Michael Douglas). Fox tells Gekko: "I think you're an incredible genius. I'd like to do business with you." Responding to Gekko's "Tell me something I don't know," Fox discloses information about the expected FAA ruling and expansion of his father's Blue Star Airlines company. Gekko acts on the insider tip, and when the court ruling comes to pass, Fox is given $1 million by Gekko for an investment account, along with the challenge, "I don't like losses." To tantalize his new "partner," Gekko one night sends a limousine for Fox; the car comes equipped with a prostitute and a supply of champagne and cocaine.

Sometime later, following a game of racquetball, Bud Fox admits a $100,000 loss on the investment of Gekko's money. Gekko, who has also learned how the Blue Star information was gained, decides Fox isn't as smart as he thought and makes a move to drop him. Fox asks for another chance, and Gekko assigns him the task of tailing archrival investor Larry Wildman (Terence Stamp), an Englishman.

Fox learns that Wildman intends to purchase an Erie, Pennsylvania, steel company, causing Gekko to act to prevent the takeover by buying heavily into the company so that Wildman cannot take a controlling interest. Fox also encourages other brokers to push the steel company with their customers. Wildman comes to Gekko's home to buy his block of shares, and Gekko jumps at the chance to sell at a huge profit.

Fox takes up his illegal doings full-time, continuing to seek insider tips and even resorting to burglary to get needed information. His profits from the dealings make him suddenly wealthy—so much so that he is able to acquire a $950,000 penthouse apartment; win Gekko's ex-girlfriend, interior decorator Darien Taylor (Daryl Hannah); and, as his company's top gross commision broker, get a private office.

To help him cover his illegal holdings and large profits, Fox convinces lawyer Roger Barnes (James Spader) a former college friend, to sign share transfer documents for him. Tensions mount for Fox, who loses his temper at the office and who, after making love to Darien in the "perfect" world that is his expensive, new condo, asks from his balcony, "Who am I?"

In one of the film's most brazen, impassioned scenes, Gekko is seen at a shareholders meeting of Teldar, Inc., where he hopes to engineer a takeover. In response to a charge that his efforts are motivated by greed, Gekko rises and, in a tirade of financial philosophy, says: "The point is greed is good . . . greed is right . . . greed works. Greed clarifies, cuts through and captures the essence of the evolutionary spirit. Greed, in all of its forms—greed for life, money, love, knowledge—has marked the upward surge of mankind. And greed, mark my words, will save not only Teldar, but that other malfunctioning corporation called the USA."

In the meantime, Bud Fox has devised a plan for turning around Blue Star Airlines ("an unpolished gem") and making a fortune for himself and Gekko. Fox argues that through modernization, advertising, and expansion, Blue Star will in time be able to compete with and beat the other major airlines. In a meeting attended by Gekko, Fox, his father, and receptive union representatives, Gekko tells how they all can make big money and asks for an increased employee workload and a 20 percent across-the-board wage cut.

Carl Fox, skeptical and wishing to keep the company as it is, reacts to Gekko's greed and leaves the meeting. His son goes after him, saying to his father, "What I see is a jealous old machinist who can't stand that his son is more successful than he is. You never had the guts to go out into the world and stake your own claim." To this Carl Fox replies, "What you see is a guy who's never measured a man's success by the size of his wallet." The son retorts: "Your men—all my life—your men have been able to count on you. Why have you never been there for me?"

With Securities and Exchange Commission officials aware of in-house fraud and beginning to breathe down his brokerage company's neck, Bud Fox learns that Gekko intends to liquidate Blue Star's assets and cash in the company's pension fund for a take of $60–70 million. Fox accuses Gekko of using him and asks, "How much is enough?"

Realizing that his father, who has suffered a heart attack, will lose his job along with his men, Fox decides to make a break with Gekko, giving up Darien—who's still loyal to Gekko—in the process, but finding the courage to confess his love for his hospitalized father and tell him: "You're the only honest man I know . . . the best." To prevent Blue Star's takeover by Gekko, Bud Fox enlists Wildman's assistance in winning control of the company by buying stock shares sold by Gekko when their cost is driven up, then falls.

The revengeful deception works, but the following day, in his company's offices, Fox is arrested by SEC officials for "conspiracy to commit securities fraud and for violating the insider traders' sanction act." Lou Mannheim (Hal Holbrook), a senior investor who had been advising Fox against the corrupting lure of money, offers the thought that Fox might be gaining his "character." As Fox is led away by a policeman, he cries.

Wall Street concludes in Central Park during a thunderstorm, where Gekko is seen approaching Bud Fox. Gekko batters Fox with his fist, knocking him to the ground and saying: "I gave you everything. You could've been one of the great ones, buddy. I look at you and I see myself. Why?" Fox answers: "I don't know. I guess I realized I'm just Bud Fox. As much as I wanted to be Gordon Gekko I'll always be Bud Fox." Gekko turns and leaves, and Fox, wiping blood from his face, goes to a nearby restaurant men's room, where he turns over a hidden tape recorder to waiting SEC agents—the evidence needed to destroy Gekko.

Final shots are of Carl Fox dropping his son off at a New York court building. On the way he has instructed his repentant son to "create, instead of living off the buying and selling of others." As Bud Fox (knowing he's going to jail) enters the courthouse, the camera booms up to reveal the New York City skyline. An end title appears, reading "Dedicated to Louis Stone, Stockbroker (1910–1985)."

The narrative similarities between *Wall Street* and *Platoon* were immediately apparent. Nigel Floyd of *Monthly Film Review* wrote:

The innocent GI played by Charlie Sheen in *Platoon* volunteers for service in Vietnam, undergoes a baptism of fire, is forced to choose between two surrogate father figures (Sergeants Barnes and Elias), and, at the end, leaves for home a disillusioned but wiser and humbler man. In *Wall Street*, Bud Fox is already tainted with ambition when he gate-crashes Gekko's office in the hope of joining his team, but his bullish enthusiasm is laced with a moral naivety. Inducted into the combative world of financial dealing, Bud is later forced to choose between surrogate father Gekko and his real father Carl (played by Sheen's own father), and at the end of the film—his dreams of power and wealth shattered—he is redeemed.[3]

Wall Street, while similar in structure to *Platoon,* had its narrative differences. The idea of a lost soul reclaimed, as Stone himself had stated it, was treated more directly than in *Platoon* through the presence of a real father rather in competition with a surrogate one. The biological father character complicated the narrative conflict of someone caught between two opposing moral forces by also revealing a poignant drifting away from one's own flesh and blood. The idea of choosing good over evil and redeeming oneself—an act of symbolic choice in *Platoon*—had a more human edge to it in *Wall Street,* in effect a moral choice too, but adding the decision of the prodigal son to return home. Both films offered a lesson-learned denouement, but *Wall Street* was also about spiritual reunion within one's innermost circle—the family.

Stone's final gesture of dedicating *Wall Street* to his father came from a belief that the nature of financial dealing had changed so dramatically, become so speculative, that it had sapped the "creative purpose" his father felt in his own work in the business in another time. In a line to Fox, Gekko says, "I create nothing. I own." Stone uses Senior Investment Director Lou Mannheim (Hal Holbrook) to speak as his father when the supervisor tells Fox: "The main thing about money, it makes you do things you don't want to do." Later, just before Fox is arrested, Lou talks about finding one's character when one stares "into the abyss and nothing looks back." In his act of dedication, Stone was directly standing his father beside people like Lou Mannheim and Carl Fox—men who were not seduced by the lure of money and who knew what character was. This added further texturing to

Michael Douglas (Gordon Gekko) advises Charlie Sheen (Bud Fox) in
Wall Street (1987). Copyright © 1987 Twentieth Century Fox Film
Corp. All rights reserved. Photo by Andy Schwartz. Courtesy The
Museum of Modern Art/Film Stills Archive.

the ideas of father–son relationships and knowledge gained with regard
to moral bankruptcy. Stone was personalizing his ideas.

Wall Street was yet another Oliver Stone film that bristled in its
maleness. There were the father–son conflicts, and there were also the
forceful male socializing rituals and the warlike rhetoric used by men
doing battle ("raiding," "kill zone," "lock and load," "total liquida-
tion"). The rituals and corrupted language of *Wall Street* were those
born of a higher level of social class than the one depicted in *Platoon,*
but the resonations were quite similar. Gekko views drugs and alcohol—so evident in *Platoon*—as appropriate rewards for Fox once the
naive young broker has joined him in his financial warring.

Gekko also articulates a self-sufficient, independent male position
in discussing his philosophy of love. On learning that Darien has
fallen for Fox, Gekko warns: "We are smart enough not to buy into
the oldest myth running—love. A fiction created to keep people from

Charlie Sheen (Bud Fox) and Martin Sheen (Carl Fox), fictional and real-life son and father, in *Wall Street* (1987). Copyright © 1987 Twentieth Century Fox Film Corp. All rights reserved. Photo by Andry Schwartz. Courtesy The Museum of Modern Art/Film Stills Archive.

jumping from windows." On the other hand, Gekko says to Fox: "If you need a friend, get a dog."

Jack Boozer, Jr., writing in the *Journal of Popular Film and Television,* notes that Gekko's language, used in his instructions to Fox on how to succeed as an investment raider and market speculator, is "uncompromisingly militaristic and aggressive" in nature: "The desire to 'make a killing' spills over in Gekko's orders to his assistant, called 'The Terminator': 'Rip their . . . throats out. Stuff 'em in your garbage compactor. . . .' Gekko's methods also imitate those of covert warfare, as he explains to Bud [Fox] how he once kept a "mole" in Larry Wildman's operation who could supply inside information. This is free-market profiteering gone berserk, a complete battle zone at the heart of an economic system that asserts freedom and opportunity but lives by the warrior code of Sun Tsu."[4]

Boozer's last reference was to the fact that Stone's script, in a voice-over by Bud Fox, incorporated elements of war philosophy as posited by Sun Tsu, a sixth-century B.C. Chinese strategist: "All warfare is based on deception. If your enemy is superior, evade him. If angry, irritate him. If equally matched, fire. And if not, split. Reevaluate." Sun Tsu's philosophy is espoused just after Gekko has sold his steel company share block to Wildman for instant huge gain. Fox recognizes that in pulling off the deal and "making a killing," Gekko has shown himself to be the superior warrior strategist of Sun Tsu's tactical inspiration.

The maleness of *Wall Street* and its aggressive tone had its impact on female characterization. Lisa, the limo prostitute, and Darien, an interior decorator, are perks—corporate acquisitions—for male entrepreneurship. Wives are background shadows. The Darien Taylor character—played by Daryl Hannah—is particularly suspect. The character appears to be designed for the purpose of fleshing out ideas rather than intended as a real flesh-and-blood human being. Her style of interior decoration serves as a calculated narrative device for poking fun at the instantly manufactured but empty lifestyle of the male nouveau riche; her rejection of Fox—in an act of loyalty to Gekko—serves in the end to reaffirm the dominating power of a male who has arrived and can hold his place. This utilitarian shaping of female characters neutralizes their credibility as people of dimension; they are more representative than real.

At the same time that *Wall Street* was diminishing its women's roles, the film was realizing in the presence of Gordon Gekko's bigger-than-life, reptilian character a screen persona of classic proportions. More than any other element, the compelling boldness of the Gekko characterization carried the film and electrified its macho drama.

Not only was Stone able to draw Gekko as a powerful, single-minded man of action, but he did so with titillating dialogue and riveting details. Gekko says that making a killing on a deal is "better than sex." He urges that "the sperm count" be raised on a deal. Fox is told to follow Wildman and find out "what's going down." Gekko's desire to display his "arrival" through modern art acquisition is such that he does not blink in the shocking act of paying more than $1 million for an abstract painting. As an uncompromising spokesman for greed, Gekko startles with his statements: "The richest 1% of this country owns half our country's wealth." "We make the rules, pal." "If you're not inside, you're outside." "It's all about bucks. The rest is just conversation." "Lunch is for wimps." "Greed works; greed is good." "What's worth doing is worth doing for money." Even the name

Gekko—derived from the tenacious I-can-climb-anywhere-I-want gecko *(Gekkonidae)* lizard—is meant to titillate.

So outrageously amoral and effectively nasty was Gekko's persona—and Michael Douglas's rendering of it—that *Wall Street* succeeded as character drama when it did not work as social analysis. The real-life story of insider trader Ivan Boesky (sentenced to three years in jail in 1987 at the very moment *Wall Street* went into release) had commanded world attention as a brazen account of greed gone berserk in the bullish 1980s. An inevitable association of Boesky with Gekko triggered the imagination of filmgoers, who could relish in the fact that in the end both men—real and fictional—got their due (perhaps a bit too easily to be convincing in Gekko's case). Michael Douglas's performance as Gekko was so gleefully affective that it earned him the year's Best Actor Academy Award.

In typical Stone fashion, *Wall Street* was also made compelling by its energy and camera dynamics. Recalling earlier work, David Sterritt of the *Christian Science Monitor* said of *Wall Street:* "Much of its strength comes from Stone's walloping visual style, which seems more controlled in the indoor settings of *Wall Street* than amid the outdoor locations of *Platoon* and the anarchic *Salvador.* Stone's ever-moving camera prowls relentlessly through the action, restless and nervous like the money-hungry characters as they follow the scent of huge, but forbidden profits."[5]

Stone had again used a prowling camera to portray moral chaos in physical as well as textual terms. He had also done the same kind of research and "realism gesturing" for *Wall Street* he'd done for *Platoon* and *Salvador*—hiring a knowledgeable ex–investment partner as an adviser, talking with dozens of assorted people from the investment world, including prosecutors of inside traders; and sending his actors to "boot camp" in the financial district as a way of researching their roles. Some $500,000 was spent converting a New York trading room to make it look as authentic as ones Stone had seen at Solomon Brothers and other investment firms. Stone hoped to convey a true sense of how Wall Street worked and what the system meant to both the people working there and the country at large.

As a film with intended social and political implications, *Wall Street* produced a number of different, often conflicting responses—nothing new for an Oliver Stone film, as *Salvador* and *Platoon* had shown.

There had been strong doubts that *Wall Street*—however realistic—would have much at all to say to filmgoers in general. Judith Williamson of the *New Statesman* found reason to agree, arguing that the way the film's value system came down in the end in favor of the hard-working, blue-collar Carl Fox would have been broadly appealing to filmgoers in an earlier time but in this case produced an anachronistic effect: "If Bud's father creates value, nevertheless he has no part to play in its shiny surface, where our present-day dramas take place. Stone's '60's morality is ineffectually acted out in the imagery of the '80s."[6]

On the other hand, James Flanigan, writing for the *Los Angeles Times*, surmised that *Wall Street* would possibly attract filmgoers through its indirect blue-collar representations and the way it spoke to certain contemporary economic realities:

Theater owners say the film won't attract the common man. But they could be wrong because the common man is an important off-screen character. He's the fall guy who took a pay cut or lost his job because of restructuring deals conceived on Wall Street. Working people everywhere will recognize the union leaders who go from one takeover artist to another, pledging that their members will take 20% pay cuts if only the financier will keep the company in operation. Right there the film captures better than any academic treatise what restructuring is all about, getting people to work harder for less money.[7]

Jack Boozer, Jr., saw in *Wall Street* a meaningful allegory for contemporary American youth—one coming through the presentation of high-finance manipulation as a metaphor for the displacement of realities by appearances. Boozer writes:

On the market exchanges in particular appearances rule. There is little sense of reality behind the image. There is mainly a continuous recirculation and recombining of images. Gekko is the consummate post-modern man. He doesn't confuse means with ends . . . but lives fully in the means. . . . The strength of this particular text is that it does manage to capture something of the aggressive longing and disappointment, the economic insecurity and fear of the mainstream of American youth. Bud can't make ends meet on $50,000 a year. And so the dominant economic order is shown to elicit a growing price, inevitably increased by a growing debt against the future. It is in this way that *Wall Street* serves as a political-economic allegory of America in the 1980's.

(Boozer, 99)

The stimulation that *Wall Street* provided had to be ferreted out of the film's many complexities and viewed among its strengths and obvious weaknesses. The film won praise as a value-oriented morality play and as a fast-paced melodrama. Stone was lauded for a position on capitalism that was not sanctimoniously one-sided. Money and its lure could not be denied. It was the excesses Stone had attacked.

Wall Street as intended social commentary, however, had its problems. Perceived flaws were primarily focused on Stone's intended but—critics said—"unrealized" analysis of the Wall Street system to which he had attached the archetypal "war story" framework. Richard Combs of the (London) *Times Literary Supplement* implied that in its combined efforts at both archetypal drama and system analysis, the analysis suffered: "An artist, of course, may constantly rework the same theme or subject, but Stone often seems to be skimping or caricaturing the setting in order to play out his own psychodramas."[8]

In a similar line of argument, Sean French of *Sight and Sound* claimed that *Wall Street* was most problematic when it asked to be taken seriously as an indictment of the Wall Street system: "Stone's *j'accuse* is confused at its very heart: is it the system itself or the abuse of the system that is wrong? Oliver Stone pretends to be a moralist, but at his best he's really a sort of Darwinist. What really interests him is the battle for survival."[9]

Other criticisms of the film also floated around the claim that the script contained increasingly formulaic, sometimes obvious plotting that acted to diminish initial excitement and ultimate impact. There were charges that in dramatic terms, the scripting suffered from an ever-widening credibility gap between Gordon Gekko's well-drawn, single-minded character and the one that evolves for Bud Fox in the movement toward conversion. The script challenged one to accept the sudden realization by Fox that Gekko's intention of using Blue Star Airlines—the way he had used other companies—was an act of greed that simply went too far. The realization seemed to be more dramatically convenient than logical.

Also, the son's confession of love for his father, along with the statement "You're the only honest man I know," was considered glib, pat, and improperly motivated. With regard to honesty, the statement seemed to belie knowledge of other honest, hardworking people—Marv, Lou Mannheim—and therefore did not ring true. The effect of all this, according to *Cineaste* critic Elayne Rapping, was to reduce "the real crisis of capitalism—moral and economic—to a matter of family ties and the resurrection of the heart."[10]

In a larger dramatic context, these recognized script flaws significantly affected the symmetry Stone had sought in his narrative conflict of a soul being pulled by the forces of good and evil. So powerful and exacting was Gekko's ruthless character spine that only dramatic contrivance could work to cause the more limp Carl Fox to come out the winner in his son's suddenly moral eyes. Many called Stone's concluding tricks of climax and resolution cheap. Carl Fox's final charge to his son to "create instead of living off the buying and selling of others" was said by some to be heavy-handed and preachy.

For all its defects, its penchant for preaching, its injustices to female characters—*Wall Street* was undeniably the creation of Oliver Stone, reaffirming his growing status as a "maverick film man." Once more he had moved boldly—and with unexpected timeliness—into controversially ripe dramatic territory; the filmic properties of *Wall Street* were again charged by both a kinetic camera and engrossing dialogue that brilliantly matched themselves to setting and enterprise. And perhaps most revealingly, Stone had once more shown his greatest strength to be in a narrowed vision of stories involving men—what they do and how they function.

This kind of auteur instinct had been noted earlier, but it took on greater credence with *Wall Street*. Tom O'Brien wrote in *Commonweal:*

Stone understands male ambition—and views it with both sympathy and moral distance. As a result, he evokes performances from male actors—not only the older leads (Dafoe and Berenger in *Platoon,* Douglas here), but from supporting actors in "loser" positions (Kevin Dillon as a sadistic soldier in *Platoon,* here John C. McGinley as Marv, a young broker). McGinley gets some sprightly lines (the best an early one about one investor's "ethical bypass at birth," a good foreshadowing of the theme).

But Marv is a loser; he has Bud's ambitions but not his brains and lacks any perspective on his own life of quiet, driven desperation. Stone understands such characters extremely well; his moral power in treating their compulsions is that much greater *because* he knows them from the inside out—the way Tolstoy understood the rakes and rascals of Russia. The comparison is not overstated. Stone's promise as a filmmaker is in reaching real-life men with a realistic and fair view of themselves, one that might lead them to question their values. Stone the moralist is most powerful not when he lectures such men, but when he shows pity for what they put themselves through. He speaks their language—a sexist trait, perhaps, but one that allows him to be heard by a part of the population often deaf to moral address. True, his populism has a chromosomal flaw, but the flaw is linked to his films' great virtue: they don't speak to the already converted. I'll take this film even if flawed."[11]

As the auteur elements of the Oliver Stone text continued to manifest themselves—and to do so with greater clarity—the "loser," "rascally," "rakish" male character of uncommon appeal and value clearly held his place. Amid the polemics and the goody-good morality, he was sustaining what really mattered in Stone's work, what gave it its life: gritty male analysis.

7

Talk Radio

I'm not afraid, see. . . . I come in here every night. I make my case, I make my point. I say what I believe in; I tell you what you are. I have to—I have no choice.

—Barry Champlain to his listeners in *Talk Radio*

For what was to be his most intimate and contained film to date, Oliver Stone chose a theater piece that had been written and first performed by Eric Bogosian in New York at Joseph Papp's Public Theatre in 1987. The play, *Talk Radio,* was a 90-minute, bombastic tour de force vehicle of nonstop verbal harangue in which a shock-prone call-in radio host, Barry Champlain, abuses his listeners mercilessly.

The "shock" style of broadcast debate had become widespread in America in the 1980s through the efforts of Morton Downey, Jr., Bob Grant, Howard Stern, Alan Berg, and a variety of imitators. Alan Berg had so incensed right-wing factions (neofascists) in his listening audience that they retaliated by shooting and killing the controversial Denver radio personality outside his studio building.

The sudden rise, popularity, and invective response of the shock forum on radio resulted from the call-in host's willingness to engage in challenging, often hostile dialogue with listeners on the most controversial of issues—religion, sex, race, politics, societal frustration. The confrontational nature of the programming—with the host serving as a calculating provocateur—worked to raise both ire and broadcast ratings. It also challenged the limits of First Amendment free speech protection.

On the one hand, Bogosian's fascination with the media phenomenon of the shock host was directed at analysis of the peculiar rhetorical world such a person lives in when railing from behind an open microphone; on the other hand, it sought to reveal a stark, subcultural landscape populated by faceless, frustrated, often lonely and vulnerable people who use the call-in talk-radio program as an outlet. *Talk Radio* as a stage play offered a pathological account of public arrogance in exploit of invisible, sad collaborators.

Edward R. Pressman, a producer on earlier Stone pictures, had bought the option on Bogosian's play, and asked Stone to consider helping with the development of a screen script. Stone was also asked to serve as coproducer of the project. Stone's eventual interest in filming *Talk Radio* developed from his response to the play's central character, Barry Champlain, an antihero protagonist of complexity and moral ambiguity—at once repugnant, ideologically conflicted, obnoxious, and cocky while at the same time compelling. As with earlier protagonists of similar ilk, Champlain promised Stone yet another way of looking at America and the misuse and abuse of its systems.

Stone agreed to direct *Talk Radio* in mid-1987, following a Los Angeles premiere screening of *Wall Street* that Bogosian had attended. Stone immediately took a liking to Bogosian and instructed him to begin converting his stage play into a filmscript, incorporating into the adaptation elements of the book *Talked to Death*—Stephen Singular's account of the life and death of Alan Berg, for which movie rights had been purchased. In October 1987 Stone met with Bogosian in New York to critique the work in progress, and in February 1988 the two finalized a shooting script. Bogosian—an intense, talented actor—agreed to re-create Barry Champlain for the screen.

Talk Radio was budgeted by Pressman at $6 million and filmed in Dallas in late 1988 over a 25-day period. The end result was a film more expansive in concept than Bogosian's play, in which the compact action had occurred in a single evening with a single character. The film had been "opened up" to incorporate additional time (a weekend) and more characters; in the process greater attention had been paid to developing a biographical and psychological profile of Barry Champlain and to shaping the story to resemble more closely Alan Berg's life, particularly through the film's climax and actual dialogue taken from recordings of Berg's broadcasts.

In making a film about a near-manic media personality who cajoles his audience, Oliver Stone said he came to see similarities between himself and his own films and Barry Champlain and his "aggressive, obsessive" radio methods. Indeed, when one of Champlain's radio colleagues—added to the film—says of the acerbic talk-show host "He's all alone out there," Stone was probably thinking of Martin Scorsese's comments about him when *Platoon* was released in 1986. Perhaps Barry Champlain and *Talk Radio* gleefully signaled Oliver Stone willing to wear his artistic heart on his sleeve.

Synopsis of *Talk Radio* (1988)

Cast: Eric Bogosian, Ellen Greene, Leslie Hope, Alec Baldwin, John C. McGinley, John Pankow, Michael Wincott, Linda Atkinson, Robert Trebar, Zach Grenier, Anna Levine, Rockets Redgare, Tony Frank, Harlan Jordan.

Credits: Director: Oliver Stone. Producer: Edward R. Pressman. Screenplay: Eric Bogosian and Oliver Stone, based on the play *Talk Radio,* by Eric Bogosian, and the book *Talked to Death: The Life and Murder of Alan Berg,* by Stephen Singular. Photography: Robert Richardson. Music: Stewart Copeland. Production design: Bruno Rubeo.

As the camera sweeps across the Dallas evening landscape, Barry Champlain (Eric Bogosian)—phone-in host of KGAB radio's "Night Talk"—is heard priming his audience with comments about how America has gone to pot. There are references to rampant pornography, insider trading, crack, and married couples who prefer television to sex. Champlain declares, "Talk radio—the last neighborhood in town," as he begins to field the evening's first calls from his slick penthouse studio high above Dallas. A transvestite, a lonely young woman, and a caller named Rhonda, who's concerned about giving clean needles to New York City addicts, phone in to solicit Champlain's advice. Champlain's responses—one by one—are unsympathetic. He interrupts Rhonda to ask doesn't she know that tobacco is the country's most dangerous drug, and hangs up as he refers to her as "Rhonda Q. Sucker."

On this particular evening, a representative of Metrowave, a Chicago broadcast corporation, is at KGAB to offer national syndication to "Night Talk" if Champlain will tone down his comments—particularly on subjects like homosexuality, blacks, and drug abusers. Champlain learns that syndication on Metrowave's 357 stations can begin as early as the following week if agreements are reached. Champlain, surprised by the news, continues to take calls, then during a break challenges his station manager, Dan (Alec Baldwin), on the syndication deal and phones ex-wife Ellen (Ellen Greene) to tell her the news. He invites her to come visit him in Dallas for the weekend without letting his current girlfriend, Laura (Leslie Hope), also a station employee, know of his plans to see Ellen.

As Champlain completes the evening program, racist caller Chet (Earl Hindman) phones for a second time to ask Champlain if he's received the package sent him at the station. Noticing for the first time the package on his console desk, Champlain nervously but bravely opens it against the advice of station staff. The box contains a death-threat note, a dead rat, and a small Nazi flag. Champlain signs off with: "Remember, sticks and stones can break your bones, but words cause permanent damage."

During his weekend off, Champlain attends an SMU basketball game as a guest of honor but is wildly booed down as he attempts to speak to the crowd. Ex-wife Ellen arrives and phones from the airport for a ride—upsetting Laura, who's at Champlain's apartment. On the way into the city, Ellen and Champlain talk and realize that they still have strong feelings for each other; in the course of their conversation, she tells her former husband he has to start loving himself, has to find someone with a soul and not "just fall in love with some girl's body."

These comments trigger a flashback sequence that traces Barry Champlain's rise from a clothing store clerk named Barry Golden to an acerbic-mouthed talk-show host. Ellen, happily married to Champlain, is shown assisting the climb, faking phone-in calls to draw attention to her husband's program. Champlain's success is accompanied by sexual dalliance, which destroys his marriage when Ellen one day catches him unexpectedly in the midst of a house sex party.

On Monday, the day of the national hookup, Metrowave suddenly announces a two-week postponement because Champlain has not agreed to curtail his abusive ways. As Ellen observes, a disappointed, angry Champlain goes on the air and is more outrageous than ever, questioning one caller on her opinions about "lesbian priests" and "masturbation." Kent (Michael Wincott), a regular caller and a spaced-out junkie, is invited to the studio to sit in on the program as a special guest. The station manager, Dan, objects—fearful that Metrowave will think Champlain undependable and withdraw its offer altogether. Ellen and Laura side with Dan, but Champlain—now insecure and paranoid—insists: "Get the kid."

Calls from a man who admits to abusing his children, and from an alleged rapist who says he's about to strike again, as well as the hysterical appearance of the drugged Kent, act to further addle Champlain's sense of control. A female phones to ask: "Are you as ugly-looking as you sound? Do you not love yourself? I'm sorry for you because you don't know how to love." Another death threat arrives in the mail.

Ellen realizes that Champlain is about "to go under" and attempts to pull him back by phoning in as "Cherylanne"—a fake name she had used as a caller when the two were married and his radio career just beginning. On the air she expresses her love for her ex-husband and the desire to take care of him. Champlain retorts: "You blew it. . . . Your ex doesn't want you. . . . He doesn't need you. . . . We reap what we sow. Follow me, Cherylanne?" He hangs up on Ellen and she leaves.

Champlain turns his sign-off into a lengthy confession, admitting his hypocrisy by saying that he does what he does strictly for money and success. He expresses disdain for his audience: "You're pathetic. I despise each and every one of you. You've got nothing, absolutely nothing—no brains, no power, no future, no hope, no God. The only thing you believe in is me. What are you if you don't have me?" Listeners phone in to sympathize with Champlain.

Metrowave representative Chuck Dietz (John Pankow) is impressed by Champlain's openness and announces he's ready to go with the show. Champlain says he isn't sure he wants to continue the program and leaves the studio. In the parking lot outside, he tells Laura he's too old for her and admits that his greatest fear is being boring. The two part. As Champlain approaches his car, a heavyset man, silhouetted in the dark, steps forward to ask for an autograph. Ready to respond, Champlain is gunned down. The screen washes to white.

The film ends with a camera tilt up of a radio transmitter, followed by a long aerial scan of Dallas at night. On the soundtrack phone-in callers and studio engineer Stu (John C. McGinley) are heard reacting to Barry Champlain, his show and his death. The final shot is of a motionless studio tape deck.

In terms of a cinematic adaptation *Talk Radio* presented unusual challenges for Oliver Stone. His reputation had been earned as a writer-director of what he liked to refer to as "broad canvas" films—films with episodic plots, rapidly changing locations, and large casts. *Salvador, Platoon,* and *Wall Street* were all films in which narrative conflict had been admirably supported by a cinematic style that immediately created a corollary between idea and chaotic, unsettled space. The arenas of action in these films were unusually intense—Central America in the early 1980s, the combat jungles of Vietnam, and the bedlam world of investment trading. All three films carried a militaristic tone.

Talk Radio was entirely different. The film's primary location, a broadcast studio, held little apparent visual interest. Intensity was essentially verbal, and dramatic conflict was provided for the most part by faceless voices. Although the script had been opened up to include additional locations and characters, the heart of the plot resided in one person in one place: Barry Champlain behind a live microphone in a radio station. The original play was created as a dramatic piece for the ear and the imagination. Space was important only in the sense of a two-way response between voices carried by airwave and telephone line. *Talk Radio* did not appear in need of or susceptible to filmic embellishment.

Stone's visual translation of Barry Champlain's world was realized through several aesthetic choices. Especially notable was the film's lighting design. Night scenes and interiors in *Salvador* and *Platoon* had shown Stone capable of achieving a strong noir quality in his work. Even darker toning for *Talk Radio* would permit intensification of the film noir look and serve as appropriate visual styling for a story with heavy psychological overtones.

Cinematographer Robert Richardson employed extensive low-key lighting schemes to achieve this effect. Interior scenes often carried strong expressionistic value through the dark, low-key toning of images. Nighttime aerial shots of Dallas effectively conveyed the mystique of a hidden, faceless universe of radio listeners. Champlain's midnight shooting death in a city parking lot offered a model view of ambiguously rendered space—perfectly toned—through the arrangement of light and shadow.

Stone also decided to free his camera in the radio studio scenes— letting it arc, dolly, zoom, and leap to overhead bird's-eye positions while the film's central character remained in a static position at his microphone. As the audio reels spin, so too does the filmgoer's view of Champlain. In one shot Stone placed Champlain's chair on a dolly so that it could turn with the camera. The studio walls seem to move in a circle while Champlain appears to remain stationary. Extreme closeups and sharply oblique camera angles supplied additional visual variety, and in the most intense, paranoid scenes, camera angling helped convey the alternating quirkiness and insecurity in Champlain's radio demeanor.

Through the use of studio control room glass and lighting, Stone found a way of employing character reflections to link in the same shot Champlain's radio talk to its impact. Full facial reaction in the glass images added sobering weight to Champlain's increasingly abusive, confrontational manner. This foreground/background effect had its greatest impact in the scene where Ellen phones as Cherylanne in an attempt to salvage Champlain's ego and he bluntly rejects her. The psychic pain of the scene was expressed in both aural and visual confrontation.

Eric Bogosian (Barry Champlain) is cautioned by Alec Baldwin (Dan, the station manager) to tone down his on-mike barbs in *Talk Radio* (1988). © 1988 Cineplex Odeon Films, Inc. All rights reserved. Photo by Joyce Rudolph. Courtesy The Museum of Modern Art/Film Stills Archive.

As another Stone film about the abuse and misuse of an American system, *Talk Radio* held a special irony by following on the heels of *Wall Street*. Barry Champlain could toss out the practice of rampant insider trading as evidence that America had gone to pot at the very moment he himself was exploiting—hypocritically—a system and its users strictly for financial gain. In the end, like Gordon Gekko, Champlain reveals himself as someone who has not really created anything meaningful but has achieved solely through bravura calculation and deception. Also like Gekko, Champlain is taken down by someone he has exploited—an ally in the deception who feels forced to act.

The differences, of course, between *Wall Street* and *Talk Radio* as statement films about corruptible systems had to do with the approaches to moral closure. A lost soul is redeemed and old-fashioned values win out at the end of *Wall Street*. In *Talk Radio*, Barry Champlain gets his due but does so through the action of not someone redeemed but a revenger matching hate with hate. In an act aimed at moral justice, Bud Fox uses words (and a tape recorder) to trap Gordon Gekko; in *Talk Radio* when words don't work for the killer as a way of getting back at Champlain, a gun is used to commit what amounts to a political assassination. The latter is an act born of bigotry, insult, frustration—not of moral lessons learned.

Talk Radio had drawn heavily on Eric Bogosian's dramaturgical vision, and with Stone's input as coauthor touched on a variety of contemporary ideas beyond system abuse: the arrogance and contempt of celebrity, the First Amendment stretch, race hatred, increased public voyeurism, social and political frustration.

Where Stone's textual presence was most felt was in the expansion of plot to include additional biographical details and characters, including a flashback insert—all meant to develop Champlain as a flesh-and-blood human being with a past. On the stage Champlain had been merely a quirky, oddball isolate who becomes totally lost in his voice and its ability to rule over its listeners.

By turning Champlain into someone who no longer seems capable of committing to love (to the point of self-loathing) and someone whose idealism seems to be failing him, *Talk Radio* became less a study of individual nihilism and more a psychodrama. While the film tosses around a number of provocative ideas, its dramatic core is shifted more significantly toward the analysis of professional and personal male identity crisis. A certain schizophrenia followed. *Chicago Tribune* critic Dave Kehr wrote: "Issues are raised and dismissed with dizzying, dismaying speed. At one moment the movie seems to be about the marital problems of show biz types; at another, it's about the true artist's need to resist the pressures of compromise."[1]

Stone also went with a decision to attach to the film an ending that would recall the fate of talk-show host Alan Berg. The attachment clearly was meant to supply a climax that would return Champlain's story—after his pained personal confession—to that of a martyred idealist. Given the dramatic construction of *Talk Radio,* the device of an assassin was found to be troublesome. Of Champlain's shooting death, Pam Cook argued that "the film would have done better to let its hero stand as the monstrous personification of a society whose ideals have gone rancid."[2]

Other critics raised questions about *Talk Radio*'s effectiveness in developing through its verbal exchanges convincing evidence of a neo-fascist race hatred—the impulse behind Berg's death, and implied in Champlain's. Berg was depicted in Singular's book *Talked to Death* as a troubled, fallen-away member of the Jewish faith (also plagued by marital problems) whose on-air comments invited the hatred of a neo-fascist cult known as "The Order." The cult members, religious fundamentalists and anti-Semitic, hired a hit squad to kill Berg for his attacks on their beliefs.

Talk Radio's narrative incorporated elements apparently designed to suggest both a Jewish-fundamentalist tension and a kind of religious hypocrisy on Champlain's part. Phone-in callers refer to Champlain as "Jew boy" and question the origin of his name; one challenges the accuracy of Holocaust death figures, calling the Holocaust a Zionist guilt ploy directed at getting U.S. tax dollars. Champlain puts down this thesis. A black calls to say he likes Jews. Champlain responds by saying no one cares for blacks. The death-threat package contains a miniature Nazi flag designated by a swastika. These verbal and visual references are meant to signify an undercurrent of racial/religious animosity.

Champlain's own conflicted response to his Jewish heritage comes early in the film, when he tells a sentimental tale to his listeners of a visit he supposedly made to the concentration camp at Dachau. He claims to have found there on the campgrounds an old Star of David. He tells his audience he's holding the Star of David in his hands even at that moment, to give him courage against bigoted callers. As he speaks these words, the camera tilts down to reveal Champlain holding a cup of coffee.

Had these racial/religious intimations been strong enough to credibly link Champlain's fate with Berg's? critics asked. Could Champlain be viewed as some kind of martyr, or was he simply the victim of his own unfortunate character flaws? These questions offered valid inquiry into what exactly *Talk Radio*'s text was saying. Clearly Champlain was generally disliked by the public at large, as his appearance at a college basketball game confirmed. The film's final voice montage of listeners reacting to Champlain's death, however, suggested confusion about how to assess the talk-show host and what he stood for. One caller says vaguely that Champlain got what he deserved. Kent—the druggie studio guest—calls in to say, simplistically, that his life was blessed by his personal appearance with Champlain on "Night Talk."

Reaction to *Talk Radio*'s schematic play on racism and anti-Semitism and the ensuing assassination of Champlain took different angles of address. Film critic J. Hoberman of the *Village Voice* commented that in spite of "all the Jew-baiting and Biblical prophesies Champlain endures," *Talk Radio* "is not so much a movie of ideas as mental images. Champlain takes his leave with a celestial white out, disembodied voices fluttering around the glittering radio town like so many angels. There's a cosmic quality to *Talk Radio*'s claustrophobia—as though Bogosian and Stone were playing grand opera in a space capsule."[3]

Richard Porton of *Cineaste* maintained that the linkage attempt with Alan Berg's life had moved *Talk Radio* into "muddled territory" and that "Bogosian's de-ethnicized presence does not really correspond to Berg's unvarnished psychic pain."[4]

Janet Maslin, *New York Times* critic, agreed: "[Barry Champlain] is a startling figure but not a terribly emblematic one. His scathing monologues, his personal ambitions, his fits of self-loathing and glimmers of self-knowledge finally have no larger implications at all. Yet the film, directed in a chillingly portentous style by Oliver Stone, is a stick of dynamite in desperate need of a fuse. So the clumsily grafted-on ending supplies the explosiveness that ought to grow out of the story itself but never really does."[5]

Other attempts were made to point out that the film's troubling ending was a result of the script's vacillating way of making Champlain both hero and villain, both tormentor and victim. The pull, it was said, left the film with no stable center and in effect resulted in an ambivalence that worked against support of the ending.

At least one critic saw the ending as an act perhaps less concerned with specific motivations than with a more generalized societal reflection: "Stone may have given us an off-handed etiology of the assassination syndrome that nearly became a national pastime at one point in our history. The Dallas of the mid-to-late '80's harbors sadistic urges never too distant from deep-seated illiteracy, especially when updated with new right-spawned anti-intellectualism"[6]

What critics also saw in Stone's tailoring of Barry Champlain was another attempt at a male protagonist along the lines of other Stone protagonists. Michael Wilmington of the *Los Angeles Times* observed that "Champlain is the same mixture of honesty and sleaze, high aspiration and character as James Woods' reporter in Stone's *Salvador*. Like that character, Champlain is a catalyst; he drags out the truth, the dark sides. But he's become a beast in public to win his ratings. And he's become a beast in private as well. He tears his life and his ideals to shreds. Honesty becomes a gig and cynicism a crutch."[7] Pam Cook termed Champlain "a classic Stone anti-hero: cynical, selfish, aggressive, insensitive to women, yet somehow saved by a vestigial idealism, a product of the worst and the best in American society" (Cook, 285).

Eric Bogosian's intensely compelling interpretation of Champlain was distinguished by its punchy, often humorous way of dealing with invisible listeners for whom he held absolutely no respect. A gift for timing in delivering one-liner retorts and for elongating words and phrases to give them nagging impact made his manner of playing provocateur engrossingly creepy. The special timing was evident when Bogosian, after ranting for drug law changes, caps his argument with "Legalize it today . . . right after these messages." Bogosian played well a true "rascally" Oliver Stone character.

Stone's success in rendering the sleazy male character and using him as a means of achieving knowledge and insight had been illustrated in the Dr. Rock character created by Jim Belushi in *Salvador*. Stone had envisioned the grungy Dr. Rock as a sideline figure whose observations of El Salvador would provide a different, common man's view of specific realities.

A similar opportunity was exploited in *Talk Radio* through the presence of Kent—the vacuous, stoned youngster who likes to play cat-and-mouse games with Champlain and who becomes the only caller allowed to enter the studio for face-to-face dialogue. Kent phones in frequently with fake scenarios about a drug overdose by girlfriend Jill, crying and appealing for help, then later gleefully calling back to admit the hoax. He says he made up the story because he had nothing else to talk about.

By OK'ing Kent's request to come to the radio station, Champlain had agreed to come from behind the anonymity of his microphone and "meet" his audience. What he sees is a long-haired, giggling, incoherent freak who babbles on about the wives of other celebrities, about revolution and fascists. As directed by Stone and played by Michael Wincott, Kent is an enervated, screaming animal who goes to pieces in the presence of a media star and who offers no evidence of intellectual substance. Champlain calls Kent an idiot and tells him that if he represents the future of the country, "we're in sad shape." Kent can only respond with "You're so funny, man."

Kent becomes the frightening source of Champlain's self-knowledge about the quality of the audience he's been dealing with, increasing the talk-show host's paranoia and driving him toward his confessional summary of his listeners' and his own faults. As he had done with Dr. Rock, Stone breathed life—sleazy life—into Kent's character and did so with benefit to narrative strategy.

It was in its projected view of the hidden audience, their hunger and their voyeurism in speaking and listening to others speak in the presence of someone famous, that *Talk Radio* had taken its firmest hold. The film depicted the callers feeding off such programs as "Night Talk" while at the same time building up the celebrity of the host. Celebrity supplies the essential ingredient that keeps the psychodynamics of so-called trash radio working. On his arrival at the studio Kent screams, "I can't believe I'm here," and later says his life was blessed, transformed by his momentary contact with Champlain.

Reviewer G. Jones pushed the implication of *Talk Radio*'s ideas of voyeurism and audience analysis into a larger media arena that included television talk shows of the type represented by "Oprah" and "Geraldo" as well as the type that docudramatize sensational, real-life events: "Oliver Stone's *Talk Radio* takes some giant steps to identify and explain this new voyeuristic culture mushrooming into respectability all around us, the crowd that is likely making up much of the audience for "A Current Affair," "America's Most Wanted," "The Reporters," "Cops," and other shows pandering to the voyeur's fascination with death and crime dramatized" (Jones, 26). In this analysis Jones refers to these types of television programs as "TV tabloid reality," which, like supermarket tabloids themselves, "incite the quintessential consumer urges, turning potential critical controversy—the stuff of productive debate—into melodrama" (Jones, 26). The consumerism aspect of what Barry Champlain does—his talent for turning serious issues into entertaining melodrama—may not be as evident to him as it is to others, but it is a significant part of *Talk Radio*'s subject. Station manager Dan says to Champlain, "You're a suit salesman with a big mouth," doing so in an attempt to jolt some reality into Champlain's head regarding his commercial appeal, which is being wooed with a potentially lucrative syndicated deal. Dan sees Champlain's act only for what it is—not salvation fare but money-generating show business enterprise that has already lifted KGAB's offices and studios to penthouse status. More money looms ahead.

Some critics felt strongly that the consumer theme of *Talk Radio* could have been even more pointed and the hero-idealist framing pushed further to the side. By emphasizing the latter and by appropriating the Alan Berg story, the film had attempted to do too much, perhaps, and in the process had lost its satiric edge as a statement about American consumer taste represented by shock radio.

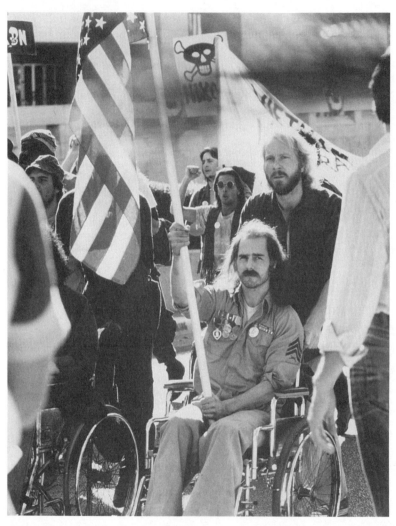

Tom Cruise as Ron Kovic in *Born on the Fourth of July* (1989). Copyright © 1989 Universal City Studios, Inc. All rights reserved. Photo by Roland Neveu. Courtesy The Museum of Modern Art/Film Stills Archive.

8

Born on the Fourth of July

I wrote a sequel [to *Platoon*], based on my own personal problems. But I felt this story [*Born on the Fourth of July*] was the bigger story. I thought it would cut across more class lines, would be much more effective, but would, at the same time, encompass my own story in many ways.
——Oliver Stone, during the filming of *Born on the Fourth of July*.

Oliver Stone found in Vietnam veteran Ron Kovic and his autobiography, *Born on the Fourth of July*, an ideal story to use as a bookend with *Platoon*—the latter being a classic study of youth initiation into war and Kovic's study offering an opportunity to look beyond war's experience to its aftermath. *Platoon* had left open the question of precisely what happens to the combat soldier who suffers the emotional and physical traumas of war and then must reintegrate into civilian life.

Also, *Platoon* had been essentially apolitical. Chris Taylor, the film's hero, comes to the knowledge of his own willingness to act in evil ways, and his epiphany as a war survivor leads him to the conclusion that he must return home and "build again" by teaching others what has been learned. But beyond these somewhat abstract realizations, *Platoon* remained detached from any political inquiry into what the Vietnam War meant to the men who fought there. The fact that the war had caused a bitter divisiveness back in the United States was not a consideration; nor had *Platoon* sought to emphasize to any significant degree the combat soldiers' confusions about their purpose in being in Vietnam or about the U.S. policy that sustained the war.

These were areas of discourse touched on in Kovic's accounting of his prewar, war, and postwar life. Kovic, a native of the Long Island town of Massapequa, New York, had detailed in his book (published in 1976) how boyhood experiences—through church, school, play, family, John Wayne movies, John F. Kennedy's idealism—had contributed to his thinking about himself and the world around him. The details recalled a developing patriotism, symbolically underscored by the fact that Kovic's birthday fell on the Fourth of July. It was this sense of duty that had caused him and other hometown high school buddies to volunteer for military service in 1964.

Kovic went to Vietnam twice during his enlisted duty in the Marine Corps—returning home at age 21 a paraplegic after gunfire entered his right shoulder and shattered his spinal column. The injury left him paralyzed from the chest down. He had also accidentally killed a fellow marine during his second tour, an incident that had added the burden of guilt to the agony of paralysis.

Kovic depicted his postwar experience as a time of great pain and confusion—stemming from numbness of body, guilt, and the antiwar dissent he found on returning to the United States. His book told how the psychological weight of the confusion led to alcoholism and despondency, followed by political conversion in the early 1970s and eventual membership in the Vietnam Veterans against the War organization.

Born on the Fourth of July held opportunity not only for political discourse on the Vietnam War but also for expanded analysis of its personal impact. Chris Taylor's call to military duty in *Platoon* was expressed as the simple desire to live up to the models of his father and grandfather and to escape a sheltered life for knowledge and adventure. Ron Kovic's story carried, on the other hand, an empirically built rationale for patriotism that derived from the cultural and ideological conditioning of young American men who grew up during the 1950s and early 1960s.

Naïveté followed both Taylor and Kovic into war, but Kovic's naïveté was explained in terms that increased the tragedy. Kovic's disillusionment and sense of loss came not simply through knowledge of what war makes people do and what it wreaks but through accompanying knowledge, Kovic argued, that could shatter faith in one's country and leave one depressed by its deception. Kovic said that the first film he saw after release from a VA hospital in the Bronx in 1968 was *The Green Berets*—the moment when his "fantasies of John Wayne finally died" and when he decided he would one day write an autobiographical account of war's realities from his own perspective.

Oliver Stone was hired to write a screen draft of Kovic's book in 1977 (with Kovic as coauthor), just after he completed writing his own Vietnam story, *Platoon*. Plans for production were outlined in 1978, with William Friedkin to direct and Al Pacino scheduled to play Kovic. Kovic began consulting with Pacino on the realities of his experience. The same luck that had befallen Stone's efforts to get *Platoon* up and running, however, befell *Born on the Fourth of July:* four days before shooting was to begin, production was suddenly canceled, probably because Pacino withdrew as the lead. It took Stone 10 years to bring *Platoon* to the screen; *Born on the Fourth of July* would have to wait 12.

Although Stone never really gave up on his intentions of realizing a film from Kovic's book (the two remained friends during the 1980s), only after the success of *Platoon*—which showed that downbeat Vietnam stories could make money—did Hollywood and investors agree to back *Born on the Fourth of July*. The other element in the turnaround was actor Tom Cruise's interest in playing the role Pacino had abandoned. In 1985 Cruise had encountered phenomenal success with *Top Gun*—a fairy-tale account of military heroism—and afterward wanted to find an acting vehicle with a more realistic point of view. He chose Kovic's story, agreeing to work for union scale and a percentage of the film's profits.

Production of the project was revitalized and in 1988 squeezed by Stone into the year's work, along with *Talk Radio*. For the Vietnam scenes, Stone returned to the Philippines to shoot; the American sequences were shot largely in Texas (Dallas), with Kovic acting as a consultant—advising on the treatment of personal incidents taken from the book and on the accuracy of medical details in scenes set in military hospitals. To add to the desired authenticity, Stone cast residents of Kovic's hometown, Massapequa, in minor roles and flew in members of Kovic's family to observe the filming. Kovic recalled the shooting of the film—with Cruise reenacting his life—as a fully cathartic experience.[1]

Oliver Stone's compulsion to make *Born on the Fourth of July* was impelled by his own underlying need to see the Vietnam story worked through fully. Kovic and Stone had experienced many of the same feelings on coming back home from the war—the sense of being disconnected and of dislocation and rejection, together with restlessness and depression. Both had resorted to self-degradation through drugs and alcohol abuse, and both had moved forward to see the war as personally and politically tragic. Ron Kovic's autobiography was partly Stone's—the lessons learned (and their urgency to be told) also as much his own as Kovic's. In this sense the film offered the opportunity of catharsis for Stone as well.

The outrage in Kovic's story of struggle and political growth, coupled with Stone's passion for retelling it, resulted in a film that was emotionally complex and also very "loud" in its construction of an antiwar message. *Born on the Fourth of July* carefully pointed its ideological position as it presented a drama of patriotic-fervor-turned-to-the-heroics-of-dissent; at the same time, it delineated personal heartbreak and disillusionment through a no-holds-barred approach that sought and won a deeply felt response.

Synopsis of *Born on the Fourth of July* (1989)

Cast: Tom Cruise, Kyra Sedgwick, Caroline Kava, Raymond J. Barry, Jerry Levine, Frank Whaley, Willem Dafoe, Tom Berenger, Bryan Larkin, Josh Evans, Tony Frank, Jayne Hayes.

Credits: Director: Oliver Stone. Producer: A. Kitman Ho. Screenplay: Oliver Stone and Ron Kovic, based on the book by Ron Kovic. Photography: Robert Richardson. Production design: Bruno Rubeo. Editor: David Brenner. Music: John Williams.

The film opens in a nostalgic, evocative manner—lyric music plays on the soundtrack while the camera roams about a patch of Long Island woods; tree branches refract the sun's rays into gentle patterns of light. Ron Kovic (Tom Cruise) is heard voice-over:

> It was a long time ago. Sometimes I can still hear their voices. . . . There was Billy, Steve, Tommy, and the tall kid from down the street, Joey—yeah it was Joey Walsh. And my best friend was Timmy Burns who lived two blocks away from me. And we'd turn the woods into a battlefield and dream that someday we would become men.

Young boys are seen playing at making war—shouting "You're dead!" "No, I'm not." A supered title appears indicating "Massapequa, Long Island, 1956."

The scene shifts to a Fourth of July street parade, which is realized in softened imagery and slow motion to sustain the nostalgic look at a time past. As opening credits roll, a montage consisting of parade elements—bands, floats, clowns, majorettes, war veterans (some in wheelchairs), curbside observers—appears to depict a typical American Independence Day celebration. An older veteran marcher glances knowingly toward a young Ronnie Kovic (Bryan Larkin), who sits on his father's shoulders, holding a small American flag. A young girl, Donna, runs up to Ronnie Kovic and hands him a New York Yankees baseball cap, saying: "Happy birthday, Ronnie Kovic." As the montage continues, the two youngsters are seen kissing during the evening's fireworks display and later, during a Little League baseball game, Donna reacts with elation when Ronnie hits a home run.

The Kovic family—a large, blue-collar family of eight—is seen at home watching television and reacting to John F. Kennedy's 1961 inaugural address, in which the newly elected president challenged national spirit with "Ask not what your country can do for you, but what you . . . , etc." Mrs. Kovic (Caroline Kava) wistfully recalls a dream she's had in which Ronnie is speaking before a large group, "saying great things."

The action shifts to a later time, when Ron Kovic (Tom Cruise)—now a high school wrestler—is being pushed by his coach to "pay the price of victory" through rigorous training and sacrifice. The physical punishment and cajoling language ("Come on, ladies. I want you to kill") have the feel of military indoctrination. In a competitive match that follows, Ron loses—greatly disappointing his mother and girlfriend, Donna (Kyra Sedgwick). Kovic, lying on his back, grimaces and cries.

In the next scene, a Marine Corps sergeant (Tom Berenger)—on a recruiting mission to the high school—tells an awed Kovic and others in attendance: "We have never lost a war." Afterward Kovic and his high school buddies gather in a local ice cream parlor, where they debate the issues of their lives: college, communism, joing the military, "staying home and taking care of the women," and so on. Kovic announces that he's signed up for the marines, saying, "I'm not not waiting. . . . This is our chance to do something."

Kovic prepares to leave Massapequa for his military duty. On his last night home, packing, he watches a television report on the VC's long history of military success against outsiders. He becomes confused, but says he loves his country and is willing to make the sacrifice. His mother, who has professed a hatred of communism, says: "It's God's will you go." After kneeling by his bed and praying for help, Kovic runs in the rain to his senior prom at the school gym for a final dance with Donna. To the lyrics of "Moon River," the two dance and kiss farewell.

As a transition to dramatized scenes in Vietnam, television news footage on the Tet Offensive and the effectiveness of the forest canopy in getting the Vietcong through is inserted. Defoliation efforts by American forces through the use of agent blue are said to have been futile, resulting only in widespread contamination of the land. The news report says elephants—used as transport by the VC—have become the targets of U.S. forces.

From a fade to black to a slow fade-in on American soldiers silhouetted against an orange-rich Vietnam horizon, the plot begins to recount Kovic's final, traumatic experiences as a combat NCO. A superimposed time-and-place title reads "Near the Cua Viet River, Vietnam, October, 1967." As Kovic's patrol moves forward, he reassures a frightened young PFC from Georgia—Willie Wilson (Rocky Carroll)—with the statement that it's his second tour of Vietnam and he hasn't "seen a Georgia boy hurt yet."

A scene of pandemonium erupts when firing begins before the order is given. The soldiers confuse villagers for the enemy. Kovic comes upon dead Vietnamese civilians, including women and children in the thatched huts of the village on which they've fired. Hand-held Steadicam shots reveal the frantic action as confused troops are instructed to "Move out! Move out!" The soldiers become more disoriented and begin to fire without certainty at ill-defined targets. Images are blurry details on the Vietnamese landscape. When Wilson, the Georgian PFC, is shot and dies, Kovic thinks he may have accidentally killed one of his own men. The action had been so fast and the image at which he shot so indistinct that Kovic at first cannot be sure he is responsible. Later he decides he is.

Back at the camp base, Kovic asks to see one of the company officers, expresses his concern about the dead civilians, and admits that he is probably responsible for Wilson's death. The officer refuses to acknowledge his confession.

On a subsequent seek-and-destroy patrol mission, Kovic is struck in the foot by an enemy bullet fired from a camouflaged straw bunker, but continues to fire back until his automatic rifle jams and another sniper bullet tears through his right shoulder. In a MASH medical unit, a priest administers the last rites after urging Kovic: "Try to stay alive."

A title super places Kovic in a rat-infested Bronx VA hospital, where a roving camera uncovers the disorderly and humiliating reaction of severely wounded bodies in the process of recovery and rehabilitation. The time is 1968, the year of the Chicago Grant Park student activist riots, which Kovic watches with disgust on a hospital television set. During his lengthy therapy, Kovic reacts to the news that he'll probably never walk again or be able to have children by undertaking dangerous and futile exercises to make his legs work. He experiences nocturnal sexual fantasies that leave him even more frustrated. Kovic's anger at his treatment and condition builds. Some medics seem more concerned about their own politics than the care of their patients.

Back home in 1969 with his family, Kovic experiences the difficulties of social and domestic reintegration as a Vietnam veteran who is also a paraplegic. Neighbors look at him suspiciously, and friends tell him he made a mistake; his brother asks him what he got out of being in the military, admitting he doesn't believe in the war. Family arguments break out; his mother—a devout Catholic—chastises him for his angered profanity.

Kovic finds his moment as a hero in the annual Massapequa Fourth of July parade, then immediately feels more isolated and a failure for whom living has lost all meaning. He shares his feelings of frustration, confusion, and loss in his backyard with longtime friend and fellow Vietnam vet Timmy Barnes (Frank Whaley). Kovic visits Donna at Syracuse University, where campus antiwar demonstrations and student-police confrontations are the order of the day. He is more perplexed than ever.

The plot leaps ahead to show Kovic as a surly, long-haired pool-hall alcoholic. Confronted by his mother for his late-night drunkenness, he shouts obscenities at her, professes knowledge that Vietnam was a lie, then rips the catheter from his penis—lamenting the loss of his potency. In the hysteria of this scene, Kovic's genteel father (Raymond J. Barry) urges that his son leave on a planned vacation trip to Mexico.

In a Mexican resort, Kovic befriends Charlie (Willem Dafoe), another paraplegic veteran, and Maria Elena (Cordelia Gonzalez), an attractive barroom hostess who introduces Kovic to the pleasures of nongenital sex. Kovic's spirits momentarily soar. In an all-out desert fight, Charlie and Kovic vent their Vietnam rage on one another. They exhaust themselves.

Kovic travels from Mexico to Georgia, the hometown of Willie Wilson, the PFC he accidentally killed in the Cua Viet Valley. He stops at the cemetery where Wilson is buried, then goes on to the parents' rural home to confess to them how their son died and to admit other mistakes and atrocities of the war. The pain of the confession is complicated by the unexpected presence of Wilson's wife and young son. Kovic cries, and Wilson's mother (Jayne Haynes) comforts him with "We understand, Ron. We understand the pain you've been going through."

Next Kovic appears in the middle of a peace demonstration at the 1972 Republican National Convention in Miami. As he attempts to push his way onto the convention floor, he tells a television news reporter: "This war is a crime." Kovic is now a fully converted member of the Disabled Vietnam War Veterans against the War, leading the demonstration with impassioned commitment. Police in a brute-force putdown of the antiwar activists haul Kovic off to jail with the other demonstrators.

Born on the Fourth of July concludes four years later at the 1976 Democratic National Convention, where Kovic waits in the wings to address the delegates—telling reporters he's "just going to tell the truth." He signs a copy of his recently published autobiography. The last shot before actor credits is one taken from behind, as Kovic wheels himself up a ramp to the speaker's podium to the applause of the waiting delegates. Mrs. Kovic is heard, voice-over, repeating her dream about her son speaking before a large group, saying important things.

The script of *Born on the Fourth of July* took a well-developed approach to narrative construction. It applied a straightforward chronological structure to its ordering of the biographical details of Kovic's life from childhood to antiwar hero, making it a less symbolic story than Stone's earlier youth initiation and conversion films of archetypal framing—*Platoon* and *Wall Street*. Without an archetypal design, *Born on the Fourth of July* was less artistically pretentious, but more plot-obvious as it worked its way to an explicitly derived message.

The more direct chronology permitted the easy placement of key points meant to define Kovic's development as a product, then victim-hero, of a specific time and cultural environment. Signification for an emerging patriotic/sacrificial attitude on Kovic's part comes through a variety of forms, but all were easy to grasp. As the film opens, Kovic and his elementary school friends play at war in a wooded area as they dream of becoming men—suggesting that even at so early an age, fighting had been planted in their thinking as a natural means of attaining manliness and all that the concept promised.

The war playing is followed by a dreamlike, child's-eye observance of a 1950s Fourth of July parade—an event set in a time when war veterans are seen as larger-than-life figures possessing knowledge and mystery that a child could only wonder at and wait for. Later the same day, a home run by young Ron Kovic in a Little League ballgame serves to indicate that being a hero—helping the team win—can result in female adoration, which is part of every would-be man's dream.

Viewed in a 1950s and 1960s cold war, small-town-America context, a statement like the one made by Kovic's mother in her dining room—"Those Communists have to be stopped"—is rhetorically credible, if overloaded, and acts to signify other conditioning of her son's thinking. The mother's dismay over Kovic's defeat in a high school championship wrestling match, plus his girlfriend's and his own dismay, reinforces the idea of a "have-to-win" philosophy that is to be seen as all-pervasive.

Like a well-made syllogism, the text of *Born on the Fourth of July* arranges its premises of argument about winning in such a way that when the marine recruiter announces "We have never lost a war," Kovic is totally persuaded and immediately signs up for four years of duty. It is the force of these mythical beliefs—winning is everything, America cannot lose, therefore I can go to war and become the winner that I must be—that propels the tragedy for Kovic. He must learn to live not only with the fact that "three-quarters" of his body has been taken from him by war but also with the devastating realization that he has been victimized by war's myths.

In its explicit development of theme, Kovic's story remained for the most part that of one man's eyes, one man's anger turned toward the American political landscape over a 20-year period, 1956–76. The innocent vision that sees war in romantic terms in 1956 is replaced by an angered vision in 1972 as Kovic declares: "War is a crime." This statement acts as the film's ideological climax, and it is also the truth that will be shared with Democratic candidates at the 1976 convention as the film ends. The denouement comes in the revelation that Kovic has been able to work through the myths and possesses the courage to announce the deceptions publicly.

Because it was such an emotionally intense, explicitly shaped film, *Born on the Fourth of July* generated an intense critical response. Kovic's personal anguish and political conversion were recognized as valid, inspired themes. The film also attracted attention in its effort to analyze the conditioning process of ideological formation. Christopher Sharrett of *Cineaste* commented on the film's attempts to use elements of myth, for example, "winning is everything," to empower its message:

Oliver Stone's *Born on the Fourth of July* may be the most incisive indictment to date of the American adventure in Vietnam because it spends little time on scenes of battlefield atrocity and focuses instead on the ideological character underlying not just American policy in Vietnam but American society overall, particularly in the decade or so before the war. . . . Stone's expansive approach succeeds in showing that the dilemma is not just Kovic's (and America's) innocence in the recuperative climate of post–World War II suburbia, but the American insistence on myths over history, and its refusal to confront political and moral assumptions supported by myth.[2]

Born on the Fourth of July also achieved critical acclaim as the first statement film about a real Vietnam veteran experiencing the political- and self-doubting that many other returned soldiers from the war had also obviously experienced. As Sharrett pointed out, only a small portion of the film (20 minutes of 143) had taken place in Vietnam—the script fixing its plot instead mainly on preentry and reentry profiles of Ron Kovic. This attempt to put the personal history of a Vietnam vet on the screen bestowed a certain social validity on the effort, as had the attempt to analyze the character and his environment from an ideological base.

While Kovic and Stone had avoided any tendency toward large symbolic rumination in their screenplay, the film was not without symbolic interpretation. The impotency, for example, that resulted from Kovic's paralysis lent itself to a variety of symbolic associations and interpretations. Pauline Kael of *New Yorker* magazine argued that "the core of the movie is Ron's emotional need to make people acknowledge what he last lost," that is, his potency. She added:

This kid's outrage at losing his potency is more graphic and real to us than anything else. It affects us in a cruder, deeper way than Ron's sloganeering and his political denunciation of the war. . . . But what really reaches us is that Ron finds his lost potency when the Convention cameras are on him. He finds it in forcing the country to recognize what it did to him and others like him. He's saying "You owe me this" or "Activism is all you've left me and you can't take it away." And he's saying "I paid for what I did over there and I go on paying for it. You haven't paid—your shame is greater." He doesn't really say that, but it's what filmgoers hear and respond to. The movie, having presented him as the innocent Catholic boy going to war for the glory of God, now reaps the reward: the audience—some of the audience—experiences a breast-beating catharsis.[3]

Kovic's graphically shocking removal of a catheter from his penis while he laments the loss of his sexuality—screaming "Penis! Penis!" at his mother, then asking his dad "Who again will ever love me?"— also carried the possibility of a symbolic connection with maternal repression and conditioning, which are a subtext of the plot. Christopher Sharrett maintained: "While men propel Kovic into all manner of evil (including covering up the death of his comrade), it is a woman who is seen as the principal conditioning force. Kovic's mother is even portrayed as a castrator, when at one point he associates his impotence with his mother's Catholic distaste for words like 'penis,'" (Sharrett, 50).

Pauline Kael questions the dramatic truth of the catheter scene, although she recognizes its implications: "We're supposed to see that [Kovic's] mother denies the realities of war and every other kind of reality—that this repressive mom who told him the Communists had to be stopped was part of the system that deluded him" (Kael, 123).

The ultimate symbolic irony of Kovic's impotence was that it meant the loss of the very thing he had dreamed of since a child—manhood. The war, expected to be the vehicle to his dream, had cost him the dream—something greater than any of his ideals, as Kovic recognizes when he says to his friend Timmy: "I was paralyzed, castrated that day. . . . I think I'd give everything I believe in, everything I got, all my values, just to have my body back again, to be whole again." The wholeness Kovic longs for is symbolically realized when, as Pauline Kael suggested, he discovers and is allowed to use his activist voice to tell the world of his loss.

Much of the unqualified critical praise for the Stone-Kovic view of war's aftermath was given to the VA hospital sequences, which had been treated so as to disgust and repel—so effectively doing so, said one critic, that they redefined the meaning of hell. David Ansen of *Newsweek* called the sequences "harrowing and filled with fury."[4] Stone's approach to filming the squalor, the neglect, and the medical sloppiness in the infamous Bronx VA hospital—which other patients on seeing the film validated as accurate—was so uncompromisingly intense that it served both to debunk the fable of war's glories and to act as a tract for the causes of social justice.

The fight scene between Cruise and Dafoe in Mexico's dusty terrain also held its own special powers of incisive observations about the effects of war. Norman Mailer labeled it "one of the best scenes ever filmed in an American move." Mailer wrote:

Willem Dafoe and Tom Cruise, marooned in their wheelchairs on a clay-dirt road in clay-red Mexican mountains, commence to argue over who has actually shot a baby in Vietnam and who is merely pretending to have it on his conscience. Before the verbal duel is over, each is spitting in the other's face. The wheelchairs tangle, fall over, and the two paraplegics wrestle on the ground, enraged that the other will not believe that, yes, I am guilty of a greater horror than you. Tumbling down together into a gully, they lie half-conscious in the dust, helpless to move, and never are we more aware of their broken spines. That scene captures as much of the war in Vietnam as did Coppola's Valkyrie ride of helicopters in *Apocalypse Now*.[5]

Another part of the film singled out for its impact, partly because it was the film's quietest, most introspective passage, involved Ron Kovic and Timmy Barnes, two wounded veterans, drinking beer and engaging in dialogue in 1969 in a Massapequa backyard. Sheila Benson, *Los Angeles Times* film critic, noted that the two veterans' irreverent joking about war casualties, their pained comments about the stupidity of the men who went to Vietnam—themselves included—and the fate that befell them were spoken by men using the same language. Benson said the "casually profane byplay" of the language—

Willem Dafoe (Charlie) and Tom Cruise (Ron), two paraplegics, meet in Mexico in *Born on the Fourth of July* (1989). Copyright © 1989 Universal City Studios, Inc. All rights reserved. Photo by Roland Neveu. Courtesy The Museum of Modern Art/Film Stills Archive.

now a well-established Stone gift—brought the film and Kovic's character to life.[6]

Stone's work in evoking the 1960s counterculture also won critical praise: "The external trappings of the sixties and seventies, such as the anti-war demonstrations, were so crudely stereotyped by television images that they're almost never convincing on film. Stone gets it right, not just the look but the mental atmosphere. Once again, as in *Salvador,* Stone's adrenalin, his emotional extremity pitches him in the right direction."[7]

The fundamental premises on which dramatic conflict and theme were based in *Born on the Fourth of July* raised a number of responses. Two centrally located questions challenged the film on its projection of Kovic's patriotic naïveté and on its effort to discourse on the politics of dissent. Were young men, critics asked, really so militaristically gung-ho and naively unaware of war's realities as represented by the young Ron Kovic? And to what extent, others asked, was the film a meaningful analysis of Vietnam-era political voices? Had it done more than delineate the painful anguish of a single, embittered Vietnam veteran?

In her review Pauline Kael expressed skepticism over Kovic's naive characterization:

> Ron Kovic, the hero of *Born on the Fourth of July,* believes everything he hears at the Independence Day ceremonies in Massapequa, Long Island. Pure of heart and patriotic, he trusts in Mom, the Catholic Church, and the flag-waving values John Wayne stands for. Ron thinks war is glamorous; it's how he'll prove himself a man. And so he joins the Marine Corps, goes to Vietnam, and is shocked to discover brutality, dirt and horror. It's inconceivable that Ron Kovic was as innocent as the movie and the 1976 autobiography on which it's based make him out to be. Was this kid kept in a bubble? At some level, everybody knows about the ugliness of war. Didn't he ever read anything on the Civil War—not even *The Red Badge of Courage?*
>
> (Kael, 122)

In response to the ideological premises for Kovic's naive patriotism, Christian Appy commented that the portrait painted of Kovic in the early part of the film explained little, arguing: "Most boys of that generation grew up liking John Wayne, trusting Kennedy, and loving their country. Yet fewer than half entered the military and only 12 percent went to Vietnam. . . . Most of the working-class kids sent to Vietnam were drawn into the military not because they wanted to go to war, or even because they believed the military would bring social advancement and honor. They simply regarded it as an unavoidable duty."[8]

Reactions such as Kael's and Appy's were provocative assumptions that called into question the sincerity and credibility of Kovic's own stated position, in which he claimed that from his earliest years he could remember wanting to be a war hero, and that much of his inspiration had come from reading war comic books and seeing war movies.[9] More forceful, perhaps, than setting logic-inspired assumptions against the possible singularity of Kovic's case was a critical position, argued on artistic grounds, maintaining that the development of Kovic's naively patriotic profile in the early part of the film had been too pat, too stacked, and too embedded in stock images and representative characters to be convincing as social deception.

Of this aspect of the film, Dave Kehr of the *Chicago Tribune* wrote: "There's no shading in these scenes, only a heavy, obvious didacticism, and it seems hypocritical of Stone to deny the mother any warmth and humanity while using her prescient dream of her son giving a big speech to pump up a sentimental finale."[10] *New York* magazine's David Denby commented: "Stone makes every line, every moment, part of Kovic's conditioning, as if the boy had no secret life, no *self*. Trying to show us the perfect American dummy-hero (Mom's victim), Stone holds the movie in too tight a grip."[11] David Ansen of *Newsweek* said, in reaction to the opening childhood sequence, "You can't connect to the characters because they've been deprived of personality; they're simply white-bread symbols of deluded American patriotism" (Ansen, 74).

With near-universal agreement, criticism of *Born on the Fourth of July* took the position that no matter how much or how little sociological truth the patriotic-building sequences held, they were the least subtle and the most pedantic in a motion picture in which subtlety and reserved ideas were not prevalent qualities.

The explicit loudness in the Kovic story as told on the screen—the rhetorical stacking of imagery and a bombastic directing style—was attributed to Stone's cathartic involvement with the material and to an artistic decision in writing and filming that kept the story tightly focused, for at least two-thirds of the film, on Kovic's embittered rage. Charging camera, poundingly brassy music, an abundance of highly sentimental popular music, war, heavy atmospherics in dens of iniquity, student–police confrontations, screaming matches, shocking medical details—all were part of the viscera of *Born on the Fourth of July* as it translated Kovic's experiences. Commenting on the film's intentions and effect, David Denby said: "What Stone wants, of course, is not only to recreate Kovic's experiences from the inside, but to bring us closer to mess and suffering—the blood and puke and disorder—so we can't escape into consoling 'aesthetic' responses" (Denby 1989, 102).

It was often argued that Stone, by opting for a viscerally compelling film experience, shortchanged the film's political message. David Ansen said: "What gets lost in all the visceral pyrotechnics is any clear understanding of Kovic's political conversion. Stone is conversant only in the politics of emotionalism. Anyone too young to have lived through the '60's will come away from this movie with only the vaguest sense of the issues" (Ansen, 74).

Others pointed out that Kovic's political antiwar conversion occurred without articulation or motivation, other than that derived from self-pity. It was noted that the activist scenes at Syracuse Uni-

Tom Cruise (Ron Kovic) struggles to find his political "voice" in *Born on the Fourth of July* (1989). Copyright © 1989 University City Studios, Inc. All rights reserved. Photo by Roland Neveu. Courtesy The Museum of Modern Art/Film Stills Archive.

versity had left Kovic silently unresponsive, as had scenes with Donna—ex-girlfriend-turned-activist-leader. Kovic is seen for the first time as an antiwar demonstrator at the 1972 Republican National Convention, just after confessing his "sins" to the Wilson family in Venus, Georgia. Critics maintained that this latter gesture was an act necessitated by psychological release rather than political movement.

Film critic Stanley Kauffmann reasoned that without political ideation, without seeing the change in Kovic—a flaw he blamed on scripting—the film had lost its thematic rationale as a story about a gung-ho-patriot-turned-antiwar-activist. Kauffmann said that without an ideational capstone, "the film is a series of segments, without architectural completion."[12]

A particularly interesting response in political discussions of the film centered on the against-type casting of Tom Cruise as Kovic. Cruise's screen-tailored persona prior to *Born on the Fourth of July* had been that of the all-American boy—confident, cocky, graceful. He was best known as the star of *Top Gun,* a grandly heroic romance of military life. Observers claimed that in casting Cruise as Kovic, the film had effectively and progressively intervened on a popular stereotype—thus adding to the film's potential for jolting the political conscience of the viewer. Cruise won considerable praise for his performance.

For the most part, critics came down hard on Oliver Stone and *Born on the Fourth of July*. Filmgoers and peers did not. The picture had been made for the heart, Stone said in a news conference at the time of its release, and its box-office reception was impressive, probably for that reason and because of Tom Cruise's presence. For his work on the film, Stone was named Best Director of 1989 by the Directors Guild of America, an honor repeated at the annual Academy Awards presentation, at which the film won four Oscars from among eight nominations.

The remarkable thing about *Born on the Fourth of July* had not been its achievements or its weaknesses, its overwhelming emotions or its pedantic flaws. What was remarkable was what the film said, once and forever, about Oliver Stone: he intended to go on making movies his way, the way he had been making them, saying things he needed to say without intimidation of prior judgment.

He had read the criticism of character treatment of women in his previous films: commodities/representatives. Women fared no better in *Born on the Fourth of July*—maybe worse. Earlier films had brought charges of irresponsibility in the freedom Stone took in altering historical fact, characterizing real people, and changing chronology and events to serve his dramatic ends. No matter. Kovic went places in his film, for example, Georgia, doing things he never did. The presentation of a Syracuse University activist-police confrontation had not been violent in the way it was staged for the screen. Activist leader Abbie Hoffman appeared as one of the characters in the Syracuse sequence; Stone chose Hoffman to play himself—a 45-year-old portraying someone who was supposed to be in his midtwenties. And despite all the charges of emotional, didactic, and cinematic excesses in previous work, Stone once again had hammered his points home—hell-bent on realizing a fully cathartic tour de force for Ron Kovic, himself, and the audience.

Stone's undeniable aplomb was present in *Born on the Fourth of July*, along with the other familiar qualities that would not be suppressed—profane male interplay and the language that resonates it, an ability to bring unchallenged actors to new heights, the conviction of moral purpose. And there was still the fascination of the 1960s counterculture, a subject Stone thought *Platoon* and Kovic's story might put to rest. It did not. The story of Jim Morrison—1960s rock cult figure— had been eating at Stone's mind, and he saw it as an ideal way to follow Ron Kovic's story with a different kind of American-boy story.

9

The Doors

They say I'm unsubtle. But we need above all a theater that wakes us up: nerves and heart.

—Oliver Stone, 1990

A book about the 1960s rock band the Doors—titled *No One Here Gets out Alive* and written by Jerry Hopkins (with a later rewrite by Danny Sugerman)—was published in 1980, spurring the interest of Hollywood producers and actor John Travolta in movie options on lead performer Jim Morrison's story. Following Morrison's death by heart attack in a Paris bathtub in July 1971, years of legal battling began over inheritance rights to the dead star's estate, and the publication of *No One Here Gets out Alive* refueled the squabbling.

John Densmore and Robby Krieger, two of the three remaining members of the legendary Doors band, at first acted to prevent the book's conversion into a movie, although the book helped reactivate interest in the band's music and revival of popularity in the early 1980s. Densmore and Krieger were suspicious of any fictional effort to depict their life with the flamboyant Morrison. Concern came from an awareness that legend and myth—the natural result of time's passage—could overwhelm any balanced depiction of Morrison, the Doors, and the 1960s era that filmmakers and television were beginning to memorialize with romantic avidity.

Eventually the Doors's survivors agreed to sell the rights to their music (for $750,000), which would be essential to the film, and then in 1988, after nine years of haggling over movie options on the Hopkins-Sugerman book (actually sold four different times during the 1980s), the Morrison estate heirs agreed on a purchase price—offered

From *The Doors* (1990). Kyle MacLachlan as Ray Manzarek, Frank Whaley as Robby Krieger, Kevin Dillon as John Densmore, and Val Kilmer as Jim Morrison. Copyright © 1991 Tri-Star Pictures, Inc. All rights reserved. Courtesy The Museum of Modern Art/Film Stills Archive.

by the Carolco company—for all rights to the Doors's story. At this point Carolco turned to Oliver Stone, who had a contract with the company; Stone consented to making the film on the stipulation that he be allowed to write his own screenplay.

Writing the Doors's story as Stone saw it was not easy. The parents of Pamela Courson, Morrison's girlfriend who died of a drug over-dose in April 1974, sought to sanitize the image of their daughter; Stone also had to fight for access to Morrison's poetry, which had been written in the later years of the star's life and which he wanted to use as introductory and bridge material that would add depth to Morrison's character. Most significantly, Stone had to make critical artistic and narrative decisions about what was included, omitted, emphasized, or de-emphasized in his screenplay. He was well aware of the hazards involved in his film version—in terms of both production logistics (80 locations, 30,000 extras) and how his account would be received by Doors's fans.

Yet his willingness to accept the challenge—however costly—was done because Stone believed that Morrison's story had to be told—before the opportunity was lost—and that he was the one meant to tell it.

His decision to make *The Doors* sustained a preoccupation for translating the 1960s counterculture. Also, the Doors's music had been a background element in Stone's Vietnam experience, and Morrison—the central figure in the group—had obtained godlike status in his brief lifetime as a darkly compulsive and rebellious American youth who wanted to take music to new heights. Morrison was the sort of raw male character, driven to excess in both his personal life and his musical theatrics, that appealed to Stone's filmic instincts. A frequent call by Morrison to his audiences during performances to "Wake up!" might very well characterize Stone's own artistic credo. Certainly the two men shared bombastic styles in seeking to reach their audiences.

Stone's penchant for locating representative figures at different ends of an ideological spectrum supplied another part of the decision to take on a movie about Jim Morrison and the Doors. Morrison was seen by Stone as a "home front" echo to the idealistic Ron Kovic of *Born on the Fourth of July*. Each was an American boy of the 1960s for whom the decade brought different responses and different knowledge; each Stone could admire as symbols of a hellish era. Kovic represented the naive young soldier valiantly marching off to war for his country's good and for the attainment of his manhood; Morrison stood as a drug-ridden contemporary Dionysus, writing and singing lyrics whose mystical images seemed to probe better than any other the darkness of the times. Both fell victim to their enterprise: loss of potency and idealism for Kovic; drugs and death for Morrison.

Stone's reputation as an imaginative 1960s storyteller (*Platoon* had set the pace) made the Doors's story a perfect match. There was also a passionate identity with the subject. "[Morrison] was a shaman. He was a god for me, a Dionysian figure, a poet, a philosopher," Stone told a *New York Times* reporter.[1] Morrison's story was also part of Stone's story: both had been "bad boys" rebelling against their fathers and reaching for the "bottom of the barrel" (Stone's words) in the way they approached life during their youth. There were other similarities: both had attended film school (Morrison at UCLA), both had been heavy drug users, and both had gone to live in Paris when their lives and their work had become unsatisfying. Ironically, in 1971 Stone had sent a copy of his first screenplay, an abstract drama called *Break,* to

Morrison in Paris because its inspiration had come from the Doors's lyrics. In 1989 the script was located in Morrison's possessions and returned to Stone just before production of *The Doors* began.

It was his feelings of connection with Morrison ("like an older brother") and the lingering effect of the Doors's music he experienced in Vietnam ("like Homer reciting the *Iliad*") that caused Stone to tackle the film version, which, during production and postproduction, he often referred to as a "monster." As its release date approached, Stone anticipated the high expectations and skepticism that would surround a film like *The Doors* and addressed his own role in philosophical terms: "There are so many people alive who knew Jim, and knew that era, that you can't make them all happy. They don't understand it will not be the real Jim on film—it will be my poem to Jim. It's my vision, my fictional poem with the Doors' music threaded through it" (Miller, 23).

Synopsis of *The Doors* (1990)

Cast: Val Kilmer, Meg Ryan, Kevin Dillon, Kyle MacLachlan, Frank Whaley, Michael Madsen, Kathleen Quinlan, Michael Wincott, Dennis Burkley, Josh Evans, Paul Williams, Kristina Fulton, Crispin Glover.

Credits: Director: Oliver Stone. Producers: Graham Harari and A. Kitman Ho. Screenplay: J. Randal Johnson and Oliver Stone. Photography: Robert Richardson. Executive music producer: Budd Car. Production design: Barbara Ling. Art direction: Larry Fulton.

The Doors opens in a red-lighted recording studio where Jim Morrison (Val Kilmer) is alone with an engineer (and a bottle of whiskey), taping poetry written in the last years of his life. As credits roll, Morrison recites, voice-over, his poem "The Movie."

The movie will begin in five moments
The mindless voice announced
All those unseated will await the next show
We filed slowly, languidly into the hall
The auditorium was vast and silent
As we seated and were darkened, the voice continued
The program for this evening is not new
You've seen the entertainment through and through
You've seen your birth, your life and death

You might recall all the rest
Did you have a good world when you died?
Enough to base a movie on?

"Riders on the Storm" emerges on the soundtrack. The film shifts to sepia-toned images of a car carrying the Morrison family through a New Mexico desert, 1949, and passing a truck wreck involving Navajo Indians. Through his car window, young Jim Morrison (Sean Stone) observes the death scene and the weeping survivors. His mother says, "It's only a dream, Jimmy." A bald-headed death figure appears in the scene, as the Morrison car moves on.

The film skips ahead to a title super, which reads "Venice Beach, California, 1965." A college-age Morrison is seen introducing himself to Pamela Courson (Meg Ryan), after which a cut places Morrison in a UCLA film class, where his student film project is being screened and evaluated. The instructor (Oliver Stone) reacts by calling the effort "a little incoherent"; the students label it pretentious. When Morrison is asked to respond, he replies, "I quit."

At night, with Morrison and Pam Courson walking on the beach, kissing, then reading poetry to each other on a blanket, Pam learns of Morrison's obsession with death. The plot advances to reveal Ray Manzarek (Kyle MacLachlan) with Morrison on the beach at Venice. Morrison says he's been writing lyrics and reads from his notebook to Manzarek, who is very impressed. The idea for a "breakthrough" rock-and-roll band emerges. Morrison says he's got a name for the group, the Doors, inspired by Blake's verse: "When the doors of perception are cleansed, things will appear as they truly are, infinite." Manzarek replies, "I like it."

A cut shows the now-formed band—with John Densmore (Kevin Dillon) and Robby Krieger (Frank Whaley) having joined Manzarek and Morrison—rehearsing "Break on Through," followed by "Light My Fire." The incipient group is struggling to find its metier.

A super title places the Doors in a Sunset Strip club, the Whiskey à Go Go, in Los Angeles six months later, performing their music and still trying to come together as an ensemble. A drugged Morrison challenges the audience with "How many of you people know you're really alive?"

This question introduces a hallucinatory sequence with the Doors and their girlfriends in a parched desert. The curvaceous landscape, soaring birds, silhouettes of the group, their hands, shadows on desert boulders, clouds, and a figure on horseback evoke a sense of hallucinogenic camaraderie. As the song "The End" plays on the soundtrack, Morrison leaves the group. He enters a cave, comes upon an old Indian warrior, and reexperiences his childhood memory of the New Mexico highway wreck. The camera dollies in to a big closeup of the Indian's eye, into which is inserted a flash-forward shot of Morrison dead in a Paris bathtub.

An iris out brings the action back to the Doors in performance, where Morrison goes wild to the lyrics of "The End," shocking the audience with "Father, I want to kill you. Mother, I want to fuck you." Representatives of Elektra Records approach the Doors for a recording contract.

Time advances to 1967 and a concert trip to San Francisco. In home-movie-styled evocations, the Doors interact with the flower children, nudes, street performers, and ever-present policemen who populated the Summer of Love protest culture. Another 1967 super takes the group to New York City for an appearance on "The Ed Sullivan Show." Morrison's emergence as the Doors's star and chief sex symbol is conveyed in a narcissistic photo session with a beautiful publicist (Mimi Rogers), who flatters Morrison by calling him "the god of rock."

The New York trip also brings Morrison in contact with the pop subculture ruled over by Andy Warhol, and in a night-on-the-town sequence shows Morrison's compulsion for excessive drugs and easy sex. It also reveals him tantalizing reporters at a press conference with statements about living in the "subconscious" and with an untrue tale about the death of his parents in an automobile crash with a truckload of Navajos. The press conference leads to an alliance with one of the reporters, Patricia Kennealy (Kathleen Quinlan), a student of witchcraft who engages Morrison in sex, coke-taking, and a blood-drinking ritual that concludes with a romp to the choral sounds of *Carmina Burana,* followed by more sex.

Subsequent scenes alternate Morrison's domestic woes (sexual impotency, fights with Pam) with the Doors's run-ins with the police, which include a mace attack in a shower stall and an aborted concert in New Haven in 1968 for alleged violation of state obscenity laws. Morrison's arrogance grows—he urinates in the middle of a crowded bar, destroys a Thanksgiving party by killing and charring Pam's pet duck, and continues his sexual dalliances with Patricia Kennealy and other women. Pam is caught in her own affair, driving Morrison to hysterical action, as he locks her in a closet and sets fire to the room.

Tensions also mount in the Doors's group. Morrison learns that one of their songs has been sold for $75,000 for use in a television commercial; he sees the action as a sellout—a violation of the group's professed aim of creating music for "breakthrough" purposes. Prior to a 1969 Miami concert, a radio announcer charges that the Doors have become "an act," are not the Doors "we once knew." Backstage, band member John Densmore expresses concern about Morrison's excessive drug use. During the Florida concert, Morrison taunts the audience with demeaning remarks and profanity, falls constantly, pretends to expose himself, and eventually loses all control. He is arrested and in 1970 charged in a Dade County courthouse for performing four "lewd" acts, including simulated masturbation. The song "When the Music's Over" accompanies the court proceedings. Intercut between this scene and Morrison's sentencing to six months in jail and two years' probation is a brief encounter with Patricia Kennealy, who claims to be pregnant. Morrison urges an abortion, saying the child will be a monster. Kennealy cries.

After Morrison's sentencing a montage appears that juxtaposes three elements: a closeup of Morrison, shots of friends giving advice on what the convicted star should do, and a collage of television images depicting the era—youth activism, Kent State, Charles Manson, moon exploration, Martin Luther King, My Lai, Bobby Kennedy, Nixon, Vietnam. The sequence of images ends with a teary-eyed Morrison in closeup, announcing, "I think I'm having a nervous breakdown."

Agreeing with Pam that they should leave, Morrison decides to move to Paris. Before departing, he attends a birthday party for Ray Manzarek's young daughter. The youngsters are dressed as cowboys and Indians, and among them Morrison sees himself as a child, moving in a sepia-toned, slow-motion image—as if seeking a reunion with his now older, bearded self.

A shot of the plane carrying Morrison to Paris appears, followed by a return to the recording studio, where the poetry taping concludes. With his bottle of Bushmill's in front of him, he asks, "Did you get all that?" The engineer (John Densmore) replies, "Yeah, I got it, Jim."

The Doors concludes in 1971 in the Paris apartment where Pam and Jim Morrison have moved. Pam is seen in bed, restless. A voice whispers: "Death. It's not so bad." Rising to look for Morrison, Pam sees a surreal figure in a body stocking sidle past. From behind she comes upon Morrison reclining in a bathtub, his long hair cascading over the back. Recognizing that he is dead, she asks: "Are you alright, Jim? Did you enjoy it when it came? Did you like it?" The camera dollies in to a closeup of Morrison's face.

A moving camera montage reveals tombstones of the famous buried at Père-Lachaise Cemetery in Paris, ending with a shot at Morrison's graffiti-covered crypt. Final lines of "An American Prayer," the last of Morrison's poems set to music on a recorded album in 1978 by the surviving Doors, is heard voice-over as supered end titles appear: "Jim is said to have died of heart failure. He was 27. Pam joined him 3 years later."

The final catharsis intended in Stone's encapsulation of Morrison's life and death can be seen in the text's efforts to depict the rock star as a tragic icon of his times—a searching poet-turned-pop-idol who is consumed by his fans and by the self-fulfilling extremes of his actions. Morrison's image as a mystical shaman (looking beyond the universe) on the one hand and as a worldly counterculture figure (rejecting family, embracing drugs and free sex) on the other is meant as genius coming unhinged, then finally destroyed, like a Christ crucified. The incorporation of Morrison's poetry at the beginning and conclusion of the film offered a bookend device for conveying this idea that Morrison was someone yearning for more than his "sacrificial" role as a 1960s cult hero.

In this sense *The Doors* and its protagonist can be viewed as the third and final entry in a triptych of films by Stone about young males whose lives become inextricably and painfully tied to the dark years of Vietnam-era America. Like Chris Taylor of *Platoon* and Ron Kovic of *Born on the Fourth of July,* Jim Morrison suffers the confusions arising from an unending war, experienced this time not from within a combat platoon but from the stage of a rebellious rock concert arena. "Break on through to the Other Side" reeks lyrically of a warring effort while speaking to the same kind of desire for experimentation and new adventures that drove *Platoon's* Chris Taylor to the jungles of Vietnam.

The family disintegration, the drugs, and the loss of potency also hold as much for Morrison as for Ron Kovic. Morrison uses his lyrics' ("Father I want to kill you. Mother I want to fuck you") to shout hatred at his disowned parents, and the oedipal accusations of parental betrayal are as readily apparent, and as shocking, as Kovic's primal scream of "Penis, penis, penis!" aimed at his mother. Morrison and Elias, the "good father" of *Platoon,* are both presented as Christs crucified, another archetypal idea carried through by Stone from *Platoon* to *The Doors.*

These associations attest to the seriousness and passion with which Stone approaches his role as a 1960s translator. In the case of *The Doors,* a film held together by music performance (25 songs), Stone was calling into review both a popular culture icon and the "freedom-loving" counterculture community that sustained the icon. Success was mixed.

Restaging of the Doors's emergence as a band at the Whiskey à Go-Go Club and their later fever-pitched concerts revealed Stone at a peak in engineering the epic scene. Strobe lights, throngs of fans moving in unison, the ever-expected swirling camera—which often makes 360-degree sweeps around Morrison and his musical companions— captured the sexually charged energy that emanated from stage to audience in bombastic fashion. The re-creation of the film's music was supervised by Paul Rothschild, original producer of several of the Doors's albums. Stone and Rothschild proved themselves uncannily successful in using Val Kilmer to actually sing Morrison's songs rather

Val Kilmer (Jim Morrison) reinterprets a frenzied concert performance in *The Doors* (1990). Copyright © 1991 Tri-Star Pictures, Inc. All rights reserved. Courtesy The Museum of Modern Art/Film Stills Archive.

than lip-synch them. Kilmer also singlehandedly scored as an eerie look-alike for Morrison and removed much of the initial skepticism about visual and aural credibility.

Especially powerful and ennervating were Stone's rendering of the 1968 New Haven and 1969 Miami concerts, which together revealed Morrison's quick movement to disorder and drugged incoherence. Psychedelic in look but darkly toned in spirit, these scenes offered grating proof of a base, self-destructive instinct in mock of both fan and law. Stone brings into the Miami concert, as he often does throughout the film, the Indian shaman to appear onstage next to Morrison as he sings, "One more time." Flames are superimposed on the action, seeming to consume the event and its fading star. Chaos reigns as Morrison falls.

To supply the necessary period atmosphere, *The Doors* incorporated an interlude of historical facsimile. The simulated hand-held 16mm camera technique captures the feeling of the San Francisco Haight-Ashbury Summer of Love celebration of 1967 as the Doors mingle

Val Kilmer (Jim Morrison) is led away for lewd behavior in *The Doors* (1990). Copyright © 1991 Tri-Star Pictures, Inc. All rights reserved. Courtesy The Museum of Modern Art/Film Stills Archive.

among the participants. The Doors themselves interact playfully with the camera, offering what are the few lighthearted moments in an otherwise deadly serious screen biography.

Stone's visual authenticity and camera dynamics were managed with great skill, and earned *The Doors* a modicum of praise. At the same time, the prerelease assessment that the film would have difficulty pleasing everybody turned out to be correct. Along with praise came harsh judgments about Stone's overall success in presenting his Dionysian 1960s hero. Much of the reaction focused on issues of dimension—a particularly innate concern when a larger-than-life director tackles a larger-than-life protagonist. Given the well-known nature of Stone's previous exercises in screen sensation, no one expected less in *The Doors,* and what resulted was an overwhelming imposition of Stone's own cinematic passions onto the excesses of Morrison's personal and professional lives. A bombastic, psychedelic visual style in the music performances and a no-holds-barred accounting of Morrison's desire to self-destruct produced unrelieved intensity. The combination resulted in visceral overload, some said emotional assault.

Although Stone had paved his road to success in the 1980s with manic, sleazeball protagonists, the dark excesses that propelled Jim Morrison to fame and early death took the concept of sleaziness and self-destruction to unimagined heights and without a turnaround moment of self-redemption common to earlier Stone films. Many felt that voyeurism and hollowness rang throughout *The Doors,* and its effect was often declared more painful than insightful.

J. Hoberman of *Sight and Sound* called the film's greatest flaw its "stupendous absence of irony," adding that Stone's frequent literalness is treating Morrison, the Doors, and their era "actively punishes the imagination."[2] Stone, for example, had juxtaposed the song "When the Music's Over" against Morrison's sentencing in Miami for public lewdness, the moment his career ended. As the result of frequent references in his lyrics to reptiles, Morrison had promoted himself as the "Lizard King"; in one instant in the film, Stone cuts to a shot of a lizard to conjure up the reptilian tag. A lack of subtlety was the charge for these literal aural and visceral associations.

Paul Baumann of *Commonweal* also maintained that *The Doors* suffered from a lack of irony and saw the inherent subject matter of the Morrison saga as part of the problem: "Drugs and drug addicts are inevitably tedious subjects, especially if given to making oracular announcements on the meaning of life, the allure of death, and the fact that no one understands them. Morrison's pathetic artistic pretensions and sodden decline desperately need an ironic perspective. Stone, however, plays it straight, intent on capturing the texture more than the meaning of Morrison's life—hoping to give us myth and catharsis, not sense or sensibility."[3]

The bottom line in assessing the remaking of Jim Morrison was that a sense of the icon had been projected but not a sense of the man. People who knew the star claimed he was much less serious and also more intelligent than presented in the film. Insiders pointed out that Morrison often joked about the "act" he put on to create the sexual and mystical auras that excited his fans. Stone treats both these aspects of the Morrison persona seriously and thus adds to the myth rather than to the myth-maker.

The depiction of Morrison in *The Doors* had a strong imaginative quality that resulted from an extended play on the alleged fascination with death and a vision of transcendence—both presented in recurring motifs of highway wrecks, death, ghosts, Indian warriors, hallucinatory sequences, and a flash-forward image of Morrison's own death.

The script's dialogue also sought to support the claim of someone capable of transcendent experience and knowledge of another consciousness. Encounters with Patricia Kennealy, a proclaimed witch who easily draws Morrison into her ritualistic world, further underscored the idea of mystical obsession.

The decision to take an imaginative approach was Stone's own. Although he had read the book on the Doors, the script written with J. Randal Johnson was developed from interview transcripts with more than 100 people. Through these interviews Stone came to believe that Morrison's life was plagued by demons from within, and that these demons were the source of the strangely imagistic lyrics—about snakes, insects, lizards—that had first attracted Stone's attention in Vietnam. He was convinced that Morrison's work—songs and poetry—had been born of another "consciousness' and thus justified the narrative departures into fantasy, memory, hallucination, and witchcraft.

The imaginative explanation of Morrison's character carried forth Stone's intentions of showing the protagonist to be something other than a mere rock star, that is, an individual of rare mystique and sensitivity who excited the times and who, on dying at 27, fulfilled his own vision while gaining the mortality his specialness ("rock god") had earned. The shot of Morrison's crypt—an altar of hero worship at Père Lachaise residing among those of Balzac, Oscar Wilde, Proust, and Molière—is intended to drive the point home.

Again Stone's vision in *The Doors* became a question of dimension. Had he gone too far in seeking to memorialize an idol who may have been less the soulful poet than imagined? Some called Morrison's poetry "high-schoolish" at best. Questions of just how consistently good the Doors's music really was also surfaced to challenge Stone's perhaps too-glamorized and myopic film biography.

Further, there was a sense of a nagging dissonance at play in the script—one born of the realization that Morrison's dominant image on the screen was entirely unpleasant, whatever demons may have been tragically tormenting his mind. The drugs, alcohol, and sex and the relationships with his group, his fans, Pam Courson, and Patricia Kennealy revealed Morrison always taking, rarely giving. The picture drawn hardly represented that of an exemplar who could conjure up a cherished memory from a special time. It appeared instead a portrait of someone simply incapable of handling the success he had initially earned with a charismatic and sensuous stage presence.

Too, there was the knowledge that Jim Morrison wasn't the only one of his kind to self-destruct at a preposterously young age. Janis Joplin and Jimi Hendrix had departed in similar fashion, perhaps also "sacrificial" figures of their day. Many maintained that when the title of "rock god" was bandied about, Hendrix, not Morrison, should be the rightful recipient.

There was no denying that the Doors were a legitimate presence in their day—a viable part of a scene that celebrated such poetic and political concepts as revolution, liberation, and unfettered individuality. It was a time of questioning and a time of "happenings" of all sorts, of which the Doors were one kind. Young college-age Americans, especially—those with time and money—were the primary role players in a subcultural movement not unlike the one that occurred in liberal Paris in the 1920s.

What Jim Morrison and the Doors came to represent as a "breakthrough" group, whose lyrics celebrated freedom and light but also carried undercurrents of anxiety and darkness, fit well similar expression in all types of mediums: music, poetry, the movie. At nearly the same moment the Doors ascended, films like *The Graduate* (1967) and *Easy Rider* (1968) appeared to make their own powerful counterculture statements. *The Graduate* offered a masterful view of youthful anxiety—anxiety about corporate America, the middle-class family, sexual liberation, commitment. *Easy Rider* might well have been a variation of the Doors's charge "Take to the highway to the end of the night"; it detailed two young protagonists taking a freedom ride through America on their motorcycles to celebrate their hippiedom and to experience a country upended by Vietnam tensions. The universe presented in *Easy Rider* was a complex one, populated by the disillusioned, bigots, and those inclined to sex orgies and drug feasts.

And what was especially telling about these films were their soundtracks. Each contained a music miniconcert that added a second text or pleasure to the film's dialogue and visual imagery: the lyrics of Simon and Garfunkel in *The Graduate* and a pastiche of rock, country, and folk songs in *Easy Rider*. This innovation was a rarity for nonmusical motion pictures and a clear sign of the sensory revolution that was brought on by counterculture ferment. The films were met with the same passionate response as a Doors or Jimi Hendrix concert, because all were fulfilling similar needs for a particular audience.

A good part of the reaction to Oliver Stone's vision of the Doors's story centered on discussions of the larger arena in which the group functioned and what exactly their place had been. Was the mystique as presented by Stone, while legitimate, overblown? Did *The Doors* film accurately represent the group and the era? These discussions moved an evaluation of Stone's vision into areas concerned with the blending of drama and history—familiar targets for an Oliver Stone film since *Midnight Express* in 1976. Issues such as artistic responsibility and ethical judgment were again at work.

The Doors as film seemed to especially rattle those who claimed to have experienced firsthand the Jim Morrison era and all it represented. David Denby, film critic of *New York* magazine, had lived in the San Francisco Bay Area during the late 1960s and in reviewing Stone's version maintained, "I assumed the flagrant eroticism and diabolism were just part of the Doors' show-business persona—conscious commercial style, not a sacred mission that had to be revered. Perhaps my response was trivial, but however seriously they took themselves, the Doors are hardly great art, even great rock art, and to make a huge fuss over anything so evanescent is to engage in willful naiveté. Stone seems to be selling erotic panache and wild mumbo jumbo to today's generation of kids the way the Doors sold it to the last generation."[4]

Where Denby saw *The Doors* as commercial fuss about the evanescent, Terrence Rafferty—Pauline Kael's replacement as *New Yorker's* film arbiter— found Stone's account to be too reductive in its view of an era that he had personally found to be "truly expansive, easy going." Rafferty wrote: "In *The Doors* Oliver Stone reduces the richly contradictory experience of the sixties to the myth of Morrison, and, in the process, reduces Morrison and the Doors as well: the movie restricts the viewer's freedom to imagine the sixties culture as anything but a movement with a single voice or to imagine the Doors as anything but a metaphor."[5]

The most direct effort to discount *The Doors* based on "memory history" appeared in an 11 March 1991 *New York Times* editorial written by Brent Staples. Staples lamented the film's lack of brightness and, like Rafferty, accused Stone of a failure to convey "the sense of boundless possibility that was so deeply felt then." The editorial ended with this: "We altered art, music, love and marriage. The guys from the Hollywood history mill can do what they will with our memories. The 20-year-olds sitting across the aisle at *The Doors* think it's all groovy. But we who lived the stuff wince at the infidelities—big ones like the absence of hope and light, and even tiny ones, like too much hair on a rock star's chest."[6]

The memory-history response to films like *The Doors* struggles to set down its own definition of a time, place, or person beside that of the filmmaker. Urgency "to set the record straight" is driven by an underlying assumption that if the filmmaker's definition is left uncorrected, the naive viewer might come to believe and accept it as the official one. Stone's films are especially vulnerable to accuracy scrutiny, not simply because of the reexploration of recent history but because he allows his imagination great freedom in shaping the history to fit familiar and recurring archetypes.

The broad archetype to which Stone most frequently returns is that of the devil/angel protagonist—a man who embodies both good and evil and whose contradictions eventually either are redeemed or destroy him. The self-acknowledged fact that Stone's archetypal constructions often lack subtlety make him an even easier critical target. Caryn James of the *New York Times* attested to this fact: "No wonder so many filmgoers are measuring *The Doors* against their own memories or fantasies of Morrison and the 60's. Mr. Stone created a movie virtually inaccessible to anyone who doesn't share his assumptions."[7]

In response, Stone spoke of the challenge of screen biography and history in terms of cinematic references: "It's like *Roshomon*—out of 40 witnesses they'll all give you a different version of events in Jim's life. He was everything to everybody and no one will agree on all events. . . . Some people would say he had to be the center of attention. Other people say they hardly noticed him. A lot of people said he was the most important person in their life. Certain women called and said, 'You're doing a fake story, you have to do my story. Because he didn't love Pam (Courson), he loved me.' It's truly like [*Citizen*] *Kane*. I could have made a movie just talking to the witnesses."[8]

Cinema, Stone was suggesting, was like life and memory of it: highly impressionistic, subjective. Literalness was a moot point, and one had only one's artistic instincts to build on—a point of view that in the case of *The Doors,* Stone said, had been to keep the action focused internally on Morrison—who recounted his life directly to the camera—and on his intoxicating music. Engaging the "witnesses" would have made another film—perhaps the more expansive film some of his critics had been hoping for, but not the kind of film Stone had chosen to make.

It must have seemed ironic, then, to Stone that many of those who offered their own challenging definitions of the Doors and the 1960s

Meg Ryan (Pam Courson) and Val Kilmer (Jim Morrison), troubled companions, in *The Doors* (1990). Copyright © 1991 Tri-Star Pictures, Inc. All rights reserved. Courtesy The Museum of Modern Art/Film Stills Archive.

were presenting scenarios perhaps more subjective and romantic than the film's. Speaking philosophically to this fact and to the complexity of 1960s-era history, Stone said: "Our generation is just coming to power, and it includes the dichotomy of both Dan Quayle and Sen. Bob Kerrey [the Nebraska Democrat who lost part of a leg in combat]—two very different Vietnam soldiers. Which way are we going to go? It's too early to tell; it's just the seventh inning."[9]

The Doors was Stone's first effort of the 1990s, and its release coincided with the Desert Storm foray against Iraq, a bit of timing that seemed to make the film's entry onto the American scene a peculiarly anomalous event. The patriotic "highs" of a perceived U.S. military victory in the Middle East stood at stylistic odds with the kind of rock music, hallucinogenic highs (and lows) Stone was celebrating in *The Doors*. Simply put, the counterculture nostalgia suddenly didn't seem as important to the public—young or older—as might have been hoped for.

Still, Stone's impact on American filmmaking was not lost in the critical and personal flap generated by *The Doors*. Andrew Sarris of the *Village Voice,* comparing *The Doors* with 1991's megahit *Dances with Wolves,* said he preferred the bravado of Stone's work to the "pseudosensitivity" of Kevin Costner's.[10] Robert Horton, writing in *Film Comment,* argued, "There's so little passion informing American movies that Stone's muscular, free-swinging ways seem all the more vital. It is possible, and useful, to note the excesses and overstatements of Stone's films, but one at least comes away from *Salvador,* and *Platoon* and *The Doors,* feeling . . . well, having had *some* kind of experience."[11]

Stone himself said of his work and his critics at this time simply, "I won't ever make boring movies ever!" Indeed, *JFK,* his next project, reached for new heights as nervy, "wake-us-up theater" presented in the form of screen entertainment.

10

JFK

Some people will say we're fiction. I would have avoided all this bullshit if I'd said this is fiction from the get-go.

—Oliver Stone, director-coscenarist, *JFK*

Since nobody agrees on anything, nobody is distorting history. The only official history is the Warren Commission report, and that nobody believes.

—Zachary Sklar, coscenarist, *JFK*

Oliver Stone earned a place in motion picture history with *JFK* (1991). No film before this one had spurred the kind of sustained media attention and controversy that befell Stone's three-hour, eight-minute dramatization of assassination theories concerning President John F. Kennedy's sniper murder in Dallas on 22 November 1963. D. W. Griffith's *The Birth of a Nation* (1915)—a pro–Ku Klux Klan story of the South during Reconstruction—had its vociferous opponents (and still does), but never in its day underwent the public and journalistic scrutiny given *JFK*.

Major newspapers approached *JFK* as front-page news. The *New York Times,* seemingly obsessed with the film, deemed the picture worthy of editorials, a run of op-ed pieces, political columns, cartoons, dozens of letters to the editor, and two lengthy reviews—one early (Vincent Canby) and one late (Janet Maslin) during the film's run in commercial theaters. A former president (Gerald Ford) leaped into the controversy, as did Jack Valenti, the chief executive of the Motion Picture Association of America, who likened *JFK* to the Nazi propaganda film *Triumph of the Will* (1936).

The debate over *JFK* led to public forums on the ethics of mixing drama and historical realities in motion pictures. Radio and television news programs and talk shows devoted hundreds of hours to discussions of the film's conspiracy thesis, to the voluminous assortment of assassination-buff arguments that had surfaced after 1963, and to a reexamination of the Warren Commission's published findings, which had declared Lee Harvey Oswald a lone assassin. Sixties-era historians and politicians took up the pen to defend or debunk *JFK*'s allegations that Kennedy intended to withdraw American military troops from Vietnam and thus roused military-industrial complex profiteers to eliminate him so that the war could continue.

The sustained press coverage of *JFK* was fueled by Stone's unwavering statements, which maintained with confidence a belief that the Kennedy assassination had resulted from conspiracy efforts, with Oswald acting as the "fall guy." Stone held steadfast to his position before the members of the National Press Club in Washington, D.C., before a worldwide television audience after receiving the Golden Globe Best Director Award of 1991, and in numerous letters of self-defense written to newspaper editors.

There was also the undeniable fact that *JFK* was the work of a gifted, seasoned filmmaker who knew how to manipulate his craft to powerful ends. The film offered an involving mystery tale that titillated—even stunned—as the imagery leaped between news footage and restaged scenes with facile, matched-cut precision. As in previous work, Stone aimed *JFK* at the gut as well as the mind—another variation of his "wakeup" theater, designed to jangle both thought and nerves.

JFK became a classic illustration of how a masterfully constructed motion picture—proffered as historical fact and widely challenged as "irresponsible" art—can create an event of unexpected magnitude, swelling curiosity and thus box-office receipts.

The effort to bring *JFK* to the screen was an arduous task—logistically and psychologically—for Stone. His interest in the project had been stimulated in 1988, on reading former New Orleans district attorney Jim Garrison's *On the Trail of the Assassins,* published that year. The book was a recounting of Garrison's efforts during 1967–69 to convict a New Orleans businessman, Clay Shaw, for conspiracy in the assassination of Kennedy. Word of a conspiracy reportedly had come to Garrison following a drunken argument in New Orleans between a private detective, Jack Martin, and a former member of the

FBI, Guy Banister, who allegedly was acquainted with Lee Harvey Oswald. Oswald had spent the summer of 1963 in New Orleans propagandizing for Cuba and passing out pro-Castro leaflets, a stack of which were found in Banister's desk after his death in 1964, before Garrison began his investigation.

Other rightist conspirators implicated in time by Garrison included a homosexual and former Eastern Airlines pilot named David Ferrie, and an unnamed and "protected" playwright living in New Orleans who was singled out as the conspiracy engineer. Ferrie died during the investigation, leaving Shaw alone to stand trial in 1969. According to Garrison's book, media and government forces had intervened to undermine his case, which implicated more than a dozen groups—including anti- and pro-Cuban agitators, military-industrial-complex profiteers, and the CIA—in the plot to kill Kennedy. The jury, after less than an hour of deliberation, declared Shaw not guilty.

Stone, who had said the world and idealism stopped for him the day Kennedy died, saw in Garrison's book "the kernel of a very powerful movie" about individual courage in the face of an alleged massive coverup. From *On the Trail of the Assassins,* Stone moved on to other books and theories by assassination buffs who had sought to discount elements of the Warren Commission report, especially the number and origin of bullets fired at the presidential limousine. He also studied the numerous writings arguing against the commission's conclusion that Oswald was a deranged loner, motivated by a desire for attention. Many had claimed that Oswald's move to Russia in 1959 and easy return to Texas three years later hinted at double-agent involvement with U.S./KGB intelligence units rather than defection to a Communist country. Such theories fanned the conspiracy flames that implied CIA spy connections with the Kennedy assassination.

Stone also read the claims of Peter Dale Scott's 1972 essay, "Vietnamization and the Drama of the Pentagon Papers," which first asserted Kennedy's intention of withdrawing U.S. forces from Vietnam. Scott's claims had been picked up by Major John Newmann in his book *J.F.K. and Vietnam,* the eventual "authoritative" source for Stone's Vietnam withdrawal thesis. This revelation jolted an awareness that had Kennedy not been killed, Stone's participation in a war in which he was wounded twice would probably not have occurred.

By the end of 1988, even before beginning *The Doors,* Stone was fully inspired to make *JFK*—to tell the "truth" of the Kennedy assassination by embodying all the uncovered evidence (highlighted by Jim

Marrs's book *Crossfire: The Plot That Killed Kennedy*) in the sleuth-hero character of Jim Garrison. In writing the script, Stone would use his now-familiar ploy of telescoping events, collapsing several characters into one, and reworking historical realities to fit an unmistakable message. "I didn't want to make a movie of the Garrison book alone," Stone told a newspaper reporter. "He is the protagonist, but the book ends essentially in 1969, and I wanted to push the movie into the new ground that was uncovered after 1969 and pre-'69—the autopsies, the bullets, the work of other researchers. So I've taken dramatic license. It is not a true story per se. It's not the Jim Garrison story. It is a film called *JFK*. It explores all the possible scenarios of why Kennedy was killed, who killed him and why."[1]

Stone engaged Zachary Sklar, Garrison's book editor, as coscenarist; sought and won the financial backing of Warner Bros. ($40 million); and in April 1991 began shooting *JFK* in Dallas. A four-square-block area of downtown Dallas was restored to a 1960s look for an exact restaging of events occurring on 22 November 1963 at the Texas School Book Depository, Dealey Plaza, and the now-historic "grassy knoll" area. Every known detail of the day and the assassination was authentically re-created, including placing vintage mud-spattered automobiles in the Dealey Plaza area because it had rained in Texas during the morning of 22 November. Hair styles and clothing (short raincoats, narrow ties) worn by extras precisely matched those of old photographic images in history books.

The *JFK* assassination scene was just one of nearly 100 scenes involving more than 200 characters with speaking roles. There were other major challenges. Re-creating the required period look, plus restaging scenes to resemble black-and-white-styled documentary footage, entailed the use of special filters, lighting, and a dozen different film stocks. Some restaged scenes at Dealey Park were filmed in 8mm and 16mm gauges for an amateurish appearance. To make things even more difficult for Stone, Dallas county officials briefly tried to prevent filming inside the Texas School Book Depository's sixth-floor room, where sniper bullets allegedly had been fired. Stone won this battle and went on—amid wary skeptics, critical newspaper reporters, and an anxious Warner Brothers—to complete filming of *JFK* in Dallas, New Orleans, and Washington, D.C., in a period of 80 days.

The intricacies of postproduction editing, perhaps the most complicated ever attempted in a narrative motion picture, were unusually demanding, as was the coordination of sound, sound effects, and mu-

Recreation of the shooting of President Kennedy in Dallas from *JFK* (1991). © 1991 Warner Bros. All rights reserved. Courtesy The Museum of Modern Art/Film Stills Archive.

sic. The final editing of the film's cornucopia of assassination details was aimed at supplying a rhythmic corollary for the chaotic intensity that surrounded the assassination and its aftermath. Along with Stone's familiar searching camera, *JFK* offered filmgoers new levels of viscera and controversy when the film reached movie theaters on 20 December 1991.

Synopsis of *JFK* (1991)

Cast: Kevin Costner, Sissy Spacek, Joe Pesci, Tommy Lee Jones, Gary Oldman, Joe O. Sanders, Laurie Metcalf, Michael Rooker, Jack Lemmon, Walter Matthau, Donald Sutherland, Kevin Bacon, Edward Asner, Brian Doyle-Murray, Jim Garrison.

Credits: Director: Oliver Stone. Producers: A. Kitman Ho and Oliver Stone. Screenplay: Oliver Stone and Zachary Sklar, based on the books *On the Trail of the Assassins,* by Jim Garrison, and *Crossfire: The Plot That Killed Kennedy,*

by Jim Marrs. Photography: Robert Richardson. Editors: Joe Hutshing and
Pietro Scalia. Production design: Victor Kempster. Music: John Williams.

The plot of *JFK* begins with television news footage of outgoing President
Dwight D. Eisenhower's famous farewell speech in which he cautions against
the increasing power of the military-industrial complex in 1960. A montage
of Americana scenes of the era accompanies the speech. Serving as a prologue
while the credits continue to roll, another montage follows—one encapsulat-
ing John F. Kennedy's election and the central political events of his presi-
dency: Fidel Castro, the quarantine of Cuba in October 1963, the Vietnam
War. A news report speculates that Kennedy has "cut a deal" with Krushchev,
intimating that the president might be "soft" on communism. Kennedy is
shown in newsreel footage in a university address proclaiming his desire to
bring the world to peace.

A car is seen traveling on a rural highway, where it slows; a woman is
shoved from the car and left by the side of the road. This mysterious event is
replaced by a shot of Air Force One arriving in Texas on 22 November 1963.
From a hospital bed, the woman seen moments before being abandoned on a
country road is frantically repeating, "They're going to kill Kennedy." Air
Force One moves on to Dallas, where in a combination of newsreel and restaged footage the presidential motorcade begins its journey toward Dealey
Plaza and the fateful assassination of Kennedy. An insert of the CBS Bulletin
logo and Walter Cronkite announcing the shooting appears.

The action switches to New Orleans, where District Attorney Jim Garrison
(Kevin Costner) is informed that Kennedy has been shot. *JFK*'s narrative—
with Garrison as the protagonist—begins to develop while television covers
the events of the weekend of 22 November 1963: Cronkite's announcement
of Kennedy's death, the capture of Lee Harvey Oswald (Gary Oldman), Oswald telling the Dallas police, "I'm just a patsy," the transportation of Kennedy's body to Bethesda Naval Hospital, the killing of Oswald by Jack Ruby
(Brian Doyle-Murray), Kennedy's funeral in Washington. As Garrison and
members of his staff watch this historic drama, Garrison suggests that Oswald's New Orleans connections be checked out. Also intercut with the television coverage are two short scenes in New Orleans in which Guy Bannister
(Edward Asner) and Jack Martin (Jack Lemmon) are drinking and reacting to
the assassination. Bannister expresses no regrets, and later in the evening—
both quite drunk—accuses and attacks Martin for going through his desk files.

Garrison's staff locates David Ferrie (Joe Pesci) as an Oswald connection
and speculates that Ferrie—a former Eastern Airlines pilot—might have been
a planned "getaway" pilot for Oswald in Dallas. A very nervous and paranoid
Ferrie is brought in for interrogation and denies knowing Oswald, but admits
to having driven to Houston on the day of the assassination to go ice skating.

Garrison declares Ferrie's story unbelievable. A television voice-over announces the creation of the Warren Commission to investigate the Kennedy assassination.

A super reads "Three Years Later," and Garrison is seen on an airplane sitting with Louisiana politician Earl Long (Walter Matthau). Long questions the Warren Commission's lone-assassin conclusion, inspiring Garrison to return home and reconsider his investigation into the assassination. He avidly reads countertheory about what might actually have happened on the grassy knoll and about Oswald's defection to the USSR and "easy" return to the United States, and after checking out the geographic area in New Orleans where Oswald was a pro-Cuban activist in the summer of 1962, he imagines a possible connection of Oswald to Guy Bannister and to the FBI, CIA, and Secret Service, all of whom had offices near Oswald's area of activity.

An interrogation at a racetrack of Jack Martin—Bannister's drinking partner on the day of the assassination—brings claims that Bannister (who has since died) had dealings in the summer of 1962 with Cubans, Ferrie, pilots, black operators, and mercenaries—"all working for the CIA." Martin, who says he never heard talk of an assassination, does say that Oswald came to Bannister's offices, along with a "society guy" named Clay.

Garrison, now obsessed, reopens his investigation with fervor, interrogating an Oswald lawyer, Dean Andrews (John Candy), and a male hustler, Willie O'Keefe (Kevin Bacon), who claims to have attended parties at Clay Bertrand's (Tommy Lee Jones), where David Ferrie and Oswald, along with Cubans, were also sometimes guests. As O'Keefe talks, on-screen visualizations depict Ferrie outlining a plan for getting rid of Kennedy that involves a trio of gunmen working from three separate locations. The assassination concept is described as "crossfire." O'Keefe professes dislike of Kennedy because he was "soft on communism."

At this point some of Garrison's staff members become wary of what they are doing and the chance for success. Susie Cox (Laurie Metcalf), however, has become intensely involved in the investigation and provides Garrison with additional information that supports a possible Oswald–government intelligence conspiracy, most significantly the peculiar nature of his stay in the USSR and return to the United States with Russian wife Marina, the niece of a Soviet intelligence officer.

Garrison is convinced Oswald was used as a patsy, and goes to Dallas to interview witnesses who were at Dealey Plaza the day of the assassination. The witnesses tell of shots from behind a picket fence on the grassy knoll, of a man running from the scene, and of a man in a truck with a gun (later recognized as Jack Ruby). Two witnesses claim that testimony as published in the Warren Commission report was "fabricated." Beverly, a Dallas showgirl, describes meeting Oswald in Jack Ruby's nightclub but refuses to testify in a trial, for fear of her life.

After a visit to the Texas School Book Depository, where the fatal bullets allegedly were fired, Garrison is more certain than ever that Oswald could not have performed the feat described in the Warren Commission report. He vows to get access to the Abraham Zapruder 8mm film of the assassination, believing it might prove theories about "triangulated crossfire," with the fatal bullet coming from a "professional" rifleman and fired from the front.

Back in New Orleans, it is discovered that "Clay Bertrand" is an alias for local businessman Clay Shaw. Shaw is called in on Easter Sunday and denies knowledge of the party (described by O'Keefe as an orgy) in which David Ferrie also participated. Shaw declares himself pro-Kennedy and a "patriot" and refuses to answer a question about involvement with the CIA.

Garrison's obsession to prove a conspiracy has taken him away from his family and has upset wife, Liz (Sissy Spacek). The New Orleans press has also begun to question Garrison's propriety in using tax funds to carry out the investigation. Self-doubts begin to surface, and Ferrie—who has described the charges against him as a "death warrant"—suddenly dies, leaving Garrison with no one to bring to trial.

Garrison flies off to Washington, D.C., where he is joined at the Lincoln Memorial by a lifetime government defense employee who calls himself X (Donald Sutherland). X tells of Kennedy's intentions of withdrawing all military personnel from Vietnam by the end of 1965—a decision said to have upset military-industrial war profiteers. X outlines Kennedy's plans for ending the cold war, stopping the moon race, effecting a nuclear test ban, withdrawing from Vietnam, and refusing to invade Cuba. These decisions, X claims, angered enough people at the government's highest levels to plant the seed for a coup d'état. The Warren Commission findings are declared a fiction, and X says the Oswald-Ruby-Cuba explanations are "detractions from the real truth." X cautions Garrison not to take his word for it but to "do your own thinking." While refusing to testify, X urges Garrison to be the first to bring someone to trial in the murder of Kennedy.

After visiting Kennedy's grave at Arlington National Cemetery, Garrison returns to New Orleans, having admitted he doesn't have much of a case. He nevertheless arrests Shaw and charges him as a conspiracy accomplice. A television news documentary discredits Garrison, and crank calls aggravate tensions between Liz and her husband. She threatens to leave. In the meantime, the killings of Martin Luther King, Jr., and, eventually, Robert F. Kennedy convince Garrison he must go on.

Despite the weakness of their case and despite internal defections, Garrison and his staff take Shaw to trial. Early witnesses—O'Keefe, Dean Andrews—are brought down by the defense, and the trial judge denies admission as evidence Shaw's earlier confession of having used the alias Clay Bertrand. Without a substantive witness or allegations of deception on Shaw's part, Garrison turns to the Zapruder film as his primary piece of evidence. Supplemented by charts and pointers, critical frames of the film are slowed down, blown up, and repeated several times to disprove the lone-assassin conclusion and to reveal that a fourth bullet struck Kennedy from the front. Autopsy and medical evidence is introduced to offer further "proof" of discrepancies in the "official" assassination story; Garrison also revises the events surrounding Oswald's activities following the assassination.

In his final pleas to the jury, Garrison argues:

> We have all become Hamlets in our country, children of a slain father-leader whose killers still possess the throne. The ghost of John Kennedy confronts us with the secret murder at the heart of the American dream. He forces on us the appalling question: Of what is our Constitution made? What is our citizenship—and more, our lives—worth? What is the future, where a President can be assassinated under conspicuously suspicious circumstances, while the machinery of legal action scarcely trembles? How many political murders disguised as heart attacks, cancer, suicides, airplane and car crashes, drug overdoses, will occur before they are exposed for what they are?

Garrison espouses the coup d'état conspiracy theory and asks for release of government documents that have been withheld from the public. "The truth is the most important value we have," he concludes—ending his case against Shaw. After a brief deliberation, the jury declares Shaw not guilty—the date: 1 March 1969. The following final supers appear as Garrison leaves the courthouse with his wife and son (Sean Stone):

- In 1979 Richard Helms, Director of Covert Operations in 1963, admitted under oath that Clay Shaw had worked for the CIA.
- Clay Shaw died in 1974 of lung cancer. No autopsy was allowed.
- In 1978 Jim Garrison was elected judge of the Louisiana State Court of Appeals in New Orleans. He was reelected in 1988. To this date he has brought the only public prosecution in the Kennedy killing.
- Southeast Asia: 2 million lives lost. 56,000 American lives lost. $230 billion spent. 10 million Americans airlifted there by commercial aircraft, more than 5,000 helicopters lost, 6½ million tons of bombs dropped.
- A Congressional investigation from 1976 to 1979 found a "probable conspiracy" in the assassination of J.F.K., and recommended the Justice Department investigate further. As of 1991, the Justice Department has done nothing. The files of the House Select Committee on Assassinations are locked away until 2029.
- What Is Past Is Prologue. Dedicated to the young in whose spirit the search for truth marches on.

In one of the few amusing responses to *JFK*—published in the *New York Times,* on 8 January 1992, at the height of the film's controversial reception—cartoon-satirist Garry Trudeau of Doonesbury fame used his drawing pen to sketch through the nearly eight months of prerelease and postrelease attacks made on Stone's assassination movie. The point of the drawings, Trudeau noted, was that "significant elements of the Establishment Media do seem hellbent on destroying [Stone's] reputation." The cartoon panels depicted Stone driving his automobile down Hollywood Boulevard and coming "under fire" as early as 7 May 1991, by *Chicago Tribune* columnist Jon Margolis, who called the then in-production *JFK* an "insult to intelligence and decency." Two weeks later, on 19 May, another shot is fired by the *Washington Post's* George Lardner, Jr., who declared *JFK* a farce—a "Dallas in Wonderland." As Stone's automobile proceeds on its way in time through the summer and fall of 1991 and toward *JFK's* winter release date, shots are fired at the car by *Time* magazine, *Esquire, New York Times* political writer Tom Wicker, ex-president Gerald Ford, columnist George Will, and an assortment of others. The final panel—drawn to represent 5–6 January 1992—carries a caption reporting a two-week, $30.8 million gross for *JFK* and concludes: "Laughing all the way, Stone roars off to the bank."[2]

Much of the prerelease reporting on *JFK* came after a draft of the original screenplay was leaked to outsiders. What was particularly infuriating to journalists like George Lardner, Jr., and Jon Margolis, who read the early draft, was that Stone's film had as its protagonist New Orleans District Attorney and later elected judge Jim Garrison. Lardner had reported on Garrison's conspiracy trial of 1969 for the *Washington Post* and had come to discredit both Garrison and his investigation. Implications of underworld connections and gambling payoffs, as well as charges that Garrison cajoled and bribed witnesses, surfaced during the conspiracy trial. Observers of the trial claimed that Garrison abused prosecutorial power and at best resorted to imaginative innuendo because he had no substantial evidence to build a convincing case against Shaw, an otherwise respected businessman and community leader. According to Lardner and Margolis, Garrison was a self-serving figure of embarrassing reputation who could not possibly be taken seriously as a truth-seeking screen campaigner. The fact that the New Orleans trial jury had taken less than an hour to render a not-guilty verdict against Shaw was offered as evidence of just how little credibility Garrison mustered at the time. Rehabilitation of Garrison's image as a courageous visionary in *JFK* had to be some kind of misguided joke, prerelease attackers charged.

Oliver Stone had been made aware of Garrison's low reputation—his less-than-pristine record as a public servant. But Stone had been attracted to rascally, good/bad male screen protagonists throughout his tenure as a writer-director, and while the status of Garrison's reputation gave him momentary pause, he was not deterred from going ahead with plans to use the ex-District Attorney as a metaphoric character representing all the challenges to the Warren Commission "myth," as Stone came to call it.

After meeting with Garrison to "check him out," Stone declared his protagonist sincere and a "true American patriot." Stone said: "Garrison, I admit, made many mistakes, trusted a lot of weirdos and followed a lot of fake leads. But he went out on a limb, way out. And he kept going, even when he knew he was facing long odds."[3] Garrison, like him or not, was potentially the same kind of cynical outsider character—the antihero/hero—that Stone had preferred in earlier films. Just as the James Woods and Jim Belushi characters in *Salvador* had turned stomachs and jarred filmmakers' perceptions of the film hero, so too did anticipation of Jim Garrison as a questionable screen protagonist capable of earning admiration.

In another typical Stone move, casting of the Garrison role went against type in much the same manner as had the casting of Tom Cruise to portray Ron Kovic in *Born on the Fourth of July*. Kevin Costner, an all-American sort of Hollywood actor who projected an image of softspoken conviction, had just achieved remarkable success as the director-star of *Dances with Wolves* (1990) when approached about playing Garrison. As Cruise had done after *Top Gun*, Costner was looking to stretch himself as an actor and accepted Stone's offer. His presence in *JFK*—in part calculated to draw younger filmgoers—dramatically affected the film's tone and its style.

Stone had, from first inspiration, envisioned Garrison as a Jimmy Stewart—Capraesque figure bravely struggling to correct deficiencies in the American system and to restore the old-fashioned values of truth, honesty, and justice on which the country and its Constitution had been founded—a 1960s-era variation of "Mr. Smith," who in 1939 had gone to Washington, found rampant corruption, and filibustered until the congressional solons took heed and began to come to their senses.

Costner's screen persona in *Dances with Wolves* had been effectively charismatic, exuding an aura of sensitivity and concern for fair play. Reminiscent of Jimmy Stewart's Mr. Smith and Henry Fonda's Tom Joad character in John Ford's *The Grapes of Wrath* (1940), Costner tended to deliver lines in a monotoned but quietly determined manner. The softspoken conviction had symbolically come to be seen as "the American way" and was a well-known and appealing trademark of the Capra-Ford populist films of pre–World War II Hollywood. It had worked well for Costner in *Dances with Wolves* as he acted out his concern for injustices against nineteenth-century native Americans.

Try as he might, neither Costner nor Stone was able to alter to any significant degree the clean-cut image conveyed by Costner in earlier films—thus remaking Jim Garrison into a screen character who is essentially without the flaws he clearly embodied in real life. External elements—greased-down hair, spectacles, slightly rumpled clothing—gave Costner a different physical appearance, but the character never made the slide into moral ambiguity, bewilderment, and pained self-doubting that had given Tom Cruise's rendering of formerly "all-American" Ron Kovic surprisingly gritty human dimensions. Garrison, at his worst, was depicted upsetting his wife because the investigation had taken him away from his family.

Without the familiar Stone grit, without the flawed good/bad hero (there for the taking, but left behind on the screen), *JFK* resulted in a different kind of Stone film—one with more bathos than edge, a cause movie rather than a caustic one. Among its plethora of more interesting oddball characters, *JFK*'s Jim Garrison stood as a representational icon rather than a full-bodied human being—in the end a symbolic teacher lecturing a class and reciting with conviction, sometimes passion, his interpretation of history.

The voice speaking through Costner, of course, was Stone's, and the effect represented nothing new: Stone had used his screen people as mouthpieces before in delivering his opinions (Richard Boyle, Carl Fox, Ron Kovic), but never in so blatant disregard of the character's potential humanity. Critics referred to the Garrison screen image as "leaden," a "wooden Jesus," another variation of "True-Blue Costner," and a "milquetoast."

To have presented Garrison as someone resembling his well-known tarnished self would have run the risk of discrediting *JFK* itself, a risk

Stone obviously chose not to take. Stone implied in interviews that keeping the Garrison character "flat" did not matter that much anyway, since the film's focus should be on Kennedy and his tragic assassination.

To that end, *JFK* substituted the viscera of technique for what may have been lost in flesh-and-blood characterization. Recalling the powerful editing of postrevolutionary Russian filmmaker Sergei Eisenstein—who also played down individual heroes in favor of lessons and larger causes—Stone bombards the viewer with metronomically charged images and repetitive "sound bites" in building his conspiracy case. Eisenstein's method in the classic anticzarist film *Potemkin* (1925) had been "montage of collision," an aesthetic approach in which individual images are arranged by calculation to clash against one another so as to avoid the effect of standard continuity, which tends to be "invisible" and therefore lulling. The aim of Eisenstein's editing was twofold: to keep the audience alert (awake) and to forge a prorevolutionary message by the dialectic juxtaposition of opposing forces and images—A opposed by B equals C. Rhythmic variation, time-space manipulations, repetition, and compositional contrasts of mass and volume were part of Eisenstein's montage of collision aesthetic.

JFK also located its power in montage. The clash of imagery comes in the skillful arrangement of documentary footage with restaged action, effecting a jolting new alertness on the part of the viewer while driving the idea of a conspiracy home. History, hypothesis, and dramatic narrative are intermixed throughout the film so brilliantly that *JFK* electrifies moment after moment. It builds its effort to resemble a classic drama in much the same way that Eisenstein's *Potemkin* was constructed as a five-act Greek tragedy.

Where Eisenstein made clear his own personal identification with the causes of revolution in the "Odessa Steps" sequence of *Potemkin,* Stone made his in the 45-minute trial sequence of *JFK.* The methods were similar. Eisenstein chose to depict the massacre of Odessa citizens by czarist soldiers as extended shock analysis rather than as documentary re-creation occurring in real time. The time-space continuum was abandoned so that the full extent of the Odessa tragedy— the gunning down of men, women, and children—could be viewed from every possible damning angle.

JFK employed extended analysis in the New Orleans trial of Clay Shaw to fully showcase the conspiracy theories for which Garrison serves as a conduit, expressing his, Stone's, and others' refutations of the Warren Commission findings. The first and primary element in the analysis, also meant to shock, was the Abraham Zapruder 8mm film of the assassination—blown up, rendered in slow motion, screened several times and from different angles and vantage points, as evidence in support of the case for a second gunman (at least) at Dealey Plaza. Viewed under intense scrutiny, the film appears to show the death bullet fired from in front of the presidential limousine.

As a means of protracted analysis, the Zapruder film in *JFK* became another instance of the *Blow-Up* phenomenon, in which magnification of photographic grain—pondered at length—allows the eye (and in this case the ear too) to find in the distorted imagery what it believes to be there. (Eisenstein had depicted the czarist killing of an Odessan citizen in subjective, slow-motion revisualization as he fell to his death on the portside steps—repeating the man's fall from several angles in order to force the viewer into a protracted contemplation of the deed's horror. Following this shocking, isolated detail, the scene returned to a larger view of the massacre for further documentation.) Having stunned the audience with the apparent revelations in the Zapruder film analysis, *JFK* widened its conspiracy trial revisualizations of events on 23 November 1963 to include black-and-white renderings of the Kennedy autopsy—again meant to shock the viewer into new awareness—as well as the arrest of Oswald in a Dallas movie theater. Oswald's pleas—"I'm a patsy"—lent significant impact to the verbal montage occurring during the trial summation as Garrison dropped phrases like "coup d'état," "secret murder," "triangulated crossfire," and "military-style ambush." Oswald's "patsy" claims were juxtaposed against Garrison's intimations of conspiracy. The color-imaged frames of the Zapruder film, acquired as actuality, preceded black-and-white restagings. All in all: the clash and contrast of visual and verbal imagery, reality and imagination.

Montage of collision as displayed by Eisenstein and Stone is deemed to be particularly useful as a means of instructing the audience from the filmmaker's point of view. Image barrage, repetition, shock, and contradiction work together for a highly directive, controlling effect in the conveyance of messages, whether emotionally spurred justification for national revolution *(Potemkin)* or profferred claims of a secretive coup d'état *(JFK)*.

Gary Oldman portrays Lee Harvey Oswald being escorted by police officials, just prior to his shooting by Jack Ruby, in *JFK* (1991). © 1991 Warner Bros. All rights reserved. Courtesy The Museum of Modern Art/Film Stills Archive.

Such exercise of filmic mediums also lends itself to charges of polemical finger-wagging and propaganda. *JFK* was so charged by those skeptical of the film's thesis, while others found in the explosive technique provocative entertainment. A predominant concern aimed at the film reiterated one expressed about other Stone efforts, that is, that the narrative presented on the screen would be accepted as true and hence would affect public opinion about America's institutions. It did not matter that Stone may very well have meant to do just that.

The two *New York Times* reviews written by Vincent Canby and Janet Maslin challenged *JFK*'s "racing" montage and provided fairly accurate representation of critical positions taken against the film's technique. Canby employed phrases like "the movie rushes frantically on" and called the assortment of historical details "a jumble." He labeled *JFK* a movie that "has been unable to separate the important material from the merely colorful."[4] Two weeks later Maslin continued this line of analysis of *JFK*'s structural and visual technique, projecting herself as a hypothetical viewer who wished that "*JFK* had more pointers and more patience." Maslin wrote: "Images fly by breathlessly and without identification. Composite characters are intermingled with actual ones. Real material and simulated scenes are intercut in a deliberately bewildering fashion. The camera races bewilderingly across supposedly 'top secret' documents and the various charts and models being used to explain forensic evidence. Major matters and petty ones are given equal weight. Without a knowledge of conspiracy theory trivia to match the director's, and without any ability to assess the film's erratic assortment of facts and fictions, the viewer is at the filmmaker's mercy."[5]

The being-at-the-filmmaker's-mercy idea was more Maslin's than Canby's, but both argued that Stone had failed to sort through his material and therefore both maintained that the technique did little to benefit the viewer. Some critics, concerned about *JFK*'s technique, its elisions and mixture of actuality and re-creation, went so far as to suggest Stone should have placed a disclaimer on the film, warning of the mixture of fact and conjecture. Tom Wicker stated: "*JFK* may prove persuasive to audiences with little knowledge of the events presented. . . . In an era when mistrust of government and loss of confidence in institutions (the press not least) are widespread and virulent, such a suggestion [conspiracy and coverup] seem a dubious public service, particularly since those dark allegations are only unproven speculations and the 'evidence' presented is often a stacked deck."[6]

Not all critics worried as much about the thought-reshaping potential of *JFK* or the artistic liberties taken in the construction of its message. Norman Mailer stated: "It is amazing how powerful the film becomes. Even when one knows the history of the Garrison investigation and the considerable liberties Stone has taken with the material, it truly does not matter, one soon decides, for no film could ever be made of the Kennedy assassination that would be accurate. There are too many theories and too much contradictory evidence. Tragedies of this dimension can be approached only as myths." Mailer went on to conclude his appraisal of *JFK* with "Several generations have already grown up with the mind-stultifying myth of the lone assassin. Let cinematic hyperbole war with the Establishment's skewed reality."[7]

Much of the newspaper editorial and columnist reaction to *JFK* questioned the validity of the film on three major points: (1) The presentation by Stone of Garrison's and others' "fabrications" as though they were true, including the unproven charges against Clay Shaw. *That Stone had actually staged visualizations of Garrison's claims as he spoke them during the courtroom summation was said to have exceeded the boundaries of dramatic license in a "morally questionable" manner.* (2) The claims made in *JFK* that the media were a significant element in the coverup of a conspiracy involving the CIA, the FBI, and Vice-President Lyndon Johnson, and that the Warren Commission followed through in the widespread coverup by "framing" Oswald. *That the film so "blatantly" tarnished the image of Earl Warren and that it implicated Lyndon B. Johnson in a dastardly crime were viewed as unconvincing and vicious "smears."* (3) The sense that *JFK* was offering itself up as the "conclusive" word on the assassination. *That Stone seemed to be presenting his beliefs as an act of closure (with all challenges to the film's point of view countered by charges of further effort to keep the conspiracy under wraps) was considered an arrogant and indefensible attempt at "brainwashing."*

The outcome of such criticism was extensive discussion of how to evaluate the ramifications of *JFK* as art and as historical artifact. New labels were coined, such as "faction," "infotainment," and "fact-film," and were added to the existing tag, "docudrama," as a means of describing Stone's blend of fact and fiction.

One stimulating essay inspired by *JFK* and published in *Rolling Stone* set out to analyze changes in American journalism and the kind of information that reached people in the 1990s. A case was made for a "new information culture" that favored a type of journalism labeled as "New News." New News, according to *Rolling Stone,* came about as a result of the increasing importance of pop culture (music, television, the movies) and its steady infiltration into Old News territory—replacing more serious and traditional methods of reporting information with approaches that were "dazzling, adolescent, irresponsible, frightening, and powerful."

New News, the essay argued, made Old News increasingly "irrelevant"—in part because of decreasing newspaper readership, but also because of a concomitant emergence of tabloid television, cable television options, and an increasing number of motion pictures and made-for-television movies with political- and issue-based themes, for example, Vietnam, gender, race, child and spouse abuse, alcoholism, homosexuality.

Provocatively, the essay maintained that the New News was "often superior to the old at spotting major stories and putting them into context," and it went on to say that *JFK* represented the most "explo-

sive assault" made to date by the New News on the Old—thus the
severe criticism by journalism's Old Guard:

The Old News condemns Stone as irresponsible because he is advancing disproved theories and crackpot speculation as truth. The Old News is crying
foul, incensed that someone has crossed over into their turf.

Yet it is Stone's movie, not years of columnizing by the Old News, that is
likely to force the release of Kennedy assassination documents the government is keeping under wraps. The license Stone took—and the risk—in rein-
venting a seminal story in the country's history illustrates why the New News
is gaining dramatically on the old: It is willing to heed and explore the passionate and sometimes frightening undercurrents of American life.[8]

What the outburst of journalistic reaction often alluded to in framing its concerns about *JFK* was that the very apparent and real new
information culture resided in the young. *Boston Globe* columnist Ellen Goodman, after viewing *JFK,* responded to the controversy over
the film by stating: "It's about Washington and Hollywood, docu and
drama. It's a fuss made by a generation that reads and writes for the
minds of a generation that watches and rewinds. . . . The younger
generation gets its information and infotainment from television and
movies. Less information. More entertainment. The franchise over
reality is passing hands." Goodman's bottom-line anxiety was that for
the young she saw in the theater at *JFK,* "Oliver Stone's theory may
become the only version and Lee Harvey Oswald may forever look
like actor Gary Oldman."[9]

This questioning of the ability of the young—"nonreaders" naively
unfamiliar with the assassination—to sort through *JFK* as something
other than absolute fact became a recurring issue. The argument maintained that those not around in 1963 might be too easily swayed by
the film's vision and might be too uninquiring to be able to look beyond the film to other possible conclusions.

Some sought to debunk these claims. *Rolling Stone* called the
charges "patronizing contempt" of the young. Lisa Nesselson countered: "One objection to *JFK* that keeps cropping up is this: Grownups
with $40 million budgets should not 'rewrite' history because this is
Very Bad For Our Nation's Youth who will suddenly and irrevocably
Lose Faith In America's Great Institutions. What's more, it's disre-
spectful of a National Tragedy that should politely have faded away
by now. I maintain that Stone's pot-pourri of sometimes sickening,
often didactic, sometimes hilarious discrepancies is Good For Young

People because it gives them splendid opportunity to sharpen their Critical Thinking."[10]

The majority of pro-*JFK* letters written to newspaper and magazine editors also took as their position a belief that Stone's point of view— accurate or inaccurate—had stimulated new interest in the assassination and provided a basis for further discussion and examination. *Newsweek* magazine reported in its 13 January 1992 issue that most letter writers had sided with Stone's attack on the Warren Commission's one-assassin conclusion. Many letters to the editor also maintained that Stone had performed a "wakeup" service that should have been provided by the nation's press. A *New York Times* editorial headline on 16 January 1992 conceded that it was time to "Get the Rest of the J.F.K. Story."

JFK raised as much discussion about filmmaker obligation in creating historically based works, and revived long-standing artistic theories about the issue of fact-fiction films. Most basic was the premise that all film artists create works with points of view, and because art frames the creation, the film must be judged as such. Any attempt to control the point of view is to interfere with the artist's rights and is tantamount to censorship of the creator's vision. In defense of Stone, Andrew Kopkind wrote in the *Nation*:

Stone neither deconstructs nor debunks. His method is to substitute another myth—consistent, compelling and just a little unconvincing—for the "official" one that seems to have been a comfort so long but is so shot full of holes by now that it can barely float. Certainly he has every right to do what he does. John Ford's *December 7th,* recently remembered as the fiftieth anniversary of Pearl Harbor came around, also mixed documentary footage with reconstructions and simulations, inserted historical speculations as ironclad fact, and gave heroic (or villainous) dimensions to ordinary people. It was a great film and brilliant propaganda, which is to say, what movies ought to be.[11]

Art and journalism do not share the same obligations, it was theorized, although the film artist might step into actuality situations that are historically well known and newsworthy. Nora Ephron, coscenarist for the film *Silkwood* (1983), argued that the intention of narrative films based on biographical or factual data should be the presentation of "not the truth, but what it was like—sort of, maybe— in a way that journalism could never come close to."[12] Ephron, like Stone, had been criticized for playing loosely with the facts of heroine

Karen Silkwood's real life when bringing her antinuclear campaign story to the screen.

While others may have argued to the contrary, defenders of *JFK* cited artistic vision, thematic point of view, dramatic license, and narrative efficiency and coherence as the essential variants of the process by which film artists must necessarily respond to historical record. Theorists replied that the right to take a position and to offer it as fact, conjecture, or countermyth resided within the jurisdiction of dramatic/film art expression, even though the narrative may be seen as exploiting the historical-news-journalism account and value of its material.

Many of the most outspoken invectives against *JFK* as irresponsible art were a result of the public stance taken by Stone that the film presented not artfully presented personal vision but the truth. This brazen position served to raise ire and sustain controversy even as the text of the film itself was telling viewers that *JFK* was more an investigatory intrigue than confident fact. For example, Ferrie—being interrogated by Garrison—shouts, "It's all a mystery, a mystery!" Garrison's team of investigators preface possible assassination scenarios with "Let's speculate" and "What if . . . ?" At the film's conclusion, the summarizing Mr. X—while breathlessly spouting the claims of a widespread conspiracy—cautions Garrison, "Don't take my word. Do your own work, your own thinking."

Had Stone used his many public forums to admit outright that *JFK* was conjecture, he would have prevented the biggest coup of all—the masterminding of a brilliant ploy to engage Old News journalists in the "advertising" of a New News event. Old News writers grabbed for the bait, even before the hook, line, and sinker hit the water—proving once again that Stone's lack of intimidation in making unconventional films and in placing them in the public arena—his own way—had paid off. With *JFK,* Oliver Stone lived up to and sustained his reputation as a maverick film man.

11

Final Analysis and Ensuing Issues

Oliver Stone's reputation was earned through unusual means—what Hollywood insiders often refer to as a guerilla style of filmmaking. In both technique and idea, his motion pictures attack the filmgoer's sensibilities as they charge forcefully ahead in the manner of artistic warfare. A subtext of urgency runs through the effort, suggesting a compulsive creator with a mission. Macho characters populate the narratives; the voice that carries Stone's unveiled messages is a masculine one, and the masculinity is grittily textured by traits that encompass both good and bad, the honorable and the despicable.

Like soldiers, Stone's protagonists are at war—with themselves, with faulty systems needing "correcting," with military enterprise itself. And like the worlds in which they must operate, they are deeply flawed. In Stone's vision perfection does not exist—only the possibility of movement toward redemption that comes through self-knowledge. This knowledge is attained by a hellish descent to which the good/bad hero readily subjects himself, often for misguided reasons and with self-destructive effect. The hero descends to the darkest of pits, pulled there by all sorts of tainting lures: drugs, easy sex, money, a search for self-esteem or for the truth, the desire to win and prove oneself "worthy." The psychological spine that braces the prototypical Stone hero and compels his actions bears the weight of a strong "father complex." From Billy Hayes in *Midnight Express* to Chris Taylor in *Platoon*, from Bud Fox in *Wall Street* and Jim Morrison in *The Doors* to Jim Garrison in *JFK*, a distant father serves as the powerful force of compulsive behavior awaiting redemption. In *Platoon* and *Wall Street*, the father complex is autobiographical; in *JFK*, ideological, as

Garrison mourns Kennedy as a "slain father-leader" whose "children" must redeem their country by uncovering the "truth" of their father's death.

The obsessive father imagery in Stone's cinematic vision serves the purpose of both personal exorcism and dramatic archetype. A need to prove himself to his father prompted Stone to enlist in the army and fight in Vietnam, in effect a "guerilla" method for trying to improve a strained father-son relationship. This kind of thinking—good intentions but questionable logic—hinted at the essence of Stone's own character when he chose the turbulence of the military over college life at Yale as the means of earning acceptance. It also spoke to his preference for rascally, renegade male protagonists who often appear as morally and psychologically confused as they are dramatically compelling. Richard Boyle and Dr. Rock of *Salvador* hold kinship with Stone because their confusions and moral ambiguities were at one time his own. They are men of similar ilk who fit well into the gadfly male club invented by Stone.

The attraction to Ron Kovic and Jim Morrison can be explained for precisely the same reasons. Both were compelled to prove their worthiness—beginning as essentially well-intended men of the 1960s who offered themselves—as Stone had—as potential heroes of the decade, only to be brought tragically down in the process. For different reasons and in different arenas, they too descended into the dark pits of social, moral, and political confusion with which Stone identified. Like the dual good/evil roles played by Charlie Chaplin in *The Great Dictator,* Kovic and Morrison represented a composite alter ego for Stone's good intentions gone awry, intentions resulting in battle scars, loss of faith and potency, drug dependency, and near self-destruction. The death of one side of the composite—Jim Morrison—can be symbolically viewed as evidence of the potential self-destruction in Stone's own descent into drugs, while on the other side the reemergence of Ron Kovic's potency in *Born on the Fourth of July*—potency gained through a political voice—is metaphor for Stone's movement from stasis to action through "bold statement" motion pictures. A symbiosis exists between Stone's unique personal character and the creative expression he designs to clarify that self. The overarticulation in the films may very well result from a deep-seated fear of failing and having once again to retreat into "unworthiness." Indirection and confusion, he has said, were closely associated with the earlier, failed period of his life. Bold statement is the counterresponse.

The father-complex imagery reveals character motivation, autobiographically derived, and it also serves as a classic dramatic device for imparting knowledge of Stone's naive but educable young heroes. Archetypal framing shaped *Platoon* and *Wall Street*—two unusually symmetrical motion pictures—and allowed the development of father-opposites in the presence of Elias and Barnes and in Gordon Gekko and Carl Fox. It was again a variation of the composite concept in which both good and evil reside, with each father type tempting the imagination and self-needs of the neophyte protagonist. The pull of the powerful father figures forces options that in turn lead to knowledge about the inherent nature of humankind, about values, ethics, and the need to do good—in the case of *Platoon,* to "teach" others what was learned in Vietnam, and in *Wall Street*'s case, to "create" rather than live as greedy parasites off others.

The father-opposites, either blood-related or symbolic surrogates, act as instructors in Stone's films, much as Stone's own father had cajoled and motivated him as a disciplinarian lest his son become spoiled and lazy. In Oliver Stone's youth, the response was to take up writing ("creating"), and the imparted charge to discipline helps explain Stone's gifted efficacy in realizing broad-canvas, logistically complex motion pictures as well as his urgency to leap from one film project into another.

The father idea dominates in such a way that the concept elucidates the essential male tensions in Stone's films at the same time as it explains the tensions in his personal life. A love-hate dissonance is at work. Resentment abounds, but it is countered with the awareness that father-son relationships, however strained, can be instructive, and in valuable ways. The imitations of father resentment and family rebellion that drew Stone to see Jim Morrison as a "brother" were countered by the elevation of Lou Stone's old-fashioned ethics and values in *Wall Street.* A frustrated but caring father appeared in *Midnight Express* to assist a son imprisoned on drug charges, just as Lou Stone had bailed out his son for a drug bust on the Mexican border following the unsettling experience of duty in Vietnam. Fathers in Stone's vision can be despised and they can be honored. They are the sires and the perpetuators of the good/bad sons who, Stone argued, are more accurately the stuff of life than Hollywood's pious, idealized heroes.

In the creation of screen characters like himself and those openly meant as alter egos, a telling self-portrait of the artist emerges. The characters function in much the same manner as Stone works. They explore new territory—usually unsettled and volatile environments bound by mystery. A trip often frames the experience, leading the characters to discovery and, simultaneously, danger. The approach is innately cinematic: a flow-of-life format that lends itself to spontaneity and the excitement of an unexpected turn of events.

As the characters come in contact with new experiences that raise their moral and/or political consciousness, they move to take a stand, and they do so in "message"-carrying monologues that arrive quickly at their point, without subtlety. Dramatic spontaneity gives way to a politically charged lecture whose rhetoric is aimed at revealing the flaws of faulty systems: Turkey's penal laws, government policy in Central America, the war in Vietnam, greed in high finance, the exploitative nature of talk radio, the myth of soldier glory and counterculture rock-and-roll heroes, the Warren Commission report.

Stone's modus operandum had its inspiration in *Midnight Express* and took hold with *Salvador.* The idea of following a gadfly, off-center character, Richard Boyle, into an exotic and dangerous land began as a character study and ended up as an indictment of U.S. policy abroad. As he works, Stone's political stance evolves more fully in the course of discovering his characters. The protagonists are invariably adventurers whose personalities set them apart from others: a drug smuggler, a vagabond journalist, naive soldiers, an inside trader, a loud-mouthed broadcast personality, a self-destructive rock star, an eccentric district attorney challenger to "official" history. All are derived from real people who stir interest first as compelling characters and then as conduits of ideology through which Stone's own interpretation of sociopolitical realities can be voiced. Only Jim Garrison of *JFK* failed to convey the character vagaries expected of a Stone hero.

This approach to the conceptualization of screen drama can be both appealing and problematic. The exhilaration provided by unconventional heroes often carried Stone beyond the potentially fatal scripting of "loud," didactic climaxes and stacked-deck messages. For many the viscera acted to override obvious flaws because it provided a fresh departure from the sentiment and pseudosensitivity that characterized many Hollywood pictures of the 1980s and 1990s. Stone's appreciation for the tarnished cynic was in large part his salvation. On the other hand, for those who could not see his characters as original and engaging, Stone's efforts were deemed at best irritating. Whether damned or praised, however, the artistic approach remained self-confidently consistent picture by picture.

This is not to say that attention was not paid to the enormous amount of criticism and controversy generated by the films. Like his own heroes, Stone was educable, and he read the reviews with an eye to ferreting out what had worked so that he could repeat it in future effort. The appeal of the good/bad hero was one element seized on after *Salvador* and retained, as was the formidable way of integrating documentary footage and re-created historical facsimiles into the narrative. Early in Stone's career, bombastic camera and editing styles had been singled out for their success in electrifying the drama, and they too became standard techniques.

Stone also began to see clearer the potential of his work and the uniqueness of its impact. As evidence surfaced in reviews of a non-standardized artist capable of making films with provocative ideas, a sense of a mission developed. He began to talk of making films with a difference, and of being compelled to do so—something he had rarely done before *Salvador,* when he was turning out horror films and writing for others in Hollywood. By the time of *The Doors,* the mission was being self-defined as "wakeup" theater. *JFK* appeared to be nearly pure exercise in that direction.

It also became clearer through the texts of his films that Stone understood what had happened to the course of his career, and he was able to be wryly introspective about potential calculations and about being a "point" filmmaker—Hollywood's social awareness standard-bearer. *Talk Radio,* for example, possessed an ironic intertext that might have been Stone's way of reflecting on his work and its controversial nature. The script spoke critically and in no uncertain terms of hypocrisy and financial exploitation within the mass media by experts who achieve their success through manipulative technique and who sensationalize social and political issues to engage an audience. Talk-show host Barry Champlain may well have been another ideological "brother" in the Stone family; certainly he was a character Stone would have understood as well as any other he chose to bring to the screen.

As a reflexive exercise—a narrative media event ruminating on the media—*Talk Radio* dealt with trends as well as issues of ethics and individual responsibility in contemporary mass communication. Many were the same fringe issues raised in the controversial flap that developed over Stone's treatment of biographical and historical material in his films. Most specifically, concern was expressed about the trend, in all manner of media output, toward the appropriation and melodramatizing of critical subject matter to appeal to consumer tastes. The steadily increasing popularity of shock-talk programming, tabloid television, and issue-oriented made-for-television movies signaled popular culture's intrusion into newsworthy territory for commercial gain.

Simultaneously, media presentations were becoming slicker and glitzier—no matter how serious the subject matter. MTV—with its metronomically charged editing structures and manipulated imagery—had significantly expanded the vision of what was possible in media displays, and by the mid-1980s the MTV style of aural-visual imaging began to appear in facsimile television programming such as "America's Most Wanted" and in time in the networks' most respected weekly newsmagazine programs. Strong on viscera, the glitzier techniques added more drama to the intrigue of the stories being told. Form and content approached melodrama as factual, unembellished reporting of information was being pushed aside.

It was into this arena of change that Stone stepped when he directed his first significant film, *Salvador,* in 1986. The restaging of a panic scene that occurred after the assassination of Archbishop Romero resembled the hand-held camera imaging of an MTV interlude. Also in MTV fashion, the work made use of an explosive pace and energy, beginning with a newsreel insert depicting violence in El Salvador.

What most resembled the newer style of factually based filming was the sense of drama supplied by a constantly moving camera, one that probes fictionalized space in an apparent search for the truth within the event it explores. The frenetic camera supplants verbal investigation within the visual rhetoric of innuendo and ambiguity. Mystery resonates the information being conveyed, proving the technique a compelling one, even though little, in the end, may be clarified.

The mystery of the probing camera was well suited for an exploration into the unsettled world of El Salvador, and it worked perfectly in conveying the ambiguity of dense Vietnam jungle in *Platoon*. Stone continued to exploit the technique as though he had invented it, and by the making of *JFK* his mastery of the moving camera as a means of investigative simulation was undeniable. The device energized the murder-mystery drama within the film the way an episode of "A Current Affair" or "Call 911" redramatized actual crimes to lure audiences.

Because all of Stone's films from *Salvador* to *JFK* journeyed into historical and sociopolitical terrain, scrutiny was intense. As a self-proclaimed standard-bearer and dynamic interpreter of recent history who used sensational techniques, Stone set himself up for attacks that revealed as much about the psychology of response to factually inspired films as they did about the perceived quality of the work itself.

The immediacy of events developed in Stone's films activated the "I-was-there" critical response—a totally understandable reaction but one that seemingly did little more than set the memory of an individual's personal experiences against the imagination of the artist. From Vietnam veterans, from rock-and-roll fans of the 1960s, from antiwar activists at Syracuse University, and from Kennedy administration insiders came personal memory reaction that disputed or discounted Stone's cinematic interpretation of real people, places, and situations. An urge to set the record straight can be so fiercely felt that it can impel an "I-was-there" *New York Times* editorialist to declare the amount of hair on the chest of Jim Morrison impersonator Val Kilmer one of *The Doors*'s many "infidelities."

In the heat of the contentious response, exactly what liberty could be taken by the filmmaker who fictionalizes history—recent or distant—was never well defined, just as the parameters of imagination in documentary films also remained in question. A documentarist like Michael Moore—a Stone contemporary—was widely chastised for the staging of situations and for chronology "aberrations" in *Roger and Me* (1988), despite the long-standing acceptance of a theory that argues all worthwhile documentaries are in varying degrees creative treatments of actuality, shaped to be as compelling as possible and to convey an enlightening point of view.

Fact-and-fiction mixtures in Stone's motion pictures were certain to be discussed not just because they blended genres in their reportage but because they could skirt rules and principles that would otherwise apply. A peculiar anxiety grew from the realization that any fictionalized historical event can capitalize on what has been called its news appeal yet need not strictly adhere to "accuracy-reporting" standards. Again the debate became philosophical and theoretical, calling into question the film dramatist's right to glean a thematic point of view from the material at hand and to render it as vividly as possible.

A law of aesthetics developed as another way of thinking about Stone's films. His own stated law had been not the truth but the spirit

of the truth—a concept of artistic guidance espoused by other beleaguered docudrama filmmakers. It was said to free the imaginative
powers and permit movement beyond what would be possible in a
journalistic accounting of a story and its significance.

Once freed from the stricture of pure fact, the theory went, film
historians like Oliver Stone could yet be held accountable for both the
artistic quality and the social value of their work—elements that
should not be viewed as mutually exclusive of each other in a process
of evaluation. Often the value of a work is the quality of its presentation. This critical analysis of Stone's highly controversial film, *JFK,*
was meant to set the importance of rational aesthetic considerations
above the paranoia of critics who dwelt on the idea that, for the naive,
fact-inspired film might be accepted as the truth and therefore become
once and forever the "official" story. The latter reaction, as with the
"I-was-there" response, failed to address the innate value of the work
as a self-contained artifact of the imagination.

If one remains within the imaginary worlds created by Stone, *inside*
his films, it is possible to discover a good/bad filmmaker, an artist
who has shown himself to be at once one of the true geniuses of his
craft as well as a troubling creator. He has been deeply appreciated for
making "movie" movies—films that are propelling exercises with unusual energy. There has been a commendable "edge" in the work,
both in what Stone has to say to filmgoers and in how he has said it.
He did not make commonplace, boring motion pictures. Nor did he
fall in line with his Hollywood contemporaries when they turned increasingly to well-made feel-good entertainment that consoled and reaffirmed in uncertain times. Stone continued to raise questions and,
blusteringly, continued to do it his way. That was good, and the films
held value because they prodded as they entertained.

At the other end of the good/bad pole is Stone's major artistic sin:
excess. He has admitted "loudness" in ramming his points home
through impassioned monologue lectures and the bravura of technique that carries its own passionate emphasis. This has been good
and it has been bad. Technique in Stone's films has shown itself to be
exhilarating on the one hand (e.g., camera work, musical underscoring, closeup detail in *Platoon*), yet it can seem to be overwrought and
self-conscious punctuation on the other (e.g., sound as repetitive
exclamation points in the latter half of *JFK*). Stone can display remarkable historical/environmental simulations as cinematic strengths
(Salvador, JFK), and he can allow his imagination to turn out a film
that is severely weakened by stylistic hodgepodge *(The Doors).* The

artistic weaknesses in Stone's films have been transparent, and they have significantly detracted from the potential value that might have come through subtler, less muscularized expression.

There are also found within the body of his films problems with narrative form, and this too has diminished overall impact. The attachment of the Alan Berg scenario to *Talk Radio* caused motivation and intent to become disjointed and prevented the film from realizing its potential as a powerful statement about consumer tastes and mass-media exploitation. The conversions of Bud Fox in *Wall Street* and Ron Kovic in *Born on the Fourth of July* did not develop from credibly devised action sufficient to motivate change and were therefore diminished as value-oriented climaxes about the politics of money and war.

Close examination of Stone's output has shown a particularly nagging difficulty with making the various elements of his narratives—character, plot, motivation, climax—mesh to realize the ideas he seeks to get across, except by forcing the issue. As skillful as he has been, and as engaging as his characters and his ideas were, Stone's narrative storytelling deficiencies were his greatest weakness. The mastery of dramatic logic toward a thematic end often eluded an otherwise compelling filmmaker. Good intentions went only partly realized as Stone's narratives frequently wallowed in their own clumsy architecture.

It is probably safe to say that both the values and the harms attributed to Stone's brazen films were overestimated. *JFK* was charged with possessing the insidiousness of *Triumph of the Will,* but such a statement of indictment against a filmmaker also served to incorrectly indict intellectual curiosity in a free society. The charge presumed a recipient inertia on the filmgoer's part and the silence of other voices. Neither, of course, was the case, and *JFK* worked to dislodge the many pieces of a grand myth that had been formed over three decades and acted to bring the pieces under a microscopic scrutiny of unparalleled intensity.

As wrong-handed as the conspiracy theme may someday prove to have been and however arrogant the claims to truth in his public position on *JFK,* Stone activated a valuable process of inquiry, not a grand deception like the one staged and projected by Leni Riefenstahl. No epilogue at the end of *Triumph of the Will* urges disclosure of government documents that might have proved or disproved the film's point of view in presenting Adolf Hitler as a newly arrived god who had fully captivated Germany's people.

Stone's position was discredited even before it reached the screen, alerting filmgoers well in advance to look at *JFK* with a critical, skeptical eye. Few could have missed the warnings. The value of the film resided in its entertainment as an epic mystery, and in its subsequent prompting of medical response by attending pathologists and promoting of government officials to release the Kennedy assassination files. Negative effects lay unverified, and Stone's credibility as a self-proclaimed purveyor of the truth remained in question.

As a proponent of "wakeup" cinema, Stone has had mixed success, rallying some, irritating others. Yet final appraisal cannot and should not be made. Works of the imagination—art—can attain different responses and levels of appreciation with the passage of time. Stone's effort is no exception. Economic turgidity and recession in the early 1990s caused a backward glance at the "sins" of the 1980s, calling into reconsideration economic policies and financial practices that meant future woe. In that backward glance, *Wall Street* can now be seen as having gained in stature as a timely and prescient statement. Even the political rhetoric of the 1992 presidential campaign picked up on a call to spur the economy by "creating something" rather than living off calculation.

At the time of its release, *Born on the Fourth of July* was widely criticized for its construction of an ideology that depicted the patriot naively ready to march off to war for the glory of America and self. The discrediting of the concept as unrealistic and passé lost validity in the fervorous response to Desert Storm and the Gulf War of 1991. When *Born on the Fourth of July* was broadcast on network television early in 1992, the film's motivation and ideology held new, certified meaning.

In time, *Salvador* and *Platoon* could also be viewed more appreciatively. They were born of a hungry innocent who knew little of his potential as a filmmaker, and even with their many flaws stand as great ventures into the drama of American intervention abroad. They offer rare dramatic instruction by depicting war as a tragedy that touches all lives; compassion flows along not patriotic but human lines. In these muscular films antiheroism—not heroism—serves to pull their ideas down to life's level and in the process elevates their importance as incisive documents at the edge of the truth. *Salvador* and *Platoon* remain, nostalgically, the two certain classics of Oliver Stone's manly output, and they are incipient evidence of the talent residing in a very special kind of filmmaker.

EPILOGUE

No doubt because of longstanding reaction to his treatment of female characters, Oliver Stone once again responded to his critics and addressed the issue by bringing to the screen *Heaven and Earth*, which opened in U.S. movie theaters on Christmas day, 1993. The picture was publicized as the third entry in a trilogy of Vietnam films by Stone, and its protagonist, Le Ly Hayslip, is a woman of Vietnamese origin.

Heaven and Earth was adapted for film by Stone from two autobiographical works written by Hayslip: *When Heaven and Earth Changed Places* (1989) and *Child of War, Woman of Peace* (1993). The two books provided the narrative details for a story of Hayslip (born Phung Thi Le Ly) as a teenager growing up in a rural rice village, Ky La, in central Vietnam and experiencing the perils of chaotic guerrilla warfare. Hayslip's story includes incidents from the war that involved harrowing encounters with both the Vietcong and the Americans as they positioned themselves in every part of the country.

Travail follows the Vietnamese woman to Saigon, where she becomes a blackmarketeer, then a prostitute, and eventually the wife of an American businessman who takes Hayslip with him to the United States. Transplanted existence in southern California offers its own difficult challenges and confusions for a woman who had begun life with strong traditional values born of the Confucian and Buddhist teachings of her parents. Stone's adaptation seeks to emphasize, thematically, a life torn apart—personally and spiritually—by the Vietnam War, followed by a longing to reconnect with the past. (In 1986 Hayslip returned to her native land for such a purpose.)

Heaven and Earth, produced by Warner Bros., was filmed by Stone near Phangna, Thailand, and in Los Angeles in late fall 1992, with minor location work in Vietnam. The role of Le Ly Hayslip was portrayed by a California college student, Hiep Thi Le—a 23-year-old Vietnamese woman who fled her country at age nine with a group of boat people. The sprawling, epic requirements of *Heaven and Earth* resulted in a $23 million effort, which Stone met with the same aplomb and efficiency that guided him through *Platoon* and *Born on the Fourth of July*, the other two parts of his Vietnam trilogy.

Heaven and Earth could be seen as a historical moment both for American film and for Stone. The film's point of view moves the

Vietnam story away from a narrowed American perspective and close to the lives of the people who endured the confusions and tragedy of the war in their own land. In this regard, *Heaven and Earth* offers a larger, less provincial consideration of political realities than previous American films on the Vietnam War. And in his sympathetic treatment of a strong female character, Stone addresses some of the criticism labeling him as severely deficient as a balanced storyteller. Embracing the symbolism of the occasion, Stone dedicated *Heaven and Earth* to his mother, Jacqueline Stone, and, having done so, gave symmetry—as Stone is wont to do—to the earlier dedication of *Wall Street* to his father, Lou.

At the Los Angeles premier of *Heaven and Earth* on 15 December 1993, Stone received a career achievement award from the Writers Guild Foundation. Melville Shavelson, president of the foundation, cited Stone as an exemplar for "filmmakers whose writing talent came first and opened the way to directing and producing their own works."

NOTES

PREFACE

1. Susan Sontag, *On Photography* (New York: Farrar, Straus and Giroux, 1973); hereafter cited in text.
2. Siegfried Kracauer, *Theory of Film* (New York: Oxford University Press, 1960).
3. Rudolf Arnheim, *Film As Art* (Berkeley and Los Angeles: University of California Press, 1966), 8, 9; hereafter cited in text.
4. George C. Pratt, *Spellbound in Darkness* (Rochester, N.Y.: University of Rochester School of Liberal and Applied Sciences, 1966).
5. Thomas Schatz, *Hollywood Genres* (New York: Random House, 1981), 22.

CHAPTER 1

1. Pat McGilligan, "Point Man," *Film Comment,* January/February 1987, 16; hereafter cited in text.
2. Alexander Cockburn, "Oliver Stone Takes Stock," *American Film* 13, no. 3 (December 1987): 22.
3. David Breskin, "Oliver Stone: The Interview," *Rolling Stone,* 4 April 1991, 40; hereafter cited in text.
4. Oliver Stone, address to the National Press Club, Washington, D.C., 7 April 1987, published in *Massachusetts Review* 29 (1988): 424.
5. Russell Miller, "Rider on the Storm," *Sunday (London) Times Magazine,* 14 February 1991, 20; hereafter cited in text.
6. John Daly, "Haunted by Stone's Hell," *Stills,* no. 29 (February 1987): 18.
7. Stephen Talbot, "60s Something," *Mother Jones,* March/April 1991, 48.
8. John Wrathall, "Greeks, Trojans and Cubans—Oliver Stone," *Monthly Film Bulletin* 56 (Octboer 1989): 320.
9. Richard Brooks, "Rolling Stone," *Observer,* 24 February 1991, 20.
10. Robert Sam Anson, "The Shooting of JFK," *Esquire,* November 1991, 94.

CHAPTER 2

1. Review of *Seizure, Independent Film Journal,* 2 April 1975, 13.
2. Vincent Canby, "Who Says They Don't Make B Movies?," *New York Times,* 23 March 1975, II, 15.
3. Tim Lucas, "Seizure," Cinefantastique 4, no. 2 (1975): 33.
4. Neal Nordlinger, "The Making of *Midnight Express,*" *Filmmakers Monthly* 12 (November 1978): 19.
5. " '78'," *Films Illustrated* 7 (January 1978): 185.
6. Clarke Taylor, "Making *Midnight Express,*" *Los Angeles Times Calendar,* 22 October 1978, 6.
7. David Ansen, "Turkey Hash," *Newsweek,* 16 October 1978: 81.
8. Pauline Kael, "Current Cinema," *New Yorker,* 27 November 1978, 185.
9. Andrew Sarris, "A Little Night Kvetch," *Village Voice,* 16 October 1978, 71.
10. Chris Hodenfeld, "The Man Who Got Away," *Rolling Stone,* 30 November 1978, 18.
11. Steven Umberger, "Conscientious Exception," *Humanist* 39 (March/April 1979): 66; hereafter cited in text.
12. Charles Champlin, "Crime and Cruel Punishment," *Los Angeles Times,* 25 October 1978, IV, 1.
13. Chris Chase, "At the Movies," *New York Times,* 15 May 1981, III, 8.
14. Vincent Canby, "On Two Levels," *New York Times,* 24 April 1981, III, 3, 8; hereafter cited in text.
15. Review of *The Hand, Rolling Stone,* 11 June 1981, 11.
16. David Ansen, "Five Finger Exercise," *Newsweek,* 27 April 1981, 90.
17. Jimmy Summers, review of *The Hand, Boxoffice* 117 (May 1981): 82.
18. "Short Takes," *Christian Science Monitor,* 7 May 1981, 19.

CHAPTER 3

1. Richard Schickel, "Overkill," *Time,* 24 May 1982, 76.
2. Laurence O'Toole, "Strong Like Bull, Red Like Abattoir," *Maclean's,* 17 May 1982, 65–66.
3. Vincent Canby, "Thoughts While Held Captive by an 'Escapist' Movie," *New York Times,* 23 May 1982, II, 21.
4. Vincent Canby, "How Should We React to Violence?," *New York Times,* 11 December 1983, II, 23.
5. David Ansen, "Gunning Their Way to Glory," *Newsweek,* 12 December 1983, 109.

6. Karen Jaehne, *"Scarface," Cineaste* 13, no. 3 (1984): 49.

7. Pauline Kael, "A De Palma Movie for People Who Don't Like De Palma Movies," *New Yorker,* 26 December 1983, 51.

8. David Chute, review of *Scarface, Film Comment* 20 (January/February 1984): 67.

9. Enrique Fernandez, *"Scarface* Died for My Sins," *Village Voice,* 20 December 1983, 74.

10. Richard Combs, review of *Year of the Dragon, Monthly Film Bulletin* 53 (January 1986): 16.

11. Janet Maslin, review of *Year of the Dragon:* "Cimino in Chinatown," *New York Times,* 16 August 1985, III, 10.

12. Pauline Kael, "The Great White Hope," *New Yorker,* 9 September 1985, 73.

13. Rita Kempley, review of *8 Million Ways to Die, Washington Post Weekend,* 25 April 1986, 30.

CHAPTER 4

1. Sally Hibbin, "Blood from Stone," *Films and Filming,* no. 388 (January 1987): 19; hereafter cited in text.

2. "'*Salvador*'—Drawing a Bead on a Dirty War," *Los Angeles Times Calendar,* 1 December 1985, 28.

3. Gary Crowdus, "Personal Struggles and Political Issues," *Cineaste* 16, no. 3 (1988): 18.

4. Damien Kingsbury, "One Man's War," *Cinema Papers* (Australia), no. 60 (November 1986): 12.

5. Elizabeth Gordon, *"Salvador:* Too Hot for US Distribs," *Film Journal* 89 (April 1986): 36, 37, 40.

6. Michael Wilmington, *"Salvador* Has Action as Loud as Its Words," *Los Angeles Times,* 10 April 1986, VI, 6; hereafter cited in text.

7. Gene Siskel, "As Political Film, *Salvador* More Insult Than Message," *Chicago Tribune,* 25 April 1986, VII, A, E.

8. Pauline Kael, "Pig Heaven," *New Yorker,* 28 July 1986, 79.

9. Patricia Kluchy, review of *Salvador, MacLean's,* 21 July 1986, 50.

10. Walter Goodman, "Central America," *New York Times,* 5 March 1986, III, 22.

11. Charles Champlin, "Anti-hero as Hero in *Salvador,*" *Los Angeles Times,* 12 April 1986, 8; hereafter cited in text.

12. Paul Attanasio, "Bold, Vivid *Salvador,*" *Washington Post,* 4 April 1986, IV, 11; hereafter cited in text.

13. Christopher Hitchins, "Commentary: South of the Border," *Times Literary Supplement,* 23 January 1987, 87.

14. Floyd Nigel, "Radical Frames of Mind" (interview with Oliver Stone), *Monthly Film Bulletin* 54, no. 636 (January 1987): 11.

15. George Robert Kimball, review of *Salvador, Films and Filming,* no. 388 (January 1987): 42.

16. Tom Matthews, review of *Salvador, Boxoffice* 122 (June 1986): R-59.

CHAPTER 5

1. Oliver Stone, "One from the Heart," *American Film* 12 (January/February 1987): 19.

2. Richard Combs, "Beating God to the Draw," *Sight and Sound* 56, no. 2 (1987): 138.

3. Ed Kelleher, review of *Platoon, Film Journal* 90 (January 1987): 41.

4. Terrence Rafferty, "Films," *Nation,* 17 January 1987, 56; hereafter cited in text.

5. David Denby, "Bringing the War Back Home," *New York,* 15 December 1986, 86; hereafter cited in text.

6. Pauline Kael, "Little Shocks, Big Shocks," *New Yorker,* 12 January 1987, 95.

7. Tom O'Brien, review of *Platoon, Commonweal,* 16 January 1987, 17.

8. Sydelle Kramer, review of *Platoon, Cineaste* 15, no. 3 (1987): 50.

9. "TRB from Washington: *Platoon* and Iranamok," *New Republic,* 9 March 1987, 4, 42.

10. Charles Krauthammer, "*Platoon* Chic," *Washington Post,* 20 February 1987, I, 19.

11. Richard Corliss, "*Platoon:* Vietnam, the Way It Really Was, on Film," *Time,* 26 January 1987, 57; hereafter cited in text.

12. Paul Attanasio, "*Platoon*'s Raw Mastery," *Washington Post,* 16 January 1987, II, 4.

CHAPTER 6

1. Aljean Harmetz, "Raising the Odds," *New York Times Magazine,* 11 September 1988, pt. 2, 76.

2. Gary Crowdus, "Personal Struggles and Political Issues," *Cineaste* 16, no. 3 (1988): 21.

3. Nigel Floyd, review of *Wall Street, Monthly Film Bulletin* 55 (April 1988): 124.

4. Jack Boozer, Jr., "*Wall Street,*" *Journal of Popular Film and Television* 17 (Fall 1989): 96; hereafter cited in text.

5. David Sterritt, "The Grime beneath the Glitter," *Christian Science Monitor,* 11 December 1987, 21.

6. Judith Williamson, "Man for Our Season," *New Statesman,* 6 May 1988, 29.

7. James Flanigan, "*Wall Street*'s Disaster Was All Too Real," *Los Angeles Times,* 13 December 1987, IV, 1.

8. Richard Combs, "Father Figures," *Times Literary Supplement,* 29 April 1988, 474b.

9. Sean French, "Breaking News," *Sight and Sound* 57 (Spring 1988): 136.

10. Elayne Rapping, review of *Wall Street, Cineaste* 16, no. 3 (1988): 50.

11. Tim O'Brien, "Stoned on Greed," *Commonweal,* 12 February 1988, 89.

CHAPTER 7

1. Dave Kehr, "Oliver Stone's Angry Voice Is Worth Listening to in *Talk Radio,*" *Chicago Tribune,* 22 December 1988, 24.

2. Pam Cook, review of *Talk Radio, Monthly Film Bulletin* 56 (September 1989): 285; hereafter cited in text.

3. J. Hoberman, "Freedom Now?" *Village Voice,* 20 December 1988, 83.

4. Richard Porton, review of *Talk Radio, Cineaste* 17, no. 2 (1989): 54–55.

5. Janet Maslin, "Endings Can Really Finish a Movie," *New York Times,* 1 January 1989, II, 15.

6. G. Jones, "Trashtalk: Oliver Stone's *Talk Radio,*" *Enclitic* 11, no. 2 (Spring 1989): 32; hereafter cited in text.

7. Michael Wilmington, "Dangerous Games for Power and Fame: *Talk Radio* Takes a Savage Look under Society's Surface," *Los Angeles Times Calendar,* 21 December 1988, 8.

CHAPTER 8

1. Ari. L. Goldman, "Ron Kovic Today: Warrior at Peace," *New York Times,* 17 December 1989.

2. Christopher Sharrett, review of *Born on the Fourth of July, Cineaste* 17, no. 4 (1990): 48; hereafter cited in text.

3. Pauline Kael, "Potency," *New Yorker,* 22 January 1990, 123; hereafter cited in text.

4. David Ansen, "Bringing It All Back Home," *Newsweek,* 25 December 1989, 74; hereafter cited in text.

5. Norman Mailer, "Footfalls in the Crypt," *Vanity Fair,* February 1992, 125.

6. Sheila Benson, "Oliver Stone Goes to War Again," *Los Angeles Times,* 20 December 1989, VI, 37.

7. Morris Dickstein, "Going to the Movies: War!," *Partisan Review* 57, no. 4 (1990): 611.

8. Christian Appy, "Vietnam According to Oliver Stone," *Commonweal,* 23 March 1990, 188.

9. Robert Seidenberg, "To Hell and Back," *American Film* 15 (January 1990): 56.

10. David Kehr, "Independence Day," *Chicago Tribune,* 20 December 1989, 5, 3.

11. David Denby, "Days of Rage," *New York,* 18 December 1989, 101; hereafter cited in text.

12. Stanley Kauffmann, "The Battle after the War," *New Republic,* 29 January 1990, 27.

CHAPTER 9

1. Glenn Collins, "Oliver Stone Is Ready to Move on from Vietnam," *New York Times,* 2 January 1990, III, 20.

2. J. Hoberman, "Out of Order," *Sight and Sound* 1, ns (May 1991): 7.

3. Paul Baumann, "Sex, Drugs and Rock 'n' Roll: Oliver Stone's *The Doors,*" *Commonweal,* 3 May 1991, 295.

4. David Denby, "The Pursuit of Unhappiness," *New York,* 25 March 1991, 68.

5. Terrence Rafferty, "Stoned Again," *New Yorker,* 11 March 1991, 81.

6. Brent Staples, "*The Doors* Distorts the 60's," *New York Times,* 11 March 1991, I, 16.

7. Caryn James, "For Groupies Only . . . ," *New York Times,* 24 March 1991, II, 11.

8. Mark Rowland, "Stone Unturned," *American Film* 16 (March 1991): 43.

9. Gene Siskel, "Stone's 'Head' Trip with Jim Morrison," *Chicago Tribune,* 24 February 1991, XIII, 3.

10. Andrew Sarris, review of *The Doors, Village Voice,* 12 March 1991, 51.

11. Robert Horton, "Riders on the Storm," *Film Comment* 27 (May/June 1991): 57.

CHAPTER 10

1. Richard Bernstein, "Oliver Stone, under Fire over the Killing of J.F.K.," *New York Times,* 28 July 1991, II, 9.

2. Garry Trudeau, cartoon "Overkill" on op ed page, *New York Times,* 8 January 1992, I, 15.

3. Jennet Conant, "The Man Who Shot *JFK,*" *GQ* January 1991, 66.

4. Vincent Canby, "Oliver Stone's *J.F.K.:* When Everything Amounts to Nothing," *New York Times,* 20 December 1991, sec. 2, p. 5.

5. Janet Maslin, "Oliver Stone Manipulates His Puppet," *New York Times,* 5 January 1992, II, 15.

6. Tom Wicker, "Does *JFK* Conspire against Reason?," *New York Times,* 15 December 1991, II, 8.

7. Norman Mailer, "Footfalls in the Crypt," *Vanity Fair,* February 1992, 171.

8. Jon Katz, "Rock, Rap and Movies Bring You the News," *Rolling Stone,* 5 March 1992, 37.

9. Ellen Goodman, "*JFK* Questions OK, Answers Iffy," *Ann Arbor (Michigan) News,* 3 January 1992, I, 9 (reprinted from the *Boston Globe*).

10. Lisa Nesselson, "*JFK:* Everybody Must Get Stoned . . . ," *Paris Free Voice* 15 (February 1992): 7.

11. Andrew Kopkind, "*JFK:* The Myth," *Nation,* 20 January 1992, 41.

12. William Grimes, "What Debt Does Hollywood Owe to Truth," *New York Times,* 5 March 1992, II, 4.

BIBLIOGRAPHY

OLIVER STONE—THE MAN

Breskin, David. "The *Rolling Stone* Interview: Oliver Stone." *Rolling Stone,* 4 April 1991, 37–43, 62.

Brooks, Richard. "Rolling Stone." *Observer Magazine,* 24 February 1991, 16–17, 19–20.

Ciment, Michel. "Entretien avec Oliver Stone." *Positif,* no. 314 (April 1987): 13–17.

Cockburn, Alexander. "Oliver Stone Takes Stock." *American Film* 13 (December 1987): 20–26.

Grenier, Alexandre. "Les fievres dans le sang." *Video* 7 (April 1988): 84–87, 102–3.

Guion, Nancy. "Le monde est Stone." *Starfix,* no. 47 (April 1987): 51–53, 68.

Horton, Robert. "Riders on the Storm." *Film Comment* 27 (May/June 1991): 57–61.

Kirkland, Douglas. "Rider on the Storm." *Sunday Times Magazine,* 24 February 1991, 18–23.

Rosenfield, Paul. "A Moralist in Movieland." *Los Angeles Times,* 20 December 1987, CAL, 6.

Seblouse, Agathe. "Oliver Stone." *Tele-Cine-Video,* no. 72 (April 1987): 64–65.

Stone, Oliver. "We Were Not the Good Guys Anymore." *Massachusetts Review* 29 (1988): 423–27.

Talbot, Stephen. "60s Something." *Mother Jones* (March/April 1991): 47–49, 69–70.

Wrathall, John. "Greeks, Trojans & Cubans—Oliver Stone." *Monthly Film Bulletin* 56 (October 1989): 320.

BORN ON THE FOURTH OF JULY

Adams, Phoebe-Lou. *"Born on the Fourth of July." Atlantic Monthly* 238 (September 1976): 99.

Ansen, David. "Bringing It All Back Home." *Newsweek,* 25 December 1989, 74.

Appy, Christian. "Vietnam According to Oliver Stone." *Commonweal*, 23 March 1990, 187–89.

Behar, Henri. "L'Amérique mutilée." *Le Monde*, 15 February 1990, 27.

Benson, Sheila. "Oliver Stone Goes to War Again." *Los Angeles Times*, 20 December 1989, F, 1.

Bernstein, Sharon. "Oliver Stone Wins Directors Award, Next the Oscar?" *Los Angeles Times*, 12 March 1990, F, 1.

Biskind, Peter. "Cutter's Way." *Premiere* 3 (February 1990): 58, 60, 63.

Blake, Richard A. "The Tide of Pomp: Images of War in a Season of Peace." *America*, 27 January 1990, 62–65.

"Born on the Fourth of July." Rolling Stone, 23 August 1990, 29.

Breslin, John B. "Vietnam Legacy." *America*, 25 September 1976, 173.

Bunting, Josiah, III. "Missing in Action." *Harper's Magazine*, September 1986, 80–81.

Canby, Vincent. "How an All-American Boy Went to War and Lost His Faith." *New York Times*, 20 December 1989, III, 15–16.

Chutkow, Paul. "The Private War of Tom Cruise." *New York Times*, 17 December 1989, II, 1, 28.

Corliss, Richard. "Tom Terrific." *Time*, 25 December 1989, 75–79.

Daws, A. *"Born on the Fourth of July." Variety*, 20 December 1989, 21.

Denby, David. "Days of Rage." *New York*, 18 December 1989, 101–2.

Dickstein, Morris. "Going to the Movies: War!" *Partisan Review* 57, no. 4 (1990): 608–11.

"Directors Honor Stone." *New York Times*, 12 March 1990, III, 16.

Display Ad. *"Born on the Fourth of July." Chicago Tribune*, 20 December 1989, 5, 7.

———. *"Born on the Fourth of July." Los Angeles Times*, 20 December 1989, F, 3.

———. *"Born on the Fourth of July." Washington Post*, 5 January 1990, WE27.

Eilert, Richard. "War Movies: *Born on the Fourth*." *Washington Post*, 6 February 1990, A, 25.

Gavin, Francis X. *"Born on the Fourth of July." Best Sellers* 36 (November 1976): 257.

Harrison, Nancy. "Hollywood Is Taking Notice of the Diversity of Long Island." *New York Times*, 24 December 1989, XXI, 1.

———. "Kissing Scene a Test for Actress, 12." *New York Times*, 24 December 1989, XXI, 13.

Hinson, Hal. "'Born on the Fourth.'" *Washington Post*, 5 January 1990, B1.

Holden, Stephen. "The Image of Movie Music Changing Once Again." *New York Times*, 28 January 1990, II, 28.

Howe, Desson. "Rained Out *Fourth of July*." *Washington Post*, 5 January 1990. WW23, 1990.

Johnson, Brian D. "Romancing the Wars." *Maclean's*, 8 January 1990, 39.

Kael, Pauline. "Potency." *New Yorker*, 22 January 1990, 122–24.

Kastor, Elizabeth. "Faintings Reported at '*Born on the Fourth.*'" *Washington Post*, 10 January 1990, D1.

Kauffmann, Stanley. "The Battle after the War." *New Republic*, 29 January 1990, 26–27.

Kempley, Rita. "*Daisy, Fourth* Top Oscar Nominees." *Washington Post*, 15 February 1990, B1.

Kehr, Dave. "Independence Day." *Chicago Tribune*, 20 December 1989, 5, 1.

Klawans, Stuart. "*Born on the Fourth of July . . .*" *Nation*, 1 January 1990, 28–30.

McKinney, Devin. "*Born on the Fourth of July.*" *Film Quarterly* 44 (Fall 1990): 44–7.

Malcolm, Derek. "Raise the Flag and Dump the Dead." *Guardian*, 1 March 1990, 24.

Martin, Douglas. "For Paraplegic, Acting in a Film Is the Easy Part." *New York Times*, 6 January 1990, I, 27.

Maslin, Janet. "Oliver Stone Takes Aim at the Viewer's Viscera." *New York Times*, 31 December 1989, II, 9.

Matthews, Jack. "For the Early Line on Oscar." *Los Angeles Times*, 17 December 1989, CAL, 7.

Meyers, Jeff. "A Film Maker's War of Independence." *Los Angeles Times*, 17 December 1989, CAL, 40.

Moore, Suzanne. "Scotching the Rambo Myth." *New Statesman and Society*, 9 March 1990, 44.

"No Cause for Celebration: *Born on the Fourth of July.*" *People Weekly*, 13 August 1990, 13.

Novak, Ralph. "*Born on the Fourth of July.*" *People Weekly*, 8 January 1990, 11–13.

O'Brien, Tom. "At War with Ourselves: . . . *Fourth of July.*" *Commonweal*, 9 February 1990, 85–86.

Pitman, Randy. "Video Movies: *Born on the Fourth of July.*" *Library Journal* 115 (1 September 1990): 274.

Rainer, Peter. "*Born on the Fourth of July.*" *American Film* 15 (August 1990): 52.

Ravo, Nick. "*Fourth of July* Unfair to Syracuse Police, Some Residents Say." *New York Times*, 15 January 1990, B, 3.

Reinhold, Robert. "*Driving Miss Daisy* Wins Four Oscars, Including One for Jessica Tandy." *New York Times*, 27 March 1990, C, 15.

Scheer, Robert. "Born on the Third of July." *Premiere* 3 (February 1990): 51–53, 56.

Seidenberg, Robert. "To Hell and Back." *American Film* 15 (January 1990): 28–31, 56.

Seligman, Jean, with Larry Wilson. "Heroes with Handicaps." *Newsweek*, 15 January 1990, 59–60.

Sharbutt, Jay. "New Film Brings the Old War Home." *Los Angeles Times*, 22 January 1989, CAL, 24.

Sharrett, Christopher. *"Born on the Fourth of July."* *Cineaste* 17, no. 4 (1990): 48–50.

Siclier, Jacques. "Trop c'est trop." *Le Monde,* 27 February 1990, 18.

Simon, J. "Wildlife." *National Review,* 5 February 1990, 57–59.

Siskel, Gene. "Cruise Reborn as Actor in *Born on the Fourth.*" *Chicago Tribune,* 22 December 1989, 7, A(25).

———. "Waiting to Be *Born on the Fourth of July.*" *Chicago Tribune,* 17 December 1989, 13, 5.

Sterritt, David. "Freeze Frames." *Christian Science Monitor,* 29 December 1989, 10.

Travers, Peter. *"Born on the Fourth of July."* *Rolling Stone,* 23 August 1990, 29.

———. "Holiday Hits and Misses." *Rolling Stone,* 11 January 1990, 46.

Wall, James M. "Films of Power and Grace in '89." *Christian Century,* 24 January 1990, 67–68.

CONAN THE BARBARIAN

Arnold, Gary. "Conan." *Washington Post,* 14 May 1982, C8.

Asahina, Robert. "On Screen." *New Leader,* 14 June 1982, 19–20.

Bahnson, Tore. "Conan." *Levende Billeder,* 23 April 1982, 56–57.

Bartholomew, D. *"Conan the Barbarian."* *Monthly Film Bulletin,* July 1982, 44.

Berg (S. Ginsberg). *"Conan the Barbarian."* *Variety,* 17 March 1982, 24.

Calum, P. *"Conan Barbaren."* *Kosmorama,* August 1982, 139.

Canby, Vincent. "Film: Fighting, Fantasy in *Conan the Barbarian*" *New York Times,* 15 May 1982, 13.

———. "Thoughts While Held Captive by an 'Escapist' Movie." *New York Times,* 23 May 1982, II, 21.

"Charge U and De Laurentis Used Spain to Enjoy Lax Animal Law." *Variety,* 26 May 1982, 6.

Chase, Chris. "At the Movies." *New York Times,* 14 May 1982, III, 8.

Clarens, Carlos. "Barbarians Now." *Film Comment* 18 (May/June 1982): 26–28.

Combs, Richard. *"Conan the Barbarian."* *Monthly Film Bulletin* 49 (August 1982): 167–68.

"Crucified to the 'Tree of Woe' and Left for Dead . . ." *Cinefantastique* 12 (June 1982): 51.

Decaux, Emmanuel. *"Conan le Barbare."* *Cinématrographe,* no. 77 (April 1982): 47.

deKuyper, Eric. "Conan." *Skrien Filmscrift,* no. 119/120 (Summer 1982): 17.

Delpeut, P. *"Conan the Barbarian."* *Skrien Filmscrift,* no. 119/120 (Summer 1982): 18–21.

"Demon Ghosts Animated by Kuran's VCE." *Cinefantastique* 12 (June 1982): 63.

Denby, David. "Sweat and Strain." *New York,* 24 May 1982, 68–69.

Forshey, Gerald E. *"Conan the Barbarian."* *Christian Century,* 18–25 August 1982, 868.

Fryxell, David A. "Back to Basics." *Horizon* 25 (September 1982): 60–61.

Garel, Alain. *"Conan le Barbare."* *Revue du Cinema,* no. 373 (June 1982): 48–51.

Garsault, Alain. *"Conan le barbare:* Le jeu de la chair et de l'acier." *Positif,* no. 256 (June 1982): 61–63.

Harmetz, Aljean. "Crowded Previews Thrust Universal's *Conan* into Spotlight." *New York Times,* 16 March 1982, III, 11.

Hoberman, J. "Lost and Found in Translation." *Village Voice,* 24 May 1963, 61.

Hogan, David J. *"Conan the Barbarian."* *Cinefantastique* 12, no. 5/6, (1982): 86.

Honeycutt, Kirk. "Milius: The Barbarian." *American Film* 7 (May 1982): 32–37.

"How to Film a Giant Fighting Snake." *Cinefantastique* 12, no. 2/3 (1982): 46.

Hughes, David. "The Price of Winning." *Sunday Times London,* 29 August 1982, 30.

Kane, M. *"Conan the Barbarian."* *Film Journal,* 12 April 1982, 34.

Kempley, Rita. *"Conan"* *Washington Post,* 14 May 1982, WE, 15.

Kroll, Jack. "A Cut-up Called *Conan."* *Newsweek,* 17 May 1982, 100.

Linck, David. *"Conan the Barbarian."* *Boxoffice,* June 1982, 63.

Mann, Roderick. "An Actor Muscling in on Stardom." *Los Angeles Times,* 11 April 1982, CAL, 20.

O'Toole, Lawrence. "Strong Like Bull, Red Like Abattoir." *Maclean's,* 17 May 1982, 65–66.

"Physical Training—Saamurai Style." *Cinefantastique* 12, no. 2/3 (1982): 34.

Pollock, Dale. "Milius: Might Makes a Right." *Los Angeles Times,* 14 May 1982, VI, 1, 11.

"Postproduction Optical Effects." *Cinefantastique* 12, no. 2/3 (1982): 58.

Preston, John. "Plumbing Depths." *New Statesman,* 27 August 1982, 24.

Rainer, P. *"Conan."* *Mademoiselle,* June 1982, 48, 50.

Rickey, Carrie. *"Conan* and the Reaganauts." *Village Voice,* 18 May 1982, 54.

"The Riddle of Steel: *Conan's* Swords." *Cinefantastique* 12, no. 2/3 (1982): 39.

Robinson, David. "The Warmth and Winning Charm of a Little Old Heroine." *Times London,* 27 August 1982, 7.

Romano, Lois. "Arnold Schwarzenegger, The Incredible Hunk." *Washington Post,* 9 May 1982, M1, M6–8.

Sammon, Paul M. "Cobb the Designer: Ron Cobb on Filming *Conan the Barbarian."* *Cinemafantastique* 12, no. 2/3 (1982): 64–71.

———. "Full-Blooded Heroes and High Adventure in *Conan."* *Los Angeles Times,* 12 April 1982, CAL, 26–27.

———. "*Conan the Barbarian:* Filming Robert E. Howard's Sword and Sorcery Epic." *Cinefantastique* 12, no. 2/3 (1982): 28–35, 37–38, 40–42, 45, 47–51, 53, 59–62.

———. "Milius the Director: John Milius on Filming *Conan the Barbarian.*" *Cinefantastique* 12, no. 2/3 (1982): 22–27.

———. "There's No Doubt." *Cinefantastique* 12, no. 4 (1982): 49.

Schickel, Richard. "Overkill." *Time,* 24 May 1982, 76.

Schupp, Patrick. "*Conan the Barbarian.*" *Séquences,* no. 109 (July 1982): 44–45.

Sragow, Michael. "Three Hapless Heroes." *Rolling Stone,* 10 June 1982, 37.

"Stunt Work Was Swordplay." *Cinefantastique* 12, no. 2/3 (1982): 43.

Thomas, Kevin. "Splendor in the Grasp of *Conan.*" *Los Angeles Times,* 14 May 1982, VI, 1.

Turan, Kenneth. "The Barbarian Breaks Out of the Comics and Attacks the Movies." *Washington Post,* 9 May 1982, M1, M4–5.

"Thulsa Doom's Temple of Set." *Cinefantastique* 12, no. 2/3 (1982): 54.

Turner, Adrian. "*Conan the Barbarian.*" *Films and Filming,* no. 335 (August 1982): 26–27.

———. "Milius and Conan." *Sight and Sound* 51, no. 3 (1982): 151–52.

Wells, Jeffrey. "The Plain, Rugged Truth from Ed Summer, Assoc. Producer of Universal's $19 Million Epic." *Film Journal,* 22 March 1982, 8, 14.

Wilson, Paul. "Muscles, Swords, and Sorcery in *Conan the Barbarian.*" *Photoplay* 33 (September 1982): 30–31.

THE DOORS

Ansen, David. "Your Not-so-basic Showbiz Movie Bio." *Newsweek,* 18 March 1991, 57.

Baumann, Paul. "Sex, Drugs, and Rock 'N' Roll: Oliver Stone's *The Doors.*" *Commonweal,* 3 May 1991, 294–96.

Bowman, James. "Swinging No More." *American Spectator* 24 (May 1991): 42–43.

Brown, Joe. "Stone's Window on *The Doors.*" *Washington Post,* 1 March 1991, WW, 38.

Cart (T. McCarthy). "*The Doors.*" *Variety,* 4 March 1991, 52.

Chutkow, Paul. "Oliver Stone and '*The Doors*': Obsession Meets the Obsessed." *New York Times,* 24 February 1991, II, 1.

Cohen, Jessica. "Neomacho." *American Film* 26 (June 1991): 36–39.

Collins, Glenn. "Oliver Stone Is Ready to Move on from Vietnam." *New York Times,* 2 January 1990, C, 13.

Combs, Richard. "*The Doors.*" *Monthly Film Bulletin* 58 (April 1991): 102–3.

Corliss, Richard. "Come on, Baby, Light My Fizzle." *Time,* 11 March 1991, 73.

De Vries, Hilary. "Rider on the Storm." *Los Angeles Times,* 24 February 1991, MAG, 8.

Denby, David. "The Pursuit of Unhappiness." *New York,* 25 March 1991, 67–68.

"Doors Singer Sought on Indecency Charge." *New York Times,* 7 March 1969, 24.

D'Yvoire, Christophe, and Lavoignat, Jean-Pierre. *"The Doors." Studio Magazine,* no. 44 (December 1990): 92–97.

Goldstein, Patrick. *"The Doors* and the '60s—A Fantasy." *Los Angeles Times, 10 March 1991, CAL, 24.*

Grant, Edmond. *"The Doors." Films in Review* 42 (May/June 1991): 193–95.

Hall, Carla. "Val Kilmer, Lighting the Fire." *Washington Post,* 3 March 1991, G, 1.

Hinson, Hal. *"Doors:* The Time to Hesitate is Now." *Washington Post,* 1 March 1991, B, 1.

Hoberman, J. "Out of Order." *Sight and Sound* 1, ns (May 1991): 7.

Hochman, Steve. *"The Doors* Fires Interest in Band." *Los Angeles Times,* 11 March 1991, F, 1.

Hopkins, Jerry. "Mr. Mo Jo Rises." *American Film* 15 (October 1990): 32–39, 51–53.

Horton, Robert. "Riders on the Storm." *Film Comment* 27 (May/June 1991): 57–61.

"Indians' Ancient Cavern Is Defaced for a Movie." *New York Times,* 29 April 1990, I, 25.

Jahn, Mile. "The Doors Draw Active Audience." *New York Times,* 19 January 1970, 35.

———. "20,000 Hear Doors Give Rock Concert in a Packed Garden." *New York Times,* 25 January 1969, 24.

James, Caryn. "For Groupies Only . . ." *New York Times,* 24 March 1991, II, 11.

"Jim Morrison, 25, Lead Singer with Doors Rock Group, Dies." *New York Times,* 9 July 1971, 34.

Kauffmann, Stanley. "Music Makers and Shakers." *New Republic,* 1 April 1991, 28–29.

Kehr, Dave. "Stoned *Doors." Chicago Tribune,* 1 March 1991, 7, C(33).

Klawans, Stuart. *"The Doors." Nation* 252 (25 March 1991): 388–91.

Loud, Lance. "Can Val Do the Backdoor Man?" *American Film* 15 August 1990, 9–10.

Lydon, Michael. "The Doors: Can They Still 'Light My Fire?'" *New York Times,* 19 January 1969, II, 22.

Maslin, Janet. "Fallen Star of the Sixties: No One Here Gets Out Alive." *New York Times Book Review,* 21 September 1980, 7.

———. "Flying, Falling: Days of *The Doors." New York Times,* 1 March 1991, C, 1, 17.

"Miami Jury Finds Morrison Guilty of Indecent Exposure." *New York Times,* 21 September 1970, 56.

Miller, Russell. "Rider on the Storm." *Sunday Times Magazine,* 24 February 1991, 18–21, 23.

Moss, Chuck. "Imagine *The Doors*—Oliver Stone-Style." *Detroit News,* 27 February 1991, A, 11.

Motion, Andrew. "A Head Full of Slamming Doors." *Times Literary Supplement,* 26 April 1991, 16.

Murphy, Karen, and Ronald Gross. "'All You Need Is Love. Love Is All You Need.'" *New York Times,* 13 April 1969, VI, 36–38, 40, 42, 45, 48, 50.

Pareles, John. ". . . And Sensitive Souls." *New York Times,* 24 March 1991, II, 11.

Rafferty, Terrence. "Current Cinema: Stoned Again." *New Yorker,* 11 March 1991, 81–82.

Richardson, John H, and Judson Klinger. "People Are Strange." *Premiere* 4 (March 1991): 62–68.

Rowland, Mark. "Stone Unturned." *American Film* 16 (March 1991): 40–43.

"Singer Surrenders to F.B.I." *New York Times,* 5 April 1969, 28.

Siskel, Gene. "Oliver Stone's *The Doors* an Exciting Trip to the '60's." *Chicago Tribune,* 1 March 1991, 7, C(33).

———. "Stone's 'Head' Trip with Jim Morrison." *Chicago Tribune,* 24 February 1991, 13, 3–4.

Staples, Brent. "*The Doors* Distorts the 60's." *New York Times,* 11 March 1991, A, 16.

Talbot, Stephen. "60s Something." *Mother Jones,* March/April 1991, 46–49, 67–70.

"30,000 in Miami Join a Rally for Decency." *New York Times,* 24 March 1969, 1, 31.

Travers, Peter. "Riders on a Sixties Storm." *Rolling Stone,* 21 March 1991, 83.

"Unorthodox Behaviour." *Economist,* 16 March 1991, 91–92.

Warner, Chapin F. "Decency Rally Scored." *New York Times,* 9 April 1969, 46.

Warren, Jenifer, and Greg Braxton. "Cave Paintings for Film Attacked." *Los Angeles Times,* 26 April 1970, A, 3.

Wilmington, Michael, and Robert Hilburn. "Sex, Drugs, and *The Doors.*" *Los Angeles Times,* 1 March 1991, F, 1.

8 MILLION WAYS TO DIE

Attanasio, Paul. "*8 Million Ways to Die:* Burning Its Bridges." *Washington Post,* 25 April 1986, D2.

Benson, Sheila. "*8 Million Ways* to Kill a Bloody, Violent Film." *Los Angeles Times,* 25 April 1986, VI, 6.

Clevtat, M. *"Huit millions de façons de mourir." Positif,* no. 312 (February 1987): 75.

Denby, David. "All That Tap Dancing." *New York,* 12 May 1986, 128, 130, 132.

"*8* Ancillary Rights on Sale from PSO." *Variety,* 17 December 1986, 5, 106.

Brit (J. Galbraith). *"8 Million Ways to Die." Variety,* 23 April 1986, 16.

Godfrey, Thomas. *"8 Million Ways to Die." Armchair Detective* 20, no. 4 (1987): 16–17.

Goodman, Walter. "Stone Cold." *New York Times,* 25 April 1986, III, 17.

Hey, Kenneth R. "Films." *USA Today,* 115 (July 1986), 93–97.

Hoberman, J. "Trackies." *Village Voice,* 6 May 1986, 62.

Kael, Pauline. "Drifters, Dopes, and Dopers." *New Yorker,* 19 May 1986, 98, 101–2, 104.

Kempley, Rita. *"8 Million Ways to Die." Washington Post,* 25 April 1986, WE27, WE30.

Kolmitz, N. *"8 Million Ways to Die." Film Journal,* 18 June 1986, 18.

McGilligan, Pat. "Point Man." *Film Comment* 23 (January/February 1987): 11–14, 16.

Paul, Alexandra, "Looking . . . " *Photoplay* 37 (May 1986): 8–9.

Serceau, Daniel. *"8 millions de façons de mourir." Revue du Cinema,* no. 421 (November 1986): 31.

———. *"Huit millions de façons de mourir." Revue du Cinema* 77 (Hors Series 1987): 34.

Siskel, Gene. "*8 Million Ways* Is a Goner." *Chicago Tribune,* 2 June 1986, 5, 3.

"Steve Roth Sues PSO for *Ways to Die* Firing." *Variety,* 2 April 1986, 3, 38.

Summers, Jimmy. *"Eight Million Ways to Die." Boxoffice,* July 1986, R-73.

THE HAND

Ansen, David. "Five-Finger Exercise." *Newsweek,* 27 April 1981, 90.

Benson, Sheila. *"The Hand." Los Angeles Times,* 25 April 1981, II, 18.

Berg (S. Ginsberg). *"The Hand." Variety,* 29 April 1981, 18.

Canby, Vincent. "On Two Levels." *New York Times,* 24 April 1981, III, 8.

Chase, Chris. "Good Fortune Has Creator of '*Hand*' Nervous." *New York Times,* 15 May 1981, III, 8.

Counts, Kyle. *"The Hand." Cinefantastique* 11, no. 2 (1981): 52.

Denby, David. "The Second Time Around." *New York,* 11 May 1981, 66–67.

Eisenberg, Adam. *"The Hand." Cinefantastique* 11, No. 1 (1981): 8.

"The Hand." Rolling Stone, 11 June 1981, 39.

Lofficier, Jean-Marc. *"The Hand." L'Ecran Fantastique,* no. 20 (1981): 22.

"Oliver Stone." *Mediascene Prevue*, no. 43 (November/December 1980): 24–26.

O'Toole, Lawrence. "Stranglehold without a Grip." *Maclean's*, 11 May 1981, 54–55.

Sarris, Andrew. "The Matrix of Movie Reviewing." *Village Voice*, 13/19 May 1981, 53.

"Short Takes: *The Hand*." *Christian Science Monitor*, 7 May 1981, 19.

Summers, Jimmy. *"The Hand." Boxoffice*, May 1981, 82.

JFK

Book

"JFK": The Book of the Film. New York: Applause Books, 1992.

Articles

Abbott, Mirana Bercovici. "*J.F.K.*: Righting, Not Rewriting History." *New York Times*, 5 January 1992, II, 4.

Abella, I.D. "'*J.F.K.*' Is Only Latest History à la Hollywood: Recoil from Bullet." *New York Times*, 10 January 1992, I, 12.

Anderson, Susan Heller. "Chronicle: Dallas Gives in to Oliver Stone, Partly." *New York Times*, 14 March 1991, II, 22.

Ansen, David. "What Does Oliver Stone Owe History?" *Newsweek*, 23 December 1991, 49.

Anson, Robert Sam. "The Shooting of JFK." *Esquire*, November 1991, 93–102, 174–76.

Auchincloss, Kenneth, with Ginny Caroll, and Maggie Malone. "Twisted History." *Newsweek*, 23 December 1991, 46–49.

Barker, Adam. "Cries and Whispers." *Sight and Sound*, no. 10 (February 1992): 24–25.

Bernstein, Richard. "Oliver Stone, under Fire over the Killing of J.F.K." *New York Times*, 28 July 1991, II, 9–10.

Blanchard, Laura, Daniel Davis, and Michael L. Nardacci. "Kennedy: The Movie." *Time*, 13 January 1992, 4.

Canby, Vincent. "Oliver Stone's *J.F.K.*" *New York Times*, 20 December 1991, II, 1, 5.

Causse, Jean Max. "*JFK*: Le dit et le non-dit." *Positif*, no. 373 (March 1992): 23–24.

Cieutat, Michel. "Autopsie d'une névrose: L'assassinat de JFK et Hollywood." *Positif*, no. 373 (March 1992): 19–22.

Ciment, Michel, and Hubert Niogret. "Une Amérique déstabilisée." *Positif,* no. 373 (March 1992): 25–30.

Cockburn, Alexander. "John and Oliver's Bogus Adventure." *Sight and Sound,* no. 10 (February 1992): 22–24.

Cohen, Martin, and Joseph Cohen. "Questions Need Asking." *New York Times,* 3 January 1992, I, 10.

"Coinciding with *JFK* Opening, Documentary Adds to Doubts about Official Story." *Baltimore Sun,* 22 December 1991, 5M.

"Collector's Item." *New York Times,* 29 December 1991, V, 7.

Conant, Jennet. "The Man Who Shot *JFK.*" *GQ,* January 1992, 61–67, 137–39.

Connors, Joanna. "Critics' Choice: Film." *Plain Dealer,* 5 January 1992, 2H.

Copperman, Annie. "Le complot de Dallas." *Les Echos,* 29 January 1992.

Corliss, Richard. "Who Killed J.F.K.?" *Time,* 23 December 1991, 66–70.

"Critics' Picks." *Washington Post,* 22 December 1991, G3.

Dallek, Robert. "Why Did It Have to Take *J.F.K.* to Wake Us? Kennedy Was No Dove." *New York Times,* 3 January 1992, I, 10.

Daniels, Lee A. "Oliver Stone Faces Snarls over Texas Shoot." *New York Times,* 4 March 1991, II, 9.

de Gasperi, Anne. "'J.F.K.': La vengeance d'Hamlet." *Le Quotidien de Paris,* 4 January 1992.

Deitch, Joel. "*J.F.K.:* A Hollow Catharsis." *New York Times,* 5 January 1992, II, 4.

Denton, Tommy. "*JFK* May force Debate on Governmental Secrecy." *Ann Arbor News,* 1 January 1992, I, 14.

D'Yvoire, Christophe. "*JFK* d'Oliver Stone." *Studio Magazine,* no. 58 (February 1992): 117–22.

Epstein, Edward Jay, Bob Makarowski, and Anthony J. Mocenigo. "There's No Proof Oswald Acted Alone." *Wall Street Journal,* 6 February 1992, A15.

Ford, Gerald, and David Belin. "Kennedy Assassination: How about Telling the Truth." *Dallas Morning News,* 22 December 1991, 4J.

Frodon, Jean-Michel. "La Grande Manip'." *Le Monde,* 30 January 1992, 26.

Gauthier, Guy. "JFK 1963-2029: L'enquête continue: une ténébreuse affaire." *Le Revue du Cinema,* no. 479 (February 1992): 25–7.

Gelb, Leslie H. "Kennedy and Vietnam." *New York Times,* 6 January 1992, I, 11.

"Get the Rest of the J.F.K. Story." *New York Times,* 16 January 1992, I, 14.

Gillies, Ewen. "'J.F.K.:' Where Was the Fourth Estate?" *New York Times,* 5 January 1992, II, 4.

Gitz, James L., Ed Shifres, Robert Gonsalves, Lyn Kelly, and O. Richard Cummings. "*JFK:* The Reel Story." *Newsweek,* 13 January 1992, 12–13.

Goodman, Ellen. "*JFK* Questions OK, Answers Iffy." *Ann Arbor News,* 3 January 1992, A9.

Grimes, William. "What Debt Does Hollywood Owe to Truth?" *New York Times,* 5 March 1992, II, 1, 4.

Hilsman, Roger. "How Kennedy Viewed the Vietnam Conflict." *New York Times,* 20 January 1992, I, 14.

Hinson, Hal. "Amid the Dogs and Doomsaying, A Surprising Number of Delights." *Washington Post,* 29 December 1991, G5.

Hoberman, J. "The President's Brain Is Missing." *Village Voice,* 31 December 1991: 48, 77.

Howe, Desson. "Dallas Mystery: Who Shot JFK?" *Washington Post,* 20 December 1991, WE, 55-6.

Hunt, Conover. *"JFK Not the Final Word." Dallas Morning News,* 29 December 1991, 1J, 9J.

Isikoff, Michael. "H-e-e-e-e-r-e's Conspiracy!" *Washington Post,* 29 December 1991, C2.

Jacobson, Marie. "Oliver Stone Poses Troubling, Unanswered Questions in *JFK." Michigan Daily,* 13 January 1992, 5.

"JFK." Fiches du Cinema, 29 January 1992.

"JFK: L'assassin du Président Kennedy n'était pas seul . . . " *Cine Revue,* 30 January 1992, 25–27.

"JFK Movie Lies about Conspiracy, Lawyer Says." *Ann Arbor News,* 15 December 1991, A1, A13.

"JFK: The Movie." *Wall Street Journal,* 27 December 1991, A10.

"JFK—Un caso ancora aperto." *Segnocinema (Ital.),* no. 54 (March/April 1992): 25–26.

Kaspi, André. "L'imposture." *Telerama,* 29 January 1992, 34.

Katz, Jon. "Rock, Rap and Movies Bring You the News." *Rolling Stone,* 5 March 1992.

Kavanaugh, Tom. "Convincing, But How True?" *St. Louis Review,* 3 January 1992, 12.

Klawans, Stuart. "Films. *JFK* . . ." *Nation,* 20 January 1992, 62–64.

Kopkind, Andrew. *"JFK:* The Myth." *Nation,* 20 January 1992, 40–41.

Krauss, Clifford, "28 Years after Kennedy's Assassination, Conspiracy Theories Refuse to Die." *New York Times,* 5 January 1992, I, 12.

Lee, Stephen. "J.F.K. Is Only Latest History à la Hollywood." *New York Times,* 10 January 1992, I, 12.

Lemann, Nicholas. "The Case against Jim Garrison." *GQ,* January 1992, 68–75.

Lewis, Anthony. "J.F.K." *New York Times,* 9 January 1992, I, 13.

Luther, Casey. "J.F.K.: Overworked Dramatic License." *New York Times,* 5 January 1992, II, 4.

Martin, Bruce J. "In Wake of Movie *JFK,* Two Best-sellers Probe Fact and Theory." *Ann Arbor News,* 13 February 1992, E9.

Maslin, Janet. "Oliver Stone Manipulates His Puppet." *New York Times,* 5 January 1992, II, 15.

"The Men Who Shot *JFK*." *Time Out* (8–15 January 1992): 14–18.

Morressy, John. "*J.F.K.*: Conditioned Response." *New York Times,* 5 January 1992, II, 4.

Nesselson, Lisa. "*JFK:* Everybody Must Get Stoned. . . . *Paris Free Voice* 15 (February 1992): 6–7.

Nevers, Camille. "Le cas K." *Cahiers du Cinema,* no. 452 (February 1992): 54–55.

Newman, John. "How Kennedy Viewed the Vietnam Conflict." *New York Times,* 20 January 1992, I, 14.

Niogret, Hubert. "Vrai ou faux: *JFK.*" *Positif,* no. 372 (February 1992): 46–48.

"Oliver Stone und das Attendat des Jahrhunderts: Costner jagt Kennedy-Killer." *Cinema,* no. 1 (January 1992): 24–33.

"Oliver Stone's Patsy: *JFK* Film Revives a Malicious Prosecution." *New York Times,* 20 December 1991, I, 14.

Philippe, Claude-Jean. "*JFK.*" *France Soir,* 1 February 1992.

Potter, Christopher. "*JFK:* Conspiracy Story Earns Storm of Controversy." *Ann Arbor News,* 20 December 1991, D1, D4.

Prouty, L. Fletcher. "*J.F.K.*: An Adviser Speaks Out." *New York Times,* 5 January 1992, II, 4.

Rafferty, Terrence. "Current Cinema: Smoke and Mirrors." *New Yorker,* 13 January 1992, 73–75.

Rémy, Vincent. "*JFK.*" *Telerama,* 29 January 1992, 33–35.

Richardson, John H. "Inside the Business of Hollywood: Moguls, Movies, and Money." *Premiere,* April 1992, 29.

Rosenbaum, Ron. "Taking a Darker View." *Time,* 13 January 1991, 54–56.

Scheer, Robert. "'Guerilla Historian' Stone Fights through Film." *Ann Arbor News,* 15 December 1991, E, 1–2.

Schlesinger, Arthur, Jr. "*JFK:* Truth and Fiction." *Wall Street Journal,* 10 January 1992, A, 8.

Scott, Steve. "*JFK* Conspiracy Theories: A Moviegoers' Guide." *Dallas Morning News,* 15 December 1991, C, 9.

Sheehan, Henry. "*JFK.*" *Sight and Sound* 1, ns (February 1992): 49–50.

Sotinel, Thomas. "Une familie de complots." *Le Monde,* 30 January 1992, 27.

Steel, Ronald. "Mr. Smith Goes to the Twilight Zone." *New Republic,* 3 February 1992, 30–31.

Stone, Oliver. "*J.F.K.*: Via the Director's Viewfinder." *New York Times,* 22 December 1991, II, 4.

———. "*J.F.K.* Uproar Proves the Truth Hurts." *St. Louis Post-Dispatch,* 27 December 1991, C, 3.

———. "La polémique sur *JFK.*" *Le Monde,* 17 February 1992, 17.

Strick Philip. "*JFK.*" *Sight and Sound* 1, ns (February 1992): 48–50.

Sumner, Jane. "*JFK:* Oliver Stone's Moving Target: Bringing 1963 Back to Dallas." *Dallas Morning News,* 15 December 1991, C, 9.

————. "*JFK:* Oliver Stone's Moving Target: DA's Crusade Captured Stone's Imagination." *Dallas Morning News,* 15 December 1991, C, 1, 9.

Trudeau, Garry. "Overkill." *New York Times,* 8 January 1992, I, 15.

Weatherby, W. J. "Stone Shoots *JFK.*" *Guardian,* 30 March 1991, 21.

Weingarten, Paul. "Book Depository Likely to be Used in JFK Film." *Chicago Tribune,* 7 March 1991, I, 3.

————. "Film Seeks Dallas' Help Recreating JFK Killing." *Chicago Tribune,* 5 March 1991, I. 2.

————. "Filming *JFK* Replays a Painful Moment in History." *Chicago Tribune,* 18 April 1991, I, 2.

Weinraub, Bernard. "Hollywood Questions Studio's Role in *J.F.K.*" *New York Times,* 24 December 1991, II, 1.

————. "Valenti Denounces Stone's *J.F.K.* as a 'Smear.'" *New York Times,* 2 April 1992, II, 1.

Wicker, Tom. "Does *J.F.K.* Conspire against Reason?" *New York Times,* 15 December 1991, II, 1.

Will, George. "Stone's *JFK* Insults Both Art and History." *St. Louis Post-Dispatch,* 27 December 1991, C, 3.

Wuntch, Philip. "*JFK:* Oliver Stone's Moving Target: Film Won't Hit Screens Until Friday, but the Spectable Has Already Begun." *Dallas Morning News,* 15 December 1991, C, 1, 8.

MIDNIGHT EXPRESS

"Alan Parker." *Sunday Times,* 16 July 1978, 35.

"American Escapee from Penal Colony Leaves Turks Climbing Walls." *New Times,* 4 September 1978, 15.

"Amnesty Int'l Exits *Midnight Express.*" *Variety,* 30 August 1978, 44.

Ansen, David. "Turkey Hash." *Newsweek,* 16 October 1978, 76, 81.

Arnold, Gary. "Sensationalistic Trip on the *Midnight Express.*" *Washington Post,* 28 October 1978, B, 4.

Baskin, Edie. "*Midnight Express.*" *USA Today* 107 (January 1979): 63–64.

Bergson, Phillip. "Love among the Ruins." *Times Educational Supplement,* 25 August 1978, 12.

Calum, Per. "*Midnight Express.*" *Kosmorama* 24 (1978): 220.

"Catholics Rap Parker's '*Express.*'" *Variety,* 8 November 1978, 23.

Champlin, Charles. "Crime and Cruel Punishment." *Los Angeles Times,* 25 October 1978, IV, 3.

Coleman, John. "Her Own Mistress." *New Statesman,* 11 August 1978, 191.

Corliss, Richard. "Western Anagram." *New Times* 11 (13 November 1978): 76–78.

"Critic Siskel Considers the Endings of Current Films to be 'Manipulative.'" *Boxoffice*, 18 December 1978, C, 1–6.

De Lord, Barbara. "Alan Parker's *Midnight Express*." *Films and Filming* 24 (August 1978): 25–29.

Denby, David. "One Touch of Mozart." *New York* 11 (16 October 1978): 122–23.

"Denby *Express* Is Anti-Turkish." *Variety*, 20 September 1978, 38.

Edelman, Rob. "*Midnight Express*." *Films in Review* 29 (December 1978): 635.

Ersoy, Ahmet. "On the *Midnight Express* . . ." *Christian Science Monitor*, 24 November 1978, 1.

"*Express* Message Is Harsh but Important." *Boxoffice*, 23 October 1978, C, 1.

Gastellier, Fabien. "*Midnight Express*." *Jeune Cinéma*, no. 113 (October 1978): 42.

Gourdon, Gilles. "*Midnight Express*." *Cinématographe*, no. 39 (June 1978): 26–27.

"Hail *Midnight Express* Warning to Young U.S. Tourists on Drugs." *Variety*, 27 December 1978, 6.

Harmetz, Aljean. "*Heaven*, War Films Lead Race for Oscars." *New York Times*, 21 January 1979, III, 13.

Hodenfield, Chris, with Angela Gaudoiso. "The Man Who Got Away." *Rolling Stone*, 30 November 1978, 18.

Hoffman, Matthew. "Two for the Lonesome Road." *Sunday Times*, 13 August 1978, 38.

Kael, Pauline. "Current Cinema: Movie Yellow Journalism." *New Yorker*, 27 November 1978, 182, 185–88.

Magny, Joel. "*Midnight Express*." *Cinéma 78*, no. 239 (November 1978): 94–96.

Maslin, Janet. "Critic's Notebook." *New York Times*, 14 December 1978, III, 20.

Maupin, Françoise. "*Midnight Express*." *Le Revue du Cinema*, no. 331 (September 1978): 123.

Medville, Bruce. "*Midnight Express* Is Running Late." *Encore American and Worldwide News*, 20 November 1978, 31.

"*Midnight Express* Set for New York Opening." *Boxoffice*, 9 October 1978, E, 7.

Munroe, D. "*Midnight Express*." *Film Bulletin* 47 (August/September 1978): R-C-D.

Murf (A. D. Murphy). "*Midnight Express*." *Variety*, 24 May 1978, 27.

Niogret, Hubert. "*Midnight Express*." *Positif*, no. 208/209 (July/August 1978): 92.

Nordlinger, Neal. "The Making of *Midnight Express*." *Filmmakers Monthly* 12 (November 1978): 18–21.

O'Toole, Lawrence. "Yes, Virginia, There Is a Gulag (and Others Too)." *Maclean's*, 6 November 1978, 66.

Perchaluk, E. *"Midnight Express." Independent Film Journal* 81 (October 1978): 46.

Pym, John. *"Midnight Express." Monthly Film Bulletin* 45 (July 1978): 139.

Reed, Rex. *"Midnight Express." Vogue,* September 1978, 62.

Robinson, David. "Cannes Repeats the Miracle." *Times of London,* 26 May 1978, 11.

———. "Picking Up the Pieces." *Times of London,* 11 August 1978, 7.

Sarris, Andrew. "A Little Night Kvetch." *Village Voice,* 16 October 1978, 71.

Schickel, Richard. "Ugly Trip." *Time,* 16 October 1978, 111–12.

"See Pressure from Turkey in Israeli Ban on *Midnight Express.*" *Variety,* 30 August 1978, 23.

"78." *Films Illustrated* 7 (January 1978): 184–85.

Sterritt, David. "Actual Episode Fictionalized for Screen." *Christian Science Monitor,* 16 October 1978, 1.

Taylor, Clarke. "Making *Midnight Express." Los Angeles Times,* 22 October 1978, CAL, 6.

"Turkish Envoy to Ireland Asks Ban on Col's *Express.*" *Variety,* 13 September 1978, 39.

"Turks Feel Maligned by *Midnight Express." Detroit News,* 14 December 1978, C, 13.

Umberger, Steve. "Conscientious Exception." *Humanist* 39 (March/April 1979): 66.

Villien, Bruno. *"Midnight Express." Cinématographe,* no. 40 (1978): 79.

Williams, Michaela. *"Midnight Express." New York Times,* 6 November 1978, 54.

PLATOON

Book

Boyle, Richard. *Oliver Stone's "Platoon" and "Salvador": The Original Screenplays.* New York: Vintage Books (Random House), 1987.

Articles

Adams, William. *"Platoon." Dissent* 34, no. 3, (1987): 383–86.

Allen, Henry. "Why We Aren't in Vietnam." *Washington Post,* 25 January 1987: B5.

Ansen, David, with Peter McAleven. "A Ferocious Vietnam Elegy." *Newsweek,* 5 January 1987, 57.

Attanasio, Paul. *"Platoon's* Raw Mystery." *Washington Post,* 16 January 1987, B1.

Barrios, Gregg. "A *Platoon* without Latinos." *Los Angeles Times,* 19 April 1987, CAL, 2.

Baxter, Brian. *"Platoon." Films and Filming,* no. 391 (April 1987): 30–31.

Bennetts, Leslie. "Oliver Stone Easing Out of Violence." *New York Times,* 13 April 1987, III, 13.

Benson, Sheila. *"Platoon." Los Angeles Times,* 19 December 1986, VI, 1.

Biskind, Peter. "Stone Raids Wall Street." *Premiere* 1 (December 1987): 32–38.

Blake, Richard A. "Mind and Heart." *America,* 21 February 1987, 159, iii.

Blauner, Peter. "Coming Home." *New York,* 8 December 1986, 60–62, 64, 66, 71–76.

Block, Alex Ben. "Getting Respect." *Forbes* 6 April 1987, 170.

Bohy, Sylvain, Cognard, François, and Boukrief, Nicolas. "Completement Stone." *Starfix,* no. 39 (August 1986): 53–54.

Boukrief, Nicolas. "La guerre sans etoiles." *Starfix,* no. 47 (April 1987): 49–50.

Broeske, Pat H. "After Seeing *Platoon,* Fonda Wept." *Los Angeles Times,* 25 January 1987, CAL, 3.

———. "Drawing Flak from Norris." *Los Angeles Times,* 25 January 1987, CAL, 3.

Bruning, Fred. "A Celluloid War of Credibility." *Maclean's,* 16 March 1987, 7.

Burke, Maureen. *"Platoon* Reviews Stone's Traumas." *Stills,* no. 29 (Fall 1987): 16–17.

Bygrave, Mike. "War in Tablets of Stone." *Guardian,* 24 January 1987, 13.

Canby, Vincent. "The Vietnam War in Stone's *Platoon" New York Times,* 19 December 1986, III, 12.

———. "It Wasn't Such a Bad Year after All." *New York Times,* 28 December 1986, II, 19.

———. *"Platoon* Finds New Life in the Old War Movie." *New York Times,* 11 January 1987, II, 21.

Cardullo, Bert. "Viet Nam Revisited." *Hudson Review* 40 (August 1987): 458–64.

Cart (T. McCarthy). *"Platoon." Variety,* 3 December 1986, 19.

Champlin, Charles. "Has *Platoon* De-Escalated War Movies?" *Los Angeles Times,* 25 January 1987, CAL, 4.

Ciment, Michel. "Entretien avec Oliver Stone." *Positif,* no. 314 (April 1987): 13–17.

Cockburn, Alexander. "Oliver Stone Takes Stock." *American Film* 13 (December 1987): 20–26.

Cohen, Richard. "The Nightmare of *Platoon."* Washington Post, 3 February 1987, A21.

Comber, Michael and O'Brien, Margaret. "Evading the War." *History: The Journal of the Historical Association* 73 (June 1988): 248–60.

Combs, Richard. "Beating God to the Draw." *Sight and Sound* 56 (No. 2, 1987): 136–38.

Copin, Christian. "Good Guy, Bad Guy." *Starfix* No. 39 (August 1986): 55, 67.

Corliss, Richard. "A Document Written in Blood." *Time* 128 (15 December 1986): 83.

———. "*Platoon.*" *Time* 129 (26 January 1987): 54–61.

———. "Stone Age Battles." *Observer Magazine*, 8 March 1987, 22-5, 28.

Crawley, Tony. "Fighting Fit." *Photoplay* 38 (June 1987): 8–11.

Darnton, Nina. "Old Passions Reawakened by *Platoon.*" *New York Times*, 20 March 1987, III, 8.

———. " '*Platoon*' Cast Was Trained by Marines." *New York Times*, 2 January 1987, III, 6.

Davis, Allison A. "Peace Is Our Responsibility." *New York Times*, 12 July 1987, XXIII, 28.

Davis, Ivor. "Hanoi Comes Home." *Times London*, 12 February 1987, 8.

———. "Hollywood Praise for a Picture It Refused to Finance." *Times London*, 1 April 1987, 9.

Denby, David. "Bringing the War Back Home." *New York* 19 (15 December 1986): 86–88.

Display Ad. "*Platoon.*" *Los Angeles Times*, 19 December 1986, VI, 16.

———. "*Platoon.*" *Washington Post*, 16 January 1987, WE25.

———. "*Platoon.*" *Village Voice*, 23 December 1986, 80.

Donnelly, Gabrielle. "Behind the Vietnam Lines." *Times London*, 4 March 1987, 13.

Evans, Harold. "Parable in the Jungle." *U.S. News and World Report*, 2 March 1987, 78.

Felker, Mike. "Back to Vietnam." *Jump Cut*, no. 33 (February 1988): 28–30.

Floyd, Nigel. "*Platoon.*" *Monthly Film Bulletin* 54 (April 1987): 121–22.

———. "Radical Frames of Mind." *Monthly Film Bulletin* 54 (January 1987): 10–11.

Forestier, François. "Ma génération, hantée par le napalm et les hélicoptères." *Spotlight*, no. 8 (March 1987): 61–64.

Fuller, Graham. "Oliver's Army Routs Rambo." *Guardian*, 14 February 1987, 15.

Gans, Christophe. "Apocalypse encore." *Starfix*, no. 39 (August 1986): 53–54.

Gardner, James. "Blood and Guts." *New Leader* 70 (9 March 1987): 22–23.

Gardner, Janet. "*Platoon*, Raising Veterans' Anxieties." *New York Times*, 7 June 1987, XI, 1.

Geduld, Harry M. "The Enemy Within." *Humanist* 47 (May/June 1987): 41.

Gold, Todd. "Good-time Charlie Sheen Puts the Pow in *Platoon.*" *People Weekly*, 9 March 1987, 48–50, 53–4, 56.

Goodgame, Dan. "How the War Was Won." *Time*, 26 January 1987, 58.

Halberstam, David, and Bernard E. Trainor. "Two Who Were There View *Platoon.*" *New York Times*, 8 March 1987, II, 21.

Harmetz, Aljean. "Directors Guild Honors Stone for *Platoon*." *New York Times*, 9 March 1987, III, 11.

———. "*Platoon* Wins Oscar as the Best Movie of 1986." *New York Times*, 31 March 1987, III, 14.

———. "Unwanted *Platoon* Finds Success as U.S. Examines the Vietnam War." *New York Times*, 9 February 1987, III, 13.

"Haunted by Stone's Hell." *Stills*, no. 29 (February 1987): 18–19.

Hey, Kenneth R. *"Platoon."* *USA Today* 115 (March 1987): 94–95.

Hoberman, J. "America Dearest." *American Film* 13 (May 1988): 39–45, 54.

———. "At War with Ourselves." *Village Voice*, 23 December 1986, 79, 82.

Holden, Stephen. "Baby-Faced Soldier of *Platoon*." *New York Times*, 9 January 1987, III, 10.

Hutchinson, T. *"Platoon."* *Photoplay* 38 (May 1987): 12.

Jeffords, Susan. "Masculinity as Excess in Vietnam Films: The Father/Son Dynamic of American Culture." *Genre* 21 (Winter 1988): 487–515.

Johnstone, Iain. "A Brutal War Comes Home." *Sunday Times*, 26 April 1987, 51.

Kael, Pauline. "Little Shocks, Big Shocks." *New Yorker*, 12 January 1987, 95–96.

Katsahnias, I. "'I Am Reality': Entretien avec Oliver Stone." *Cahiers du Cinema*, no. 394 (April 1987): 17–19.

Kehr, Dave. "Reality of *Platoon* Is Steeped in Surreality." *Chicago Tribune*, 30 December 1986, 5, 3.

Kelleher, Ed. *"Platoon."* *Film Journal* 90 (January 1987): 41.

Kempley, Rita. *"Platoon:* Awesome Requiem." *Washington Post*, 16 January 1987, WE17.

Kinsley, Michael. "From *Rambo* to *Platoon*." *Washington Post*, 18 February 1987, A, 19.

Kishiyama, David. "A Reason to Reflect on War." *Los Angeles Times*, 25 January 1987, CAL, 2.

Kramer, Sydelle. *"Platoon."* *Cineaste* 15 (No. 3, 1987): 49–50.

Krauthammer, Charles. "The Fog of War Wrapped Waterloo No Less Than It Did Vietnam." *Los Angeles Times*, 22 February 1987, V, 5.

———. "'*Platoon*' Chic." *Washington Post*, 20 February 1987, A19.

Lachat, Pierre. "Lost War . . ." *Filmbulletin* 29, no. 2 (153) (1987): 48–49.

London, Michael. "De Laurentis, Stone in Lawsuit." *Los Angeles Times*, 21 December 1984, VI, 1, 24.

McCarthy, Colman. "Why Teens Should See *Platoon*." *Washington Post*, 7 February 1987, A21.

McCombs, Phil. "Veterans, Reliving the Pain." *Washington Post*, 16 January 1987, B, 1.

McGilligan, Pat. "Point Man." *Film Comment* 23 (January/February 1987): 11–14, 16–20, 60.

MacPherson, Myra. *"Platoon." Washington Post,* 25 January 1987, G1.

Maddocks, Melvin, "Vietnam: the Different War—and the Same." *Christian Science Monitor,* 11 March 1987, 21.

Malcolm, Derek. "One Hell of a Vision." *Guardian,* 23 April 1987, 11.

Mann, Roderick. *"Platoon* Just Part of Sheen's Basic Training." *Los Angeles Times,* 28 December 1986, CAL, 26.

Maslin, Janet. "Critics' Choices for a Wintry Weekend." *New York Times,* 16 January 1987, III, 26.

———. "Movie Bloodlines Lead to Rambo's Children." *New York Times,* 1 March 1987, II, 21.

———. "Unlikely Casting Can Reward Actor and Audience." *New York Times,* 4 January 1987, II, 17.

Mathews, Jack. *"Platoon*—Hollywood Steps on a Gold Mine." *Los Angeles Times,* 25 January 1987, CAL, 3.

———. "Stone Wins Top Honor from Directors Guild." *Los Angeles Times,* 9 March 1987, VI, 1.

Norman, Michael. *"Platoon* Grapples with Vietnam." *New York Times,* 21 December 1986, II, 17.

Novak, Ralph. *"Platoon." People Weekly,* 19 January 1987, 8.

O'Brien, Tom, *"Platoon." Commonweal,* 16 January 1987, 17–18.

"Oliver Stone." *Playboy* 35 (February 1988): 51–53, 56–60, 112.

"Oliver Stone's Platoon Buddies Recall the War 20 Years Later." *People Weekly,* 11 May 1987, 81–84, 87–88.

Paris, Michael. "The American Film Industry and Vietnam." *History Today* 37 (April 1987): 19–26.

Peary, Gerald. "The Balad of a Haunted Soldier." *Maclean's,* 30 March 1987, 61–62.

Perrett, B.J., and Frank Burnett. "Two Vets Reply." *Playboy,* July 1987, 45.

Pfeifer, Chuch. "Oliver Stone." *Interview* 17 (February 1987): 72–73.

"Platoon Honored." *Christian Century,* 4 May 1987, 217.

"Platoon Meets Rambo." *New York Times,* 22 January 1978, I, 26.

"Platoon Oscars on Shelf, Kopelson and Stone Prepare Next." *Variety,* 6 May 1987, 135, 334.

Rafferty, Terrence. *"Platoon." Nation* 17 January 1987, 54–56.

Ratliff, Sandra. *"Platoon* Hits Its Mark." *Detroit News,* 30 December 1986, F, 1.

Rauche, Jean-Michel, and François Forestier. "Vingt ans apres, Oliver Stone raconte sa guerre." *Spotlight,* no. 8 (March 1987): 55–60.

Reed, S. K. "After Seven Years Gleb Panfilov's Film, *Tema,* sees Daylight at Last and Wrests an Award from *Platoon." People Weekly,* 6 April 1987, 57–58.

Richman, Alan. "For His Look Back in Anger at Vietnam, *Platoon's* Oliver Stone is Bombarded with Oscar Nominations." *People Weekly,* 2 March 1987, 82–83, 85, 87–88.

Rist, Peter. "Standard Hollywood Fare: The World War II Combat Film Revisited." *CineAction!* no. 12 (Spring 1988): 23–26.

Robinson, David. "Man's Belligerence Vehemently Denounced." *Times London,* 24 April 1987, 19.

———. "The Vietnam Experience for All the World." *Times London,* 22 April 1987, 17.

Rosenbaum, Ron. "The Ultimate Horror Movie." *Mademoiselle,* April 1987, 96, 98.

Ryan, Desmond. "War's Reality Finally Comes to Hollywood." *Chicago Tribune,* 16 January 1978, 7, M(35).

Schruers, Fred. "Soldier's Story." *Rolling Stone,* 29 January 1987, 23–24, 26, 53.

———. *"Platoon's* Real Trouper." *Rolling Stone,* 21 May 1987, 49, 53, 121.

Sharbutt, Jay. "The Grunt's War, Take 1." *Los Angeles Times,* 25 May 1986, CAL, 32.

———. "Life after *Platoon." Los Angeles Times,* 19 February 1988, VI, 1, 21.

———. "Reunion: Men of a Real Platoon." *Los Angeles Times,* 7 February 1987, VI, 1, 12.

Shawcross, William. "The Unseen Enemy." *Times Literary Supplement,* 24 April 1987, 438.

Simon, John. "Found in the Mud." *National Review,* 13 March 1987, 54–57.

Sineaux, Michel. "Oliver Stone." *Positif,* 12 April 1987, 10–12.

Sklar, Robert. *"Platoon* on Inspection: A Critical Symposium." *Cineaste* 15, no. 4 (1987): 4–11.

Sorgen, Richard A. "The Morality of *Platoon." New York Times,* 12 April 1987, II, 13.

Spear, Linda. "Vietnam Veterans Look to Future." *New York Times,* 5 April 1987, XXII, 6.

Springer, Claudia. "Antiwar Film as Spectable: Contradictions of the Combat Sequence." *Genre* 21 (Winter 1988): 479–86.

———. "Rebellious Sons in Vietnam Combat Films: A Response." *Genre* 21 (Winter 1988): 517–22.

Stark, Susan. *"Platoon:* Astute Lessons in War and Remembrance." *Detroit News,* 11 January 1987, E, 1.

Sterritt, David. "Oliver Stone: Why *Platoon* Was Made So Harsh." *Christian Science Monitor,* 9 January 1987, 23.

———. "Views of Vietnam: *Platoon* vs. *Rambo." Christian Science Monitor,* 26 March 1987, 23.

Stevenson, John. "Recent Vietnam Films" *Enclitic* 10, no. 1 (1988): 41–51.

Stoddart, Patrick. "Blood Out of Stone." *Sunday Times,* 5 April 1987, 51.

Stone, Oliver. "One from the Heart." *American Film* 12 (January/February 1987): 17–19, 56.

"Stone Receives Two Writers Guild Bids." *Variety,* 11 February 1987, 6.

Strother, Shelby. "Viet War Revisited, and That's Terrifying." *Detroit News,* 30 December 1986, A, 1, 6.

Summers, Jimmy. *"Platoon." Boxoffice,* February 1987, R, 15.

Szamuely, George. "Hollywood Goes to Vietnam." *Commentary,* January 1988, 48–53.

Talbot, Stephen. "60s Something." *Mother Jones* (March/April 1991): 47–49, 69–70.

Tanner, Louise. "Oliver Stone." *Films in Review* 38 (March 1987): 153–55.

———. *"Platoon." Films in Review* 38 (March 1987): 171–72.

Terry, Wallace. "An Angry Vietnam War Correspondent Charges That Black Combat Soldiers are *Platoon's* M.I.A.s." *People Weekly,* 20 April 1987, 101–2, 104.

Tessier, Max. *"Platoon." Revue du Cinema,* no. 426 (April 1987): 30–32.

Tesson, Charles. "La planéte guerre." *Cahiers du Cinema,* no. 394 (April 1987): 12–16.

"TRB from Washington: *Platoon* and Iranamok." *New Republic,* 9 March 1987, 4, 42.

Tyrrell, R. Emmett, Jr. *"Platoon." Washington Post,* 7 April 1987, A, 17.

Wall, James M. *"Platoon." Christian Century,* 21 January 1987, 60–61.

Ward, Geoffrey C. "Hard Looks at Hidden History." *American Heritage* 38 (July/August 1987): 12, 14.

Williamson, Judith. "Exorcism of a Nation's Guilt." *New Statesman,* 1 May 1987, 23–24.

"Who Took All Those Oscars." *Christian Science Monitor,* 1 April 1987, 26.

Wilson, Jeff. "After Oscar, the Winners Unwind." *Detroit News,* 1 April 1987, D, 4.

Wong, Herman. "Viet Refugees Give *Platoon* Good Reviews." *Los Angeles Times,* 25 January 1987, CAL, 5.

Worrell, Denise. "My Brilliant Career." *Time,* 26 January 1987, 60.

Zimmer, Jacques. *"Platoon." Revue du Cinema* (Hors Series 34, 1987): 118.

SALVADOR

Book

Boyle, Richard. *Oliver Stone's "Platoon" and "Salvador": The Original Screenplays.* New York: Vintage Books (Random House), 1987.

Articles

Ansen, David, with Joseph Harmes. "Oh, What an Ugly War." *Newsweek,* 9 September 1985, 89.

Attanasio, Paul. "Bold, Vivid *Salvador" Washington Post,* 4 April 1986, D, 1.

Baxter, Brian. *"Salvador:* The Truth, the Lies, the Story." *Films and Filming,* no. 383 (August 1986): 15–17.

"Bodies of Four American Women Are Found in El Salvador." *New York Times,* 5 December 1980, III, 3.

Bosséno, Christian. *"Salvador." Revue du Cinema, Hors Serie* 33 (1986): 106–7.

———. *"Salvador:* Rambo versus Rambo." *Revue du Cinema,* no. 417 (June 1986), 26–27.

Boyer, Leonard. "Boundaries of Grief." *New York Times,* 21 December 1980, IV, 16.

Browne, David. "How to Outgun Hollywood." *Times London,* 10 September 1986, 10.

Cart (T. McCarthy). *"Salvador." Variety,* 5 March 1986, 14, 20.

Champlin, Charles. "Anti-hero as Hero in *Salvador." Los Angeles Times,* 12 April 1986, V, 1.

Combs, R. "Beating God to the Draw." *Sight and Sound* 56 (Spring 1987): 136–38.

Cooke, Bruce. "Stone's *Salvador* Lets Politics Speak for Itself." *Chicago Tribune,* 27 April 1986, XIII, 18.

Crowdus, Gary. "Personal Struggles and Political Issues." *Cineaste* 16, no. 3 (1988): 18–21.

de Onis, Juan. "U.S. Officials Fly to El Salvador to Investigate Murders." *New York Times,* 7 December 1980, 8.

———. "U.S. Suspends New Aid to Salvador till American Deaths Are Clarified." *New York Times,* 6 December 1980, 1.

Denby, David. "In Another Country." *New York,* 24 March 1986, 86, 88–89.

Edelstein, David. "The Overkilling Fields." *Village Voice,* 11 March 1986, 62.

"5,000 in San Salvador Take Part in a March for Murdered Prelate." *New York Times,* 27 March 1980, 12.

Floyd, Nigel. "Radical Frames of Mind." *Monthly Film Bulletin* 54, no. 636 (January 1987): 10–11.

"Four U.S. Women Missing: Van Is Found Burned." *New York Times,* 4 December 1980, III, 2.

Goodman, Walter. "Central America: Salvador." *New York Times,* 5 March 1986, C, 22.

Gordon, Elizabeth. *"Salvador." The Film Journal* 89 (March 1986): 11–12.

———. *"Salvador:* Too Hot for U.S. Distribs." *Film Journal* 89 (April 1986): 36, 40.

"Hell, Book, and Candle." *Guardian,* 22 January 1987, 23.

Henderson, Elaina. "Lives in the Balance: Salvador and Latino." *Stills,* no. 28 (1986): 59.

Hibbin, Sally. "Blood from Stone." *Films and Filming,* no. 388 (January 1987): 18–19.

Hitchens, Christopher. "Commentary: South of the Border." *Times Literary Supplement,* 23 January 1987, 87.

Hluchy, Patricia. "Rebels and Reprobates." *Maclean's,* 21 July 1986, 50.

"Honduran Authorities Ban the Film *Salvador." New York Times,* 8 July 1987, III, 19.

Kael, Pauline. "Pig Heaven." *New Yorker,* 28 July 1986, 77–79.

Killackey, Edward R. "Martyrdom in El Salvador." *New York Times,* 25 December 1980, 22.

Kimball, George Robert. *"Salvador." Films and Filming,* no. 388 (January 1987): 41–42.

Kingsbury, Damien. "One Man's War." *Cinema Papers* (Australia), no. 60 (November 1986): 12.

Kroll, Jack. "Hell at Close Range: El Salvador's Nightmare." *Newsweek,* 17 March 1986, 80.

Leahy, James. *"Salvador." Monthly Film Bulletin* 54 (January 1987): 9–10.

McGilligan, Pat. "Point Man." *Film Comment* 23 (January/ February 1987): 11–14, 16–20, 60.

Matthews, Tom. *"Salvador." Boxoffice* 122 (June 1986): R-59.

"Murder in El Salvador." *New York Times,* 26 March 1980, 30.

Norman, N. *"Salvador." Photoplay* 38 (February 1987): 13.

"Nun Describes Slaying." *New York Times,* 26 March 1980, I, 7.

O'Mahoney, J. B. "The Maryknoll's 'Hopeful Search.'" *New York Times,* 21 December 1980, XXII, 1.

"Outspoken Rights Advocate." *New York Times,* 25 March 1980, I, 8.

"Parting Kiss for Slain Archbishop." *New York Times,* 26 March 1980, 1.

Perry, George. "Disillusion of the Monastery." *Sunday Times,* 25 January 1987, 51.

Phelps, Timothy M. "For Two Nuns, Needs of Poor Hid the Danger." *New York Times,* 7 December 1980, 9.

Robinson, David. "Crude Vigour on an Epic Scale." *Times London,* 23 January 1987, 17.

Rosenbaum, Ron. "Curtains for Yuppies." *Mademoiselle,* 19 July 1986, 48.

"Salvador Archbishop Assassinated by Sniper While Officiating at Mass." *New York Times,* 25 March 1980, I, 1.

"Salvador—Drawing a Bead on a Dirty War." *Los Angeles Times Calendar,* 1 December 1985, 24.

"A Salvador Gunman Kills an American." *New York Times,* 18 December 1980, III, 1.

"Salvador's Military Ousts Chief Liberal from Ruling Junta." *New York Times,* 8 December 1980, 1.

Shipman, David. "Cinema: A Quarterly Review." *Contemporary Review* 249 (December 1986): 324–47.

Sineux, M. *"Salvador." Positif,* no. 305/306 (July/August 1986): 117.

Siskel, Gene. "As Political Film, *Salvador* More Insult Than Message." *Chicago Tribune,* 25 April 1986, VII, A (36).

"Slain Nun Honored in Cleveland." *New York Times,* 8 December 1980, 9.

"Three in Salvadoran Cabinet Quit and Leave Country." *New York Times,* 28 March 1980, 8.

"Two Murdered American Nuns Buried in Salvadoran Town." *New York Times,* 7 December 1980, 8.

Tucker, G. M. "*Wall Street* (Stewart Copeland); *Salvador* (Georges Delerue)." *Soundtrack!* 7, no. 26 (1988): 15.

Turkel, M. G. "Martyrdom in El Salvador." *New York Times,* 25 December 1980, 22.

Williamson, Judith. "Arms and the Men." *New Statesman,* 30 January 1987, 23–24.

Wilmington, Michael. "*Salvador* Has Action as Loud as Its Words." *Los Angeles Times,* 10 April 1986, VI, 6.

Yorke, Jeffrey. "Both Sides of *Salvador.*" *Washington Post,* 4 April 1986, WE29.

SCARFACE

Ansen, David. "Gunning Their Way to Glory." *Newsweek,* 12 December 1983, 109.

Arnold, Gary. "*Scarface.*" *Washington Post,* 8 November 1983, D1.

Baumbach, Jonathan. "De Palma's Violence: *Scarface.*" *Commonweal,* 24 February 1984, 116–17.

Benson, Sheila. "*Scarface* OD's on Drugs, Violence." *Los Angeles Times,* 9 December 1983, VI, 1.

Brown, Georgia A. "Obsession." *American Film* 9 (December 1983): 28–34.

Canby, Vincent. "How Should We React to Violence?" *New York Times,* 11 December 1983, II, 23.

————. "Screen: Al Pacino Stars in *Scarface.*" *New York Times,* 9 December 1983, III, 18.

Cart (T. McCarthy). "*Scarface.*" *Variety,* 30 November 1983, 20.

Chase, Chris. "A *Scarface* Sidekick and the Cuban Image." *New York Times,* 9 December 1983, III, 10.

Chion, M. "*Scarface.*" *Cahiers du Cinéma,* no. 357 (March 1984): 58.

Chute, David. "*Scarface.*" *Film Comment* 20 (January/February 1984): 66–70.

Coleman, John. "DePalma Ham." *New Statesman,* 3 February 1984, 28, 30.

Combs, Richard. "*Scarface.*" *Monthly Film Bulletin* 51 (February 1984): 50–52.

Corliss, Richard. "Say Good Night to the Bad Guy." *Time,* 5 December 1983, 96.

Denby, David. "Snowed Under." *New York,* 19 December 1983, 70, 73.

Display Ad. "*Scarface.*" *Los Angeles Times,* 9 December 1983, VI, 3.

Fernandez, Enrique. "*Scarface* Died for My Sins." *Village Voice,* 20 December 1983, 74.

Ferrario, Davide. "*Scarface.*" *Cineforum,* no. 24 (May 1984): 66–70.

Garsault, Alain. "*Scarface.*" *Positif,* no. 279, May 1984, 52–53.

Geduld, Harry M. "Overkill: Reaction to *Scarface.*" *Humanist* 44 (March/April 1984): 39–40.

Gran, M. "*Scarface.*" *Photoplay* 35 (March 1984): 22.

Greenspan, Roger. "Films: Hindsight." *Penthouse* 15 (April 1984): 46.

Harmetz, Aljean. "De Palma Disputes Rating for *Scarface*." *New York Times*, 26 October 1983, III, 21.

————. "'*Scarface*' Receives X Rating." *New York Times*, 30 October 1983, I, 66.

————. "'*Scarface*' Gets R Rating on Appeal." *New York Times*, 9 November 1983, III, 28.

Hey, Kenneth R. "*Scarface*." *USA Today* 112 (March 1984): 95–96.

Hirschberg, Lynn. "Brian De Palma's Death Wish." *Esquire*, January 1984, 79–83.

Jaehne, Karen. "*Scarface*." *Cineaste* 13, no. 3 (1984): 48–50.

Kael, Pauline. "A De Palma Movie for People Who Don't Like De Palma Movies." *New Yorker*, 26 December 1983, 50–53.

Kauffmann, Stanley. "The World Is Theirs." *New Republic*, 9–16 January 1984, 24–25.

Krohn, Bill. "*Scarface*." *Boxoffice*, February 1984, 20–21.

Lally, Kevin. "*Scarface*." *Film Journal* 87 (January 1984): 9.

Le Fanu, Mark. "*Scarface*." *Films and Filming*, no. 353 (February 1984): 40.

London, Michael. "Cuba-born Actor a *Scarface* Hit." *Los Angeles Times*, 16 December 1983, VI, 1.

McGuigan, Cathleen, with Janet Huck. "Should X Mark the Violence?" *Newsweek*, 5 December 1983, 122, 125.

McMuran, Kristan, David Hutchings, and Pamela Lansden. "The Famous Turn Out for (and Some Are Turned Off by) the Bicoastal Previews of Al Pacino's Bloody *Scarface*." *People Weekly*, 19 December 1983, 55–56.

Magny, Joel. "*Scarface*." *Cinéma* 303 (March 1984): 45–46.

Mann, Roderick. "Pfeiffer: Accent on Negative." *Los Angeles Times*, 22 December 1983, VI, 1.

O'Toole, Lawrence. "In Praise of the Honest Criminal." *Maclean's*, 12 December 1983, 69.

Pollock, Dale. "De Palma Takes a Shot at Defending *Scarface*." *Los Angeles Times*, 5 December 1983, VI, 1.

Romano, Lois. "*Scarface* Reprieve." *Washington Post*, 9 November 1983, D1.

Rosenbaum, Ron. "Glamour Kills." *Mademoiselle*, March 1984, 94, 98.

Sarris, Andrew. "Pacino's Cuban Capone Comes a Cropper." *Village Voice*, 20 December 1983, 77–78.

Shifren, David. "Producer Bregman Discusses His Controversial *Scarface*." *Film Journal* 86 (November/December 1983): 20.

Simon, John. "Blood Wading." *National Review*, 10 February 1984, 49–51.

Siskel, Gene. "Pacino's *Scarface* Does Have a Redeeming Feature: It Ends." *Chicago Tribune*, 9 December 1983, V, 1, 4.

Stark, Susan. "Blood and Boredom." *Detroit News*, 12 December 1983, B, 1.

Will, George F. "Doing Violence to Art." *Washington Post*, 15 December 1983, A19.

SEIZURE

Canby, Vincent. "Who Says They Don't Make B Movies?" *New York Times,* 23 March 1975, II, 15.

Eyquem, O. *"Seizure." Positif,* no. 160 (June 1974): 35–36.

Lucas, Tim. *"Seizure."* Cinefantastique 4, no. 2 (1975): 33.

McGillivray, David. *"Seizure." Monthly Film Bulletin* 43 (October 1976): 219.

"Seizure." Films and Filming 23 (December 1975): 46.

"Seizure." Independent Film Journal 75 (2 April 1975): 13.

Thomas, Kevin. "Cast of Scare Actors Populates *Seizure,"* *Los Angeles Times,* 16 November 1974, II, 6.

TALK RADIO

Ansen, David. "The Temper of Several Times." *Newsweek,* 9 January 1989, 54.

Blauner, Peter. "Word of Mouth." *New York,* 12 December 1988, 50–56.

Bogosian, Eric. "How Three Plum Movie Roles Took Shape: Barry Champlain, Sculptured by Stone." *New York Times,* 18 December 1988, II, 1.

Brennan, Mark. "Double Barrelled Disenchantment." *Sunday Times,* 18 January 1987, 49.

Brown, Geoff. "I Just Called to Say I Loathe You." *Times London,* 14 September 1989, 20.

Canby, Vincent. "The Nights of a Radio Big Mouth." *New York Times,* 21 December 1988, III, 28.

Cart (T. McCarthy). *"Talk Radio." Variety,* 7 December 1988, 25, 29.

Cook, Pam. *"Talk Radio." Monthly Film Bulletin* 56 (September 1989): 284–85.

Corliss, Richard. *"Talk Radio." Time* 132 (19 December 1988): 79.

de Blois, M. *"Talk Radio." 24 Images,* no. 42 (Spring 1989): 85.

deCurtis, Anthony. "Talking Big." *Rolling Stone,* February 1989, 95–97.

Denby, David. "Raging Bull." *New York* 21 (12 December 1988): 112–14.

Dika, Vera. "The Cave." *ArtForum* 27 (February 1989): 18–20.

Display Ad. *"Talk Radio." Los Angeles Times,* 21 December 1988, VI, 3.

———. *"Talk Radio." New York Times,* 1 January 1989, II, 11.

Dutka, Elaine. "The Latest Exorcism of Oliver Stone." *Los Angeles Times,* 17 December 1989, CAL, 38.

Gehr, Richard. "Screenings: *Talk Radio." American Film* 14 (8 December 1988): 8.

Godard, Colette, and Henri Behar. "Rififi en direct." *Le Monde,* 13 April 1989, 5.

Hoberman, J. "Freedom Now?" *Village Voice,* 20 December 1988, 83.

Jacobsen, Kurt. "Talking through the Long American Night." *Guardian,* 2 February 1989, 21.

Johnstone, Iain. "The Menace of Unstoppable Mel." *Sunday Times*, 17 September 1989, C, 3.

Jones G. "Trash talk: Oliver Stone's *Talk Radio*." Enclitic 11, no. 2 (Spring 1989): 25–32.

Kauffmann, Stanley. "Justice Collectors." *New Republic*, 13 February 1989, 26–27.

Kehr, Dave. "Oliver Stone's Angry Voice Is Worth Listening to in *Talk Radio*." *Chicago Tribune*, 22 December 1988, 1, 24.

Klawans, Stuart. "*Talk Radio*." *Nation*, 9 January 1989, 65–67.

Kogan, Rick. "Hello, Tell Me Your Nightmare." *Chicago Tribune*, 20 December 1988, J, 2.

————. "Riding the Waves." *Chicago Tribune*, 18 December 1988, XIII, 6.

Kozak, Jim. "*Talk Radio*." *Boxoffice*, February 1989, R, 1–2.

Maslin, Janet. "Endings Can Really Finish a Movie." *New York Times*, 1 January 1989, II, 15.

Masson, A. "*Talk Radio*." *Positif*, no. 338 (April 1989): 72.

Meisel, M. "*Talk Radio*." *Film Journal* 92 (January 1989): 25.

Moore, Suzanne. "It's Only Words." *New Statesman and Society*, 22 September 1989, 43.

O'Brien, Tom. "In the Line of Fire." *Commonweal*, 13 January 1989: 20–21.

Porton, Richard. "*Talk Radio*." *Cineaste* 17, no. 2 (1989): 53–55.

Pulleine, Tim. "The Sound and the Fury." *Guardian*, 14 September 1989, 29.

Simon, John. "Addled Adaptations." *National Review*, 24 March 1989, 46–49.

Stark, Susan. "*Talk Radio* Can't Find Its Purpose on the Dial." *Detroit News*, 12 January 1989, C, 1.

"*Talk Radio*." *Library Journal* 114 (July 1989): 122.

"*Talk Radio*." *People Weekly*, 9 January 1989, 15.

Wilmington, Michael. "Dangerous Games for Power and Fame." *Los Angeles Times Calendar*, 21 December 1988, 1.

WALL STREET

Amiel, Barbara. "Times Diary." *Times London*, 17 May 1988, 14.

Apple, R. W., Jr., Robert A. Bennett, and Lawrence J. De Maria. "Stocks Fall, but Avert Plunge; Reagan Says He'll 'Negotiate' with Congress on the Deficit." *New York Times*, 23 October 1987, I, 1.

Arenson, Karen W. "How Wall Street Bred an Ivan Boesky." *New York Times*, 23 November 1986, III, 1.

"Atticus." *Sunday Times*, 6 March 1988, B3.

Baker, Russell. "Oh What a Lovely Life." *New York Times*, 10 February 1988, I, 31.

Benson, Sheila. "*Wall Street* Lays an Egg." *Los Angeles Times Calendar,* 11 December 1987, 1.

Bennetts, Leslie. "Oliver Stone Easing Out of Violence." *New York Times,* 13 April 1987, III, 13.

Biskind, Peter. "Stone Raids Wall Street." *Premiere* 1 (December 1987): 32–38.

Blake, Richard A. "Dead End Street." *America,* 30 January 1988, 100, 102.

Boozer, Jack, Jr. "Wall Street." *Journal of Popular Film and Television* 17 (Fall 1989): 90–99.

Braudeau, Michel. "Rue du Mur d'argent." *Le Monde,* 12 February 1988, 19.

Brimelow, Peter. "*Platoon* . . . Fired." *Times London,* 20 February 1988, 8.

Brit (J. Galbraith). "*Wall Street.*" *Variety,* 9 December 1987, 13.

Brown, Merrill. "Murdoch Night at the Movies." *Channels* 8 (February 1988): 36.

Buss, Robin. "Devils Incarnate." *Times Educational Supplement,* 6 May 1988, 30.

Canby, Vincent. "Stone's *Wall Street.*" *New York Times,* 11 December 1987, III, 3.

Cassidy, John. "Man Called Gekko Focuses Wall Street's Ugly Side." *Sunday Times,* 27 December 1987, 15.

Champlin, Charles. "Big One on Wall Street Perfect Teaser for Film." *Los Angeles Times,* 22 October 1987, VI, 1.

Cieply, Michael. "Wall Street as a War Zone." *Los Angeles Times,* 10 May 1987, CAL, 24.

Cockburn, Alexander. "Oliver Stone Takes Stock." *American Film* 13 (December 1987): 20–26.

Cole, Robert J. "Drexel-Boesky Tie for Some Investors." *New York Times,* 19 November 1986, IV, 1.

———. "Guilty Plea Entered by Boesky." *New York Times,* 24 April 1987, IV, 1.

Combs, Richard. "Father Figures." *Times Literary Supplement,* 29 April 1988, 474.

Corliss, Richard. "A Season of Flash and Greed." *Time* 130 (14 December 1987): 82–83.

"Could There Be Greedy Gekkos at Lunch in the City?" *Sunday Times,* 1 May 1988, D, 1.

Cowan, Alison Leigh. "In the Aftermath of Market Plunge, Much Uneasiness." *New York Times,* 19 October 1987, I, 1.

———. "Making *Wall Street* Look Like Wall Street." *New York Times,* 30 December 1987, III, 16.

Crowdus, Gary. "Personal Struggles and Political Issues." *Cineaste* 16, no. 3 (1988): 18–21.

Crudele, John, and Thomas C. Hayes. "Drexel 'Junk Bond' Wizard . . . and a Jeffries Early Bird." *New York Times,* 21 November 1986, IV, 1.

————. "43.31 Drop Puts Dow at 1,817.21." *New York Times,* 19 November 1986, IV, 1.

Darnton, Nina. "After *Platoon,* Stone Turns to Wall Street Corruption." *New York Times,* 30 January 1987, III, 6.

Denby, David. "Empire Builders." *New York,* 14 December 1987, 86–88.

Dudar, Helen. "Michael Douglas, as Villain, Hits It Big on *Wall Street.*" *New York Times,* 6 December 1987, II, 23.

Edelstein, David. "Raiders of the Lost Market." *Village Voice,* 15 December 1987, 110.

Fabrikant, Geraldine. "Wall Street Reviews *Wall Street.*" *New York Times,* 10 December 1987, IV, 1.

Fiorillo, C. M. *"Wall Street." Films in Review* 39 (March 1988): 163–65.

Flanigan, James. "Wall Street's Disaster Was All Too Real." *Los Angeles Times,* 13 December 1987, IV, 1.

Floyd, Nigel. *"Wall Street." Monthly Film Bulletin* 55 (April 1988): 123–25.

French, Sean. "Breaking News." *Sight and Sound* 57 (Spring 1988): 136–37.

Fuerbringer, Jonathan. "Congress Weighs Takeover Curbs in Effort to Stem Insider Trading." *New York Times,* 23 November 1986, I, 1.

Garcia, Guy D. "In the Trenches of *Wall Street.*" *Time,* 20 July 1987, 76–77.

Gindick, Tia, and Mary Rourke. "Will the Power Look Work in Laid-Back Los Angeles?" *Los Angeles Times,* 8 January 1988, V, 4.

Goodwin, Betty. "Retailers Bracing to Take Stockbroker Look to the Bank." *Los Angeles Times,* 8 January 1988, V, 5.

Gregg, Robin. "Cashing in on the Wall Street Slickers." *Sunday Times,* 8 March 1987, 51.

Gross, John. "The New Greed Takes Center Stage." *New York Times,* 3 January 1988, II, 1.

Haller, Scot. *"Wall Street." People Weekly,* 11 January 1988, 10.

Harmetz, Aljean. "Raising the Odds." *New York Times Magazine,* 11 September 1988, pt. 2, 74.

"How Three Insider Deals Worked, as Detailed by U.S." *New York Times,* 16 November 1986, I, 34.

Howe, Desson. "For a Few Dollars More." *Washington Post,* 11 December 1987, WE45.

Johnstone, Iain. "A Modern Immorality Play of Magnetic Appeal." *Sunday Times,* 1 May 1988, C8.

Joseph, Joe. "Money out of a Stone." *Times London,* 6 May 1988, 25.

————. "Stone-faced." *Times London,* 10 November 1987, 27.

Katz, Donald R. "The Way We Are." *Esquire,* May 1988, 63–64.

Kauffmann, Stanley. "A Hazard of New Fortunes." *New Republic,* 4–11 January 1988, 24–25.

Kehr, Dave. "Director Stone Plays Options Right in *Wall Street.*" *Chicago Tribune,* 11 December 1987, 7, A(52).

Kempley, Rita. "Preachy, Punchy *Wall Street*." *Washington Post*, 11 December 1987, C, 1.

Kilborn, Peter T. "Big Trader to Pay U.S. $100 Million for Insider Abuses." *New York Times*, 15 November 1986, I, 1.

———. "Insiders Scandal Stirs Ethics Debate." *New York Times*, 28 November 1986, IV, 1.

———. "U.S. Said to Issue Subpoenas Linked to Boesky Trading." *New York Times*, 17 November 1986, I, 1.

Lally, K. "*Wall Street*." *Film Journal* 91 (January 1988): 49–50.

Lardner, James. "*Wall Street*." *Nation*, 23 January 1988, 94–98.

Leonard, Carol. "To Ensure a True-to-Life Portrayal. . . ." *Times London*, 28 August 1987, 23.

———. "Pink Stone." *Times London*, 7 July 1987, 35.

———. "Romancing the Street." *Times London*, 14 December 1987, 23.

———. "Sheen Shares Shine." *Times London*, 22 June 1987, 23.

Levine, Bettijane. "Men Are Bullish on Power Styles Seen in *Wall Street*." *Los Angeles Times*, 8 January 1988, V, 1.

Lipper, Don. "Ad Hock." *Premiere* 1 (March 1988): 10.

Lohr, Steve. "Barclays Pullout: The Pressure Grew." *New York Times*, 25 November 1986, IV, 6.

Mabrick, Jeffrey. "*Wall Street:* The Banality of Greed." *New York Times*, 17 January 1988, III, 3.

McGuigan, Cathleen, with Michael Reese. "A Bull Market in Sin." *Newsweek*, 14 December 1987, 78–79.

Malcolm, Derek. "It's Business as Usual." *Guardian*, 28 April 1988, 35.

Martin, Marcel. "*Wall Street*." *Revue du Cinema*, no. 435 (February 1988): 45–47.

———. "*Wall Street*." *Revue du Cinema* 35 (Hors Serie 1988): 116–17.

Maslin, Janet. "Morality Tales for Our Time." *New York Times*, 20 December 1987, II, 25.

Newman, Peter C. "Wall Street's Gutter Ethics." *Maclean's*, 28 December 1987, 46.

Niogret, Hubert. "*Wall Street*." *Positif*, no. 325 (March 1988): 71–72.

O'Brien, Tom. "Stoned on Greed." *Commonweal*, 12 February 1988, 88–89.

Orth, Maureen. "Talking to . . . Oliver Stone. . . ." *Vogue*, December 1987, 166, 172.

O'Toole, Lawrence. "*Wall Street*." *Maclean's*, 21 December 1987, 61.

Perry, George. "Stoned on Wall Street." *Sunday Times Magazine*, 28 February 1988, 9–24.

Philippon, Alain, "Les Repaces: *Wall Street*." *Cahiers du Cinema*, no. 404 (February 1988).

Powers, John. "The Amazing Mr. Ed." *American Film* 13 (April 1988): 44–50.

Quinlan, David. "*Wall Street*." *Photoplay* 39 (May 1988): 24–25.

Rapping, Elayne. *"Wall Street." Cineaste* 16, no. 3 (1988): 49–51.

Rattner, Steven. "From Vietnam to Wall Street." *New York Times,* 30 August 1987, VI, Special Section, 34.

———. "A View from the Trenches." *Newsweek,* 14 December 1987, 80.

Rich, Frank. "Baying for Money." *New York Times,* 31 December 1987, III, 18.

"The Rise and Fall of Bud Fox." *Time,* 2 November 1987, 53.

Robinson, David. "Where Greed Is the Creed." *Times London,* 28 April 1988, 30.

Schruers, Fred. "Michael Douglas." *Rolling Stone,* 14 January 1988, 40–42, 45, 47, 69.

Sessums, Kevin. "Banking on *Wall Street:* Edward Pressman." *Interview* 17 (December 1987): 154–55.

Silk, Leonard. "Is Wall Street as Bad as It's Painted?" *New York Times,* 3 January 1988, II, 20.

Simon, John. "Death and South-death." *National Review,* 22 January 1988, 64–66.

Smith, Adam. "At the Corner of Wall Street and Vine." *Esquire,* April 1988, 87–88.

Stark, Susan. "On the Shady Side of Wall Street." *Detroit News,* 11 December 1987, E, 1.

Sterritt, David. "The Grime beneath the Glitter." *Christian Science Monitor,* 11 December 1987, 21.

"Stocks Resume Sharp Plunge." *New York Times,* 19 October 1987, I, 5.

Troy, Carol. "Can You Imagine Them Making Love?" *American Film* 14 (June 1989): 46–51, 64.

"Turmoil on Wall St." *New York Times,* 13 February 1987, IV, 16.

Vaux, Kenneth. "The Sprigs of Hope Still Can Pierce Hearts of Greed." *Chicago Tribune,* 25 December 1987, I, 25.

Vincenzi, Lisa. "An Eye for Ideas." *Millimeter* 15 (November 1987): 85.

"Wall Street Mysteries." *Fortune,* 18 January 1988, 168, 171.

Wayne, Leslie, and Joseph Berger. "The Worlds of Ivan F. Boesky." *New York Times,* 22 November 1986, I, 41.

Weatherby, W. J. "Oliver's Twisters." *Guardian,* 12 December 1987, 11.

———. "Stone's Throw at the Yuppies." *Guardian,* 29 September 1987, 11.

Wells, Chris. "The Platoon of Pros Who Helped Out on *Wall Street." Business Week,* 21 December 1987, 38–39.

Will, George F. "With Revulsion High Corrupt Capitalists Must Be Prosecuted." *Los Angeles Times,* 28 December 1987, II, 7.

Williamson, Bruce. *Playboy* 35 (March 1988): 21–22.

Williamson, Judith. "Man for Our Season." *New Statesman,* 6 May 1988, 28–29.

Young, Jon. *"Wall Street." Video* 12 (August 1988): 55–56.

YEAR OF THE DRAGON

Anderson, Susan Keller, and David W. Dunlap. "Who Was the Mayor in the Movie?" *New York Times,* 6 August 1985, II, 3.

Attanasio, Paul. "Cimino's Gang Show." *Washington Post,* 17 August 1985, G3.

Ansen, David. "The Scourge of Chinatown." *Newsweek,* 19 August 1985, 69.

Banner, Simon. "An Obsession with the Legacy of Vietnam." *Times of London,* 8 January 1986, 8.

Behar, H. *"De L'année du dragon à Rambo II."* *Revue du Cinema,* no. 409 (October 1985): 12–14.

Benson, Sheila. "Cimino's Back, with a Fiery *Year of Dragon.*" *Los Angeles Times,* 18 August 1985, CAL, 30.

———. *"Dragon."* *Los Angeles Times,* 16 August 1985, VI, 1, 16.

Broeske, Pat H. "Chasing the *Dragon.*" *Stills,* no. 21 (October 1985): 9.

Canby, Vincent. "After *Heaven's Gate, Dragon* Doesn't Look Bad.*" New York Times,* 25 August 1985, II, 15.

Caulfield, Deborah. *"Dragon* Rourke Breathes Fire." *Los Angeles Times,* 16 September 1985, CAL, 1.

Chanko, Kenneth M. *"Year of the Dragon."* *Films in Review* 36 (October 1986): 495.

Charles, Don Hogan. "Demonstrators Protest Film about Chinatown." *New York Times,* 17 August 1985, I, 46.

Coleman, John. "Bull in a China Shop." *New Statesman,* 10 January 1986, 29–30.

Combs, Richard. *"Year of the Dragon."* *Monthly Film Bulletin* 53 (January 1986): 15–17.

Corliss, Richard. *"Year of the Dragon."* *Time,* 19 August 1985, 71.

Denby, David. "The Chinese Connection." *New York,* 26 August 1985, 101–2.

Display Ad. *"Year of the Dragon."* *Los Angeles Times,* 16 August 1985, VI, 13.

Elley, Derek. *"The Year of the Dragon."* *Films and Filming,* no. 376 (January 1986): 43–44.

Floyd, Nigel. "Radical Frames of Mind." *Monthly Film Bulletin* 54 (January 1987): 10–11.

Gever, Martha. *"Dragon* Busters." *Independent* 8 (October 1985): 8–9.

Godfrey, Thomas. "TAD at the Movies." *Armchair Detective* 19, no. 2 (1986): 173–75.

Harmetz, Aljean. "Movie to Have Disclaimer." *New York Times,* 30 August 1985, III, 6.

———. "Hungry an Hour Later." *New York Times,* 23 August 1985, III, 6.

Hart (J. Harwood). *"Year of the Dragon."* *Variety,* 14 August 1985, 16.

Horn, John. "Demonstrators Picket *Year of the Dragon.*" *Los Angeles Times,* 26 August 1985, VI, 2.

———. "*Dragon* to Get a Disclaimer." *Los Angeles Times,* 30 August 1985, VI, 1, 10.

———. "MGM/UA May Insert *Dragon* Disclaimer." *Los Angeles Times,* 28 August 1985, VI, 1, 7.

Howe, Joyce. "Chinese Women in the Movies." *Village Voice,* 27 August 1985, 60–61.

Johnstone, Iain. "No Offense Spared." *Sunday Times,* 12 January 1986, 38.

Kael, Pauline. "The Great White Hope." *New Yorker,* 9 September 1985, 72–73.

Karp, Alan. "*Year of the Dragon.*" *Boxoffice* October 1985, R115–16.

Kauffmann, Stanley. "Loose Again." *New Republic,* 16–23 September 1985, 30–32.

Larson, Randall D. "*Year of the Dragon.*" *Soundtrack: The Collectors Quarterly* 5 (March 1986): 20.

Linfield, Susan. "Cimino's Magic *Dragon.*" *American Film* 11 (April 1986): 11.

Livingston, Guy. "Mayor of Boston Blasts *Dragon.* Pickets Converge on Sack House." *Variety,* 28 August 1985, 3.

Loynd, Ray. "MGM/UA Sending '*Year*' Disclaimers Out to Exhibitors." *Variety,* 4 September 1985, 3.

Malcolm, Derek. "When the Maestro Lays It on the Line." *Guardian,* 9 January 1986, 11.

Martineau, Richard. "*Year of the Dragon.*" *Sequences,* no. 122 (October 1985): 64–66.

Maslin, Janet. "*Year of the Dragon* Cimino in Chinatown." *New York Times,* 16 August 1985, III, 10.

Mathews, Jack. "Fire and Loathing in Dens of Studio Dragons." *Los Angeles Times,* 18 September 1985, VI, 1.

"MGM/UA Defends Anti-Asian Charges Leveled at *Dragon.*" *Variety,* 21 August 1985, 3, 21.

Norman, Neil. "Rourkes Drift." *Photoplay* 37 (January 1986): 22–27.

———. "*Year of the Dragon.* *Photoplay* 37 (January 1986): 52.

Novak, Ralph. "*Year of the Dragon.*" *People Weekly,* 26 August 1985, 18.

O'Toole, Lawrence. "Streets of Blood and Vengeance." *Maclean's,* 26 August 1985, 53.

Pym, John. "After the Deluge." *Sight and Sound* 55, no. 1 (1985/86): 66–67.

Robbins, Jim. "Asian-Americans Planning *Dragon* Boycott Campaign." *Variety,* 14 August 1985, 3, 26.

Robinson, David. "Attenborough Shrewd Enough to Let Well Alone." *Times London,* 10 January 1986, 13.

Roddick, Nick. "Hell's Gate." *Cinema Papers,* no. 56 (March 1986): 74.

Rosenbaum, Ron. "The Good, the Bad, and the Boring." *Mademoiselle,* November 1985, 72.

Sarris, Andrew. "Dim Summer." *Village Voice,* 20 August 1985, 53.

Simon, John. "The Tong Wars—Chapter Two." *National Review,* 20 September 1985, 46–49.

Siskel, Gene. "Excessive, Yes, but Cimino's *Dragon* Shows His Vision." *Chicago Tribune,* 16 August 1986, 7, A(32).

Slesin, Suzanne. "Brief Luxury: An Apartment Made for a Movie." *New York Times,* 24 January 1985, III, 1.

Stark, Susan. "Cimino's Insulting *Dragon* Drags On." *Detroit News,* 16 August 1985, D, 3.

Vian, Walt R. *"The Year of the Dragon." Film Bulletin* 27, no. 4 (143) (1985): 30–31.

Wood, Robin. "Hero/Anti-Hero." *CineAction!* no. 6 (Summer/Fall 1986): 57–61.

"Year of the Dragon." USA Today 114 (November 1985): 95.

"Year of the Dragon: "Asian-Americans React." *Los Angeles Times,* 1 September 1985, CAL, 28.

"Year of the Dragon Called Libel." New York Times, 1 September 1985, I, 29.

FILMOGRAPHY

Seizure (Cinerama via American International Pictures, 1974)
Director: Oliver Stone.
Producers: Garrard Glenn and Jeffrey Kapelmann.
Screenplay: Edward Mann and Oliver Stone, based on a story by Stone.
Photography: Roger Racine.
Art direction: Najwa Stone.
Music: Lee Gagnon.
Cast: Jonathan Frid, Martine Beswick, Joe Sirola, Christina Pickles, Roger de Koven, Mary Woronov, Herve Villechaize, Richard Cox, Henry Baker, Timothy Ousey, Lucy Bingham, Alexis Kirk, Emil Meola.

Midnight Express (Columbia Pictures, 1978)
Director: Alan Parker.
Producers: Alan Marshall and David Puttman.
Screenplay: Oliver Stone, based on the book by William Hayes with William Hoffer.
Photography: Michael Seresin.
Music: Giorgio Moroder.
Cast: Brad Davis, Irene Miracle, Bo Hopkins, Paolo Bonacelli, Paul Smith, Randy Quaid, Norbert Wiesser, John Hurt, Mike Kellin, Franco Diogene, Michael Ensign, Peter Jeffrey.

The Hand (Orion Pictures released through Warner Bros., 1981)
Director: Oliver Stone.
Producer: Edward R. Pressman.
Screenplay: Oliver Stone, from the novel *The Lizard's Tail* by Marc Brandel.
Photography: King Baggot.
Music: James Horner.
Cast: Michael Caine, Andrea Marcovicci, Annie McEnroe, Bruce McGill, Viveca Lindfors, Rosemary Murphy, Mara Hobel, Pat Corley, Bill Marshall, Charles Fletcher.

Conan the Barbarian (A Dino De Laurentis presentation of an Edward R. Pressman Production, 1982)

Director: John Milius.
Producer: Edward R. Pressman.
Screenplay: John Milius, Oliver Stone.
Photography: Duke Callaghan.
Production design: Ron Cobb.
Art design: Pierliugi Basile, Benjamin Fernandez.
Music: Basil Poledouris.
Cast: Arnold Schwarzenegger, James Earl Jones, Max von Sydow, Sandahl Bergman, Ben Davidson, Cassandra Gaviola, Gerry Lopez.

Scarface (Universal Pictures, 1983)

Director: Brian De Palma.
Producer: Martin Bregman.
Screenplay: Oliver Stone.
Photography: John A. Alonzo.
Art direction: Ed Richardson.
Music: Giorgio Moroder.
Cast: Al Pacino, Steven Bauer, Michelle Pfeiffer, Mary Elizabeth Mastrantonio, Robert Loggia, Miriam Colon, F. Murray Abraham, Paul Shenar, Harris Yulin, Angel Salazar, Pepe Serma.

Year of the Dragon (MGM-United Artists, 1985)

Director: Michael Cimino.
Producer: Dino De Laurentis.
Screenplay: Oliver Stone and Michael Cimino, based on the book by Robert Daley.
Photography: Alex Thomson.
Music: David Mansfield.
Cast: Mickey Rourke, John Lone, Ariane, Leonard Termo, Ray Barry, Caroline Kava, Eddie Jones, Joey Chin, Victor Wong.

8 Million Ways to Die (Tri-Star Pictures, 1986)

Director: Hal Ashby.
Producer: Steve Roth.
Screenplay: Oliver Stone and David Lee Henry, based on the novel by Lawrence Block.
Photography: Stephen H. Burum.
Music: James Newton Howard.
Cast: Jeff Bridges, Rosanna Arquette, Alexandra Paul, Randy Brooks, Andy Garcia, Lisa Stone, Christa Denton.

Salvador (Virgin Films, 1986)

Director: Oliver Stone.
Screenplay: Oliver Stone and Richard Boyle.
Photography: Robert Richardson.
Music: Georges Delerue.
Production: Pasta Productions, Hemdale.
Cast: James Woods, James Belushi, Elepedia Carrillo, Michael Murphy, John Savage, Tony Plana, Cynthia Gibb, Colby Chester, Will MacMillan, Jorge Luke, Valerie Wilman, Jose Carlos Ruiz, Juan Gernandez.

Platoon (Hemdale, 1986)

Director: Oliver Stone.
Producer: Arnold Kopelson.
Screenplay: Oliver Stone.
Photography: Robert Richardson.
Music: Georges Delerue.
Art direction: Rodel Cruz, Doris Sher Williams.
Cast: Tom Berenger, Willem Dafoe, Charlie Sheen, Forrest Whitaker, Francesco Quinn, John C. McGinley, Richard Edson, Kevin Dillon, Reggie Johnson, Keith David, Johnny Depp, David Neidorf, Mark Moses, Chris Pedersen, Corkey Ford, Corey Glover, Bob Orwig.

Wall Street (Twentieth-Century Fox, 1987)

Director: Oliver Stone.
Producer: Edward R. Pressman.
Screenplay: Stanley Weiser and Oliver Stone.
Photography: Robert Richardson.
Art direction: John Jay Moore, Hilda Stark.
Music: Stewart Copeland.
Cast: Michael Douglas, Charlie Sheen, Daryl Hannah, Martin Sheen, Terence Stamp, James Spader, Sean Young, Millie Perkins, John C. McGinley, Hal Holbrook, Tamara Tunie, Franklin Cover, Sylvia Miles, Sean Stone.

Talk Radio (Universal Pictures, 1988)

Director: Oliver Stone.
Producer: Edward R. Pressman.
Screenplay: Eric Bogosian and Oliver Stone, based on the play *Talk Radio* by Eric Bogosian and the book *Talked to Death: The Life and Murder of Alan Berg* by Stephen Singular.
Photography: Robert Richardson.

Music: Stewart Copeland.
Production design: Bruno Rubeo.
Cast: Eric Bogosian, Ellen Greene, Leslie Hope, Alec Baldwin, John C. McGinley, John Pankow, Michael Wincott, Linda Atkinson, Robert Trebar, Zach Grenier, Anna Levine, Rockets Redgare, Tony Frank, Harlan Jordan.

Born on the Fourth of July (Universal Pictures, 1989)
Director: Oliver Stone.
Producer: A. Kitman Ho.
Screenplay: Oliver Stone and Ron Kovic, based on the book by Ron Kovic.
Photography: Robert Richardson.
Production design: Bruno Rubeo.
Music: John Williams.
Cast: Tom Cruise, Kyra Sedgwick, Caroline Kava, Raymond J. Barry, Jerry Levine, Frank Whaley, Willem Dafoe, Tom Berenger, Bryan Larkin, Josh Evans, Tony Frank, Jayne Hayes.

The Doors (Tri-Star Pictures, 1990)
Director: Oliver Stone.
Producers: Graham Harari, A. Kitman Ho.
Screenplay: J. Randal Johnson, Oliver Stone.
Photography: Robert Richardson.
Executive music producer: Budd Car.
Production design: Barbara Ling.
Art direction: Larry Fulton.
Cast: Val Kilmer, Meg Ryan, Kevin Dillon, Kyle MacLachlan, Frank Whaley, Michael Madsen, Kathleen Quinlan, Michael Wincott, Dennis Burkley, Josh Evans, Paul Williams, Kristina Fulton, Crispin Glover.

JFK (Warner Bros., 1991)
Director: Oliver Stone.
Producers: A. Kitman Ho, Oliver Stone.
Screenplay: Oliver Stone and Zachary Sklar, based on the books *On the Trail of the Assassins* by Jim Garrison and *Crossfire: The Plot That Killed Kennedy* by Jim Marrs.
Photography: Robert Richardson.
Production design: Victor Kempster.
Music: John Williams.
Cast: Kevin Costner, Sissy Spacek, Joe Pesci, Tommy Lee Jones, Gary Oldman, Joe O. Sanders, Laurie Metcalf, Michael Rooker, Jack Lemmon, Walter Matthau, Donald Sutherland, Kevin Bacon, Edward Asner, Brian Doyle-Murray, Jim Garrison.

INDEX

THE AUTHOR

Frank E. Beaver was born in Cleveland, North Carolina, in 1938 and was educated at the University of North Carolina, Chapel Hill (B.A., M.A.) and the University of Michigan (Ph.D.). He has authored three books on the art and history of the motion picture and is currently completing two others. A veteran of the Vietnam War, Beaver has focused his research on the social role of film in twentieth-century life, exploring subjects such as censorship, film and the American depression, film treatment of the Vietnam War experience, and film and politics. In 1988 he was named Arthur F. Thurnau Professor of Communication at the University of Michigan and recently completed his second term as Chair of the Department of Communication at the University of Michigan. For 20 years Beaver has served as media commentator for National Public Radio stations WUOM-WVGR-WFUM. He is General Editor for Twayne's Filmmakers Series. His current projects include *A Political History of "The Birth of a Nation"* and a revision of the *Dictionary of Film Terms.*